Beheading the Saint

Beheading the Saint

Nationalism, Religion, and Secularism in Quebec

Geneviève Zubrzycki

THE UNIVERSITY OF CHICAGO PRESS • CHICAGO AND LONDON

The University of Chicago Press, Chicago 60637
The University of Chicago Press, Ltd., London

Printed in the United States of America

25 24 23 22 21 20 19 18 17 16   1 2 3 4 5

ISBN-13: 978-0-226-39154-0 (cloth)
ISBN-13: 978-0-226-39168-7 (paper)
ISBN-13: 978-0-226-39171-7 (e-book)
DOI: 10.7208/chicago/9780226391717.001.0001

Library of Congress Cataloging-in-Publication Data
Names: Zubrzycki, Geneviève, author.
Title: Beheading the saint : nationalism, religion, and secularism in Quebec / Geneviève Zubrzycki.
Description: Chicago ; London : The University of Chicago Press, 2016. | Includes bibliographical references and index.
Identifiers: LCCN 2016015887 | ISBN 9780226391540 (cloth : alk. paper) | ISBN 9780226391687 (pbk. : alk. paper) | ISBN 9780226391717 (e-book)
Subjects: LCSH: Nationalism—Québec (Province) | Secularism—Political aspects—Québec (Province) | Church and state—Québec (Province) | Parades—Political aspects—Québec (Province) | John the Baptist's Day—Québec (Province) | Social change—Québec (Province)
Classification: LCC JC311 .Z83 2016 BL2765.Q3 | DDC 320.5409714—dc23
LC record available at https://lccn.loc.gov/2016015887

⊗ This paper meets the requirements of ANSI/NISO Z39.48-1992 (Permanence of Paper).

Pour ma mère
et
à la mémoire de ma grand-mère

CONTENTS

ACKNOWLEDGMENTS

RESEARCH FOR THIS BOOK WAS GENEROUSLY FUNDED BY GRANTS from the University of Michigan's Office of Research, the Rackham Graduate School, the Weiser Center for Emerging Democracies, and the Department of Sociology, as well as from the American Sociological Association's Fund for the Advancement of the Discipline. A leave at the University of Michigan's Institute for the Humanities in 2012–13 gave me the necessary time to complete the manuscript's first full draft.

I am grateful to Maxime Morin, Elizabeth Young, and Sami Jalbert for their research assistance as well as to several archivists who went out of their way to help me make the most of my research stay in the summers of 2007 and 2008: Estelle Brisson (Archives nationales du Québec à Montréal), André Ruest (Archives nationales du Québec à Québec), Marie-Paule Robitaille (Musée de l'Amérique francophone), and François Dumas (Centre de recherche Lionel-Groulx). I am thankful also to the Mouvement national des Québécoises et des Québécois's executive director, Gilles Grondin, for granting me special access to the organization's archives at the Archives nationales du Québec à Montréal (Fonds P161), and to Francis Mailly for sharing with me current documents of the organization in the fall of 2014. I also very much appreciated the timely assistance of Sarah Garneau and Juliette Delrieu from the Musées de la civilisation in Québec City for providing photographs of artifacts from the Museum's collection. Acknowledgment is due to *Theory and Society* for the permission to reproduce portions of "Aesthetic Revolt: The Remaking of National Identity in Québec, 1960–1969," 42 (5): 423–75, which appeared in their pages in 2013.

Thanks as well to my friends, colleagues, and students for their constructive criticism and helpful suggestions: Uriel Abulof, Barbara Anderson, Elizabeth Armstrong, Courtney Bender, Gérard Bouchard, Marian Burchardt, Geoff Eley, Kriszti Fehérváry, Anna Grzymała-Busse, Rob Jansen, Paul Johnson, Vic Johnson, Peter Hall, Michael Kennedy, Matthias

Koenig, Mary Ellen Konieczny, Greta Krippner, Michèle Lamont, Camilo Leslie, Sandy Levitsky, Peggy Levitt, Paul Lichterman, Marcin Napiórkowski, Emmanuel Peddler, Fiona Rose-Greenland, Bill Sewell, Philip Smith, and Kiyo Tsutsui.

I also benefited immensely from lively discussions of sections of the book, over the years, with members of the Yale's Center for Cultural Sociology, the Successful Societies Program at the Canadian Institute for Advanced Research, the École des Hautes Études en Sciences Sociales in Paris and Marseille, the Institute of Polish Culture in Warsaw, the Max Planck Institute for the Study of Religious and Ethnic Diversity in Göttingen, the Higher School of Economics in Saint-Petersburg (Russia), Princeton University's Liechtenstein Institute on Self-Determination, and Harvard's Weatherhead Center.

Aga Pasieka, Howard Kimeldorf, Müge Göçek, and Denys Delâge deserve special recognition for carefully reading the entire manuscript. Their comments were invaluable. So was the editing of Erika Büky, who improved the prose considerably. The book would not have come to the light of day in this form were it not for Doug Mitchell, whose vision aligned with mine and encouraged me to forge ahead.

I'm grateful also for friends and family dispersed on the North American continent and beyond for their support, good humor, and patience. I'm especially thankful to my parents and siblings for helping me keep the pulse on recent affairs through their consistent sharing of news, documents, and opinions (as well as confiding in me when family disputes would erupt over political issues). It is not always easy to feel like a foreigner in one's "home," but I firmly believe that distance combined with constant returns for research or for family visits has given me a unique vantage point to analyze contemporary debates in Québec. The reader will benefit from my between and betwixt position.

A final word of gratitude is due to Paul Christopher Johnson, who lived with me through the ups and downs of research and writing; whose constant belief in the project helped sustain mine; and whose love of Québec, a place he discovered only seventeen years ago, he manages to pass on every day to our daughter, Anaïs. Merci.

This book is dedicated to my mother, Andrée Gendreau, and to the memory of my grandmother, Rosaline Gendreau, née Jolicoeur, both intrepid pioneers. May Anaïs follow their example in making her own path, wherever it may lead.

ABBREVIATIONS

ADQ	Action démocratique du Québec
CAQ	Coalition avenir Québec
COFNQ	Comité organisateur de la fête nationale du Québec
FLP	Front de libération populaire
FLQ	Front de libération du Québec
MNQ	Mouvement national des Québécoises et des Québécois
PLQ	Parti libéral du Québec
PQ	Parti Québécois
RIN	Rassemblement pour l'indépendance nationale
SSJBM	Société Saint-Jean-Baptiste de Montréal

1 From French Canada to Québec

An Introduction

JUNE 24, 1969, A CROWD OF YOUTHFUL PROTESTERS FOLLOWING the traditional St-Jean-Baptiste Day parade in Montréal seized and overturned the float dedicated to the patron saint of French Canadians. The large statue of St. John the Baptist fell to the ground, its head breaking off from the body. In the following days, the violent gesture was interpreted and narrated following the biblical story of the saint: it was described in the media and referred to in the public sphere as the "Beheading of the Baptist." With this symbolic death of the saint, the parades disappeared, and new modes of national celebrations were institutionalized.

The attack could have been interpreted at the time as an offensive yet ultimately inconsequential act of vandalism by agitated youth, but as the destruction of the float and the saint were called in the media a "beheading"—with photojournalistic images supporting that interpretation—the incident became an "event" with transformative consequences (Sewell 1996). The attack could be analyzed today by social scientists as "merely symbolic." Yet this proverbial coup de grâce can also be seen as the last constitutive action in the articulation of a new secular, Québécois national identity, a process in which verbal and physical attacks on the patron saint's icon throughout the 1960s played an intrinsic role. The debates about, and reshaping of, the national icon were part and parcel of the Quiet Revolution, a period of far-reaching social, political, economic, and cultural transformations that significantly restructured Québec society and the identity of its French-speaking members.

Once called "the priest-ridden province" by its Protestant neighbors, during the Quiet Revolution of the 1960s, the Québécois rid themselves of Catholicism, amputating what a new generation of social activists and political figures viewed as a gangrenous limb poisoning the national body. The building of a modern provincial welfare state allowed the secularization of social services, including education, health care, and social welfare, which were until then provided and controlled by the Catholic Church. The decade was marked by aggressive criticism of the Church in the public sphere, a wholesale decline in religious practice, and a large number of priests and nuns who renounced their vows and reentered secular society.[1] Many Québécois today, as heirs of the Quiet Revolution, perceive religion as an atavistic residue of the past, surviving only at the margins of society, or else as a foreign concept imported by recent waves of immigrants.

Still, religion is far from being merely an import. To continue with the metaphor of the nation as body, we might say that religion is a skeleton in Québec's closet, or a palpable absence, like phantom limb pain. Its lingering presence became apparent in heated debates over the "reasonable accommodation" of cultural minorities' religious practices, a matter that caused the creation of a special public commission to address the issue in 2006. And the question of religion's place in a secular Québec reemerged in 2013 in a much-contested proposal for a "Charter of Québec Values" (referred to simply as the Charter of Values or the Charter of Secularism). Although framed in the media and certain political circles as contests between the secular majority and religious minorities, these debates revealed that Québec's religious past is still very much a feature

1. Hard evidence of that process is scant, since the Catholic Church does not publish data on personnel who leave religious orders. Based on total numbers of religious personnel and new vocations, Gagné, Langlois, et al. (2007) have calculated that whereas between 1901 and 1961 religious personnel grew by an average of 24% per decade, between 1961 and 1971 the Church saw a 13.9% decrease in personnel. The eminent historian of religion Nive Voisine (1984) has shown that between 1965 and 1979, 26% of priests in the archdiocese of Rimouski, a midsize town northeast of Québec City, left the priesthood. One could legitimately expect that the number of religious personnel leaving orders was at least as large, if not larger, in bigger cities. The total number of new vocations, moreover, plummeted during and after the Quiet Revolution. The decline made it difficult for the institution to recruit young Québécois into its orders, especially given the expansion of employment opportunities during and after the Quiet Revolution. See also Gagnon and Paradis Simpson (2013).

of its present religious landscape and the challenges it poses for a self-avowed secular society. The debate about the increasing visibility of religion in the public sphere became a deliberation about the very identity of Québec, which reinvented itself over half a century ago with the drastic rejection of Catholicism.

Beheading the Saint is about this shifting relationship between nationalism, religion, and secularism in a society which was, until the late 1960s, exemplary of what Charles Taylor calls the "neo-Durkheimian" link between national identity and religion, wherein "the sense of belonging to the group and confession are fused and the moral issues of the group's history tend to be coded in religious categories" (2007, 458). I examine how the relationship between French Canadianness and Catholicism was configured in the nineteenth century, how it was reconfigured as Québécois and secular in the 1960s, and why and how that transition informs recent debates over secularism in Québec. The secularization of national identity during the Quiet Revolution remains the key to understanding the role and place of religion in the public sphere in today's Québec.

Nationalism, Religion, and Secularism in Québec

In the nineteenth and twentieth centuries, Catholicism played a central role in defining the French Canadians' national identity against the Anglo-Protestants surrounding them on the North American continent. After New France was ceded to England in 1763, colonial domination by this powerful, ever-present Other further reinforced Catholicism's ability to shape and sharpen French Canadian ethno-national identity and strengthened the role played by the Catholic Church in nationalist politics. National and religious identities were tightly linked at the cultural and institutional levels, with Catholicism serving as a robust ethno-national marker and the Catholic Church performing many functions usually carried out by the state, such as providing education, health, and social welfare services (Dumont 1986, 1993; Bouchard 1999; Ferretti 1999).

This state of affairs was radically disrupted following the death of Premier Maurice Duplessis in September 1959. Duplessis had ruled the Province of Québec for almost a quarter of a century, his political tenure characterized by rabid corruption, quid pro quo relationships with the Catholic Church, and shady dealings with big business—specifically with Anglo-Canadian and American firms that owned and controlled most of the province's natural resources, like mining and minerals, forestry, and hydropower (Keating 1996, 93). Duplessis managed to remain

FIGURE 1.1 *Lazare*, circa 1941, oil painting by Jean-Paul Lemieux (1904–1990). This painting captures the centrality of the Catholic Church in pre-Quiet Revolution Québec: the institution dominates the landscape and structures both daily life and major life events (Acc. no. 2574. © Art Gallery of Ontario.).

in office for as long as he did thanks to his unscrupulous, Chicago-style, electoral-machine tactics and strong pressure from the Catholic Church, which urged the population to "vote blue," the color of his party. Priests reminded their parishioners that "the heavens are blue, and hell is red" (red being the color of the opposition). With his passing in 1959, the political landscape was leveled, and a new, progressive political elite took advantage of the change to seize power. In June 1960 the Liberal Party was elected after campaigning with the slogans "It's Time for a Change," "Now

FIGURE 1.2 Jean Lesage (center) with René Lévesque (left), minister of natural resources, and Paul Gérin-Lajoie (photo: Réal St-Jean, *La Presse*).

or Never," and "Masters in our own house."[2] These were more than empty slogans: they proposed an ambitious program of reform that Premier Jean Lesage's "thunder team" (*l'équipe du tonnerre*) brought to fruition.

The Quiet Revolution: Structural Pivot and Narrative Turning Point

Lesage's election marked the beginning of a decade of profound political, economic, social, and cultural transformations that not only brought Québec out of the Duplessis era, commonly referred to as the Great Darkness (*Grande noirceur*), but also effected a significant rupture with a traditional past.[3]

2. All translations from French are mine unless I am citing a text already translated into English.

3. That representation of history, however, is increasingly questioned. Québec historians and sociologists have in recent years engaged in a critical reexamination of the putative chiaroscuro that contrasts the Great Darkness of the Duplessis years with the "light" of the Quiet Revolution (see, e.g., Bourque, Duchastel, and Beauchemin 1994; Gagnon and Sarra-Bournet 1997; Bélanger, Comeau, and Métivier 2000; Bouchard 2005). Several studies have identified the Quiet Revolution's roots in the

Chief among the structural changes was the building of a modern provincial welfare state and the secularization of social services previously controlled by the Church. The Lesage government created a rational bureaucracy and several ministries that not only modernized and democratized Québec, but also created jobs for Francophone Québécois, whose professional advancement had been stalled because of lack of opportunity (except for members of the clergy), insufficient qualifications, or linguistic discrimination.[4] The state took over significant sectors of the provincial economy, buying out private companies and nationalizing them. The nationalization of private electrical companies and their consolidation in 1962 as the large state-owned company Hydro-Québec is a prime example. Hydro-Québec became a major actor in Québec's economy not only because it offered subsidized prices for entrepreneurs and standardized prices to its customers, but also because it provided jobs for Francophone workers. Soon it was the largest employer in the province, and by 1977 it was the second-largest public utility enterprise in North America (McRoberts, 1993, 174).

In addition, the creation of economic and financial institutions such as the Société générale de financement (1962), the Société de Sidérurgie du Québec (1964), the Société québécoise d'exploitation minière (1965), and the Caisse de dépôt et de placement (1965) rendered the Québec state the key agent in the development of the province's economy, creating thousands of jobs.[5] This gave concrete backing to Lesage's slogan "Masters in our own house." Between 1960 and 1966, new ministries, consultative councils, regulatory bodies, and public enterprises were created. The number of personnel employed in the civil service grew by 42.6%, rising from 29,298 to 41,847. Those employed in public enterprises (excluding

---

1930s and 1940s, either in liberal activism (Behiels 1985) or even in religious movements within the Catholic Church itself (Meunier and Warren 1999; Gauvreau 2008).

4. That lack of upward mobility was often explained by the lower educational level of French Canadians, but there is convincing evidence showing that the income differential between English Canadians and French Canadians could not be solely explained by educational disparities. McRoberts (1993) cites a study based on the 1961 census that showed that only 33% of the difference of income between Anglophones and Francophones living in Montréal was due to the lower educational level of the latter group. An additional 6% of the difference resulted from the different age-group composition of the two populations; the remaining 60% was attributed to a clear preference of Anglophone employers for Anglophone candidates.

5. These societies are primarily state owned: they are funded by support of the state, financial institutions, and taxpayers.

Hydro-Québec and the Société des Alcools) nearly doubled between 1960 and 1965, from 7,468 to 14, 411 (McRoberts 1993, 126).

These transformations are especially significant in light of their linguistic aspect. In 1961, Francophone-controlled businesses and institutions accounted for only 47% of all jobs in Québec (Linteau et al. 1991, 213). While employment in the agrarian sector remained largely unaffected by the Quiet Revolution—92% of jobs in that sector were provided by Francophone-controlled establishments in 1961, and this figure was unchanged 20 years later—the percentage of jobs accounted for by Francophone-controlled financial institutions rose from 25.8% to 44.8% (332). The Quiet Revolution, therefore, opened up fields of employment that had previously been closed to Francophones, including public service, business, and finance. It also initiated a significant reversal in which Francophones gradually began to assume positions of leadership in the workplace.[6] Whereas in 1959 Anglophones were overrepresented in management, holding almost two-thirds of leadership positions despite constituting only 13% of Québec's total population, by 1988 they held about 25% of managerial positions, while Francophones had assumed over 50% (Simard 2000). The same trend was evident with white-collar jobs: in 1961, nearly 50% of Anglophones occupied white-collar positions, while not even 25% of Francophones did. Thirty years later, the proportion of Francophones in those positions had doubled (Simard 2000, 57–59). There is no question that the Quiet Revolution had a significant impact on Québec's economic development, particularly in increasing the opportunities for employment and advancement for French-speaking workers.[7]

These structural transformations took place alongside a cultural revolution. National history began to follow a new narrative arc, shifting the framework of identification and affiliation from a pan–North American, ethnic French Canadian identity based on language and religion to one circumscribed by the territory of Québec and a civic and secular identity centered on language. The institutional marginalization of the Catholic Church and the cultural rejection of its national ideology was accompanied by an unusually rapid process of what Martin Riesebrodt, building

6. This ethno-linguistic division of labor was analyzed by Everett C. Hughes in his *French Canada in Transition* ([1943] 2009). In this classic Chicago School ethnography of Québec in the 1930s, Hughes showed that most factory bosses and skilled laborers in midsize manufacturing cities in the province were Anglophones born in the United States or the United Kingdom.

7. These transformations also provided greater access to employment for men and women who did not know English. See Béland, Forgues, and Beaudin (2010).

from Max Weber's key word *Entzauberung*, calls religious "disenchantment," the rationalization of consciousness. In the space of just ten years, churches that had been thronged with people several days a week now sat quiet and empty.[8] In Montréal, participation of the population over fifteen years of age in Sunday mass dropped from 88% in 1957 to 30% in 1971 (Hamelin 1984, 277; Christiano 2007, 31). Without parishioners to support the local churches financially, many churches fell into disrepair. Some were bulldozed; others were sold to developers who transformed them into condominiums or hotels. Some surviving church buildings were rededicated as sites of "cultural heritage" years later or converted to places of worship for other, often "ethnic," denominations (Baum 1991; Seljak 1996; Lemieux 2006; Christiano 2007; Zubrzycki 2012a).[9]

As religious participation tumbled, so did fertility rates: on the eve of the Quiet Revolution, in 1959, Québec had the highest birthrate of all the provinces in Canada. The average French Canadian woman gave birth to four children. By 1972, Québec had the lowest birthrate in the country, dropping to 2.09 children per woman, below the 2.1 level required for population replacement (Christiano 2007, 34; Langlois 1999, 136).

These various sociopolitical, cultural, and demographic trends were not unique among industrialized societies in that period, but the degree and rapidity at which they occurred in Québec was indeed revolutionary. The Quiet Revolution should not, of course, be viewed in isolation from social movements, political developments, and cultural transformations elsewhere in the world, such as student rebellions against entrenched social hierarchies and conservative political authority in the United States, Europe, and South America; the civil rights movement in the U.S.; anticolonial protests in metropoles and the overthrowing of colonial régimes in Africa and Asia; the women's liberation movement and the sexual revolution; and, last but not least, the Second Vatican Council reforms and the emergence of Catholic "liberation theologies." In Québec, however, these

8. For analyses of the role of Catholicism in the constitution of French Canadian society, and Catholicism's trajectory in twentieth-century Québec, see Dumont (1986); Heap et al. (1986); Lemieux (1990); Beauchemin, Bourque, and Duchastel (1991); Baum (1991); Lemieux (2006); Christiano (2007); and Dillon (2007). For an analysis of the reconfiguration of Catholicism as cultural heritage, see Zubrzycki (2012b). For an impressive comparative analysis of religious influence on policy in various societies, including Québec, see Grzymała-Busse (2015).

9. See also the document *Nos églises, un patrimoine à convertir*, published by the Conseil du patrimoine religieux du Québec (2012), available on the organization's website: http://www.patrimoine-religieux.qc.ca/fr/telechargement/Patrimoine_a_convertir_Continuite_CPRQ2.pdf, accessed January 18, 2016.

movements were entwined with the rejection of the Church's moral authority and its exercise of tight social control on the one hand, and with nationalism on the other. In their nationalist discourse, French Canadians in Québec adopted the language of civil rights movements, Marxism, and postcolonialism: The "white niggers of North America," to take an expression from an influential manifesto by the journalist and activist Pierre Vallières in 1968, were to be emancipated from English Canadian colonial ascendancy and freed from the oppression of the Catholic Church by the new government's modern state and its nationalist political project.[10] On June 30, 1961, Québec's first political group for the sovereignty of Québec, the Rassemblement pour l'indépendance nationale (RIN), took out an advertisement in *Le Devoir* that read: "In 1951 . . . Dahomey (pop. 1,700,000) was a colony, and French Canada was asking for bilingual checks [for benefits distributed by the federal government]. In 1961 . . . Dahomey is an independent Republic [Bénin], and French Canada is still asking for bilingual checks. The only solution: INDEPENDENCE." Feminism was conceived and articulated within the same broad nationalist framework; women's individual emancipation from patriarchal structures would be achieved through Québec's ideological emancipation from the Church and its national liberation from Ottawa's federal control (Lamoureux 1983; De Sève 1998). According to a slogan of feminist groups, there would be "No women's Liberation without a Free Québec, no Free Québec without women's Liberation" (Lamoureux 1983).

The early 1960s therefore marked the rise of modern Québécois nationalism on multiple institutional and cultural fronts. The new nation was defined and created in opposition to the old Catholic narrative of the nation and the entire ideological and institutional edifice that had supported it. They were replaced with a secular identification based on language and territory, soon to be mobilized by the prospect of political independence (Breton 1988; Mann 1988; Balthazar 1986; Dumont 1993). Yet the new national configuration still very much depended on Catholicism to serve as its foil. One of the principal challenges this book undertakes is

10. Québécois nationalism is often cited as a case of "internal-colonialism nationalism," broadly defined as resulting from and responding to structural political and economic inequalities within a polity (see Hechter 1975; McRoberts 1979; O'Sullivan See 1986; Pettinicchio 2012). If an economically exploited minority group is sufficiently different from the majority (with respect to language, religion, or physical appearance), class conflicts become expressed in (ethno)national terms. Internal-colonialism nationalism is also related to Gellner's thesis of uneven development (1964, 1983).

to trace and document this ghostly presence as it haunts new social projects, from "cultural heritage" to "reasonable accommodation" to the Charter of Values.

Secularizing French Canadians, Building Québécois Identity

Although its radical nature and significance have been disputed, the Quiet Revolution has a quasi-sacred status in Québec (see Létourneau 1997). If it occupies such a central place in the Québécois national narrative, it is not merely because it brought about Québec's modernization and created its welfare state—as significant as those transformations were—but also because it marked a shift in the way French Canadians conceived of themselves and their nation. No longer a "little people born for a small piece of bread" (*un petit peuple né pour un petit pain*), as a popular saying proclaimed, French Canadians reimagined the borders of their nation. Instead of seeing themselves as a mere drop in the ocean of Canada, they now understood themselves as a large majority of, and the legitimate heirs to, the territory of Québec, the cradle of their civilization (see Breton 1988; Balthazar 1986; Lamont and Bail 2005). After the Quiet Revolution, Québec was no longer called "la Province de Québec" but "l'*État* du Québec." That new state, although not independent, affirmed its legitimacy in the international sphere by seeking recognition and representation abroad, opening a Maison du Québec in Paris (1961), and Québec Government Offices in London (1963) and later in the United States, South America, and Asia.[11]

In the wake of that shift in self-image and its attendant institutional backing, French Canadians living in Québec in the early 1960s adopted a new name to describe themselves: *Québécois*. The significance of this nominative turn requires explanation. Despite their frequent conflation in (non-Canadian) English, the terms *French Canadian* and *Québécois* were and are not synonymous. They represent distinct identities, visions, and even histories of the nation. As early as the eighteenth century, descendants of French settlers in Canada called themselves *Canadiens*, an ethnonym expressing their budding national identity, discrete from their French ancestors. When Alexis de Tocqueville traveled Lower Canada in the 1830s, he noted that "the English and the French merge so little with each other that the latter use exclusively the name of *Canadiens*, while the

11. There are currently 21 Québec Government Offices on four continents. See "Voici le Québec," http://www.international.gouv.qc.ca/fr/general, accessed June 15, 2015.

others continue to call themselves English" ([1831] 2003, 163). The Canadiens started calling themselves "Canadiens *français*" only in the second half of the nineteenth century, when the British who settled in Canada after the Conquest (1759–63) began describing themselves as "Canadians" (Frenette 1998, 9). The term *Canadiens français* fell out of use in Canada during the 1960s, when the French Canadians in Québec started thinking of themselves as *Québécois*.

The territorial narrowing of Québécois identity set off a ripple effect throughout Canada, causing other French-speaking Canadian groups to redefine their own identities along provincial lines: Franco-Ontarians, Franco-Manitobans, Saskatchewan's Fransaskois, Franco-Albertans, Franco-Columbians, and so on.[12] But whereas Francophones in Québec constitute approximately 80% of the province's population, they constitute only 14% of all other Canadian provinces' populations; hence their common designation as "Francophones outside Québec."[13] Over the last four decades, Québec has therefore become the entity through which—and sometimes against which—Francophone Canadians are defined and define themselves. In sum, despite the pervasive use of the term in (non-Canadian) English, no "French Canadian" identity has been operative since the 1960s. To wit, the opening sentence of *Brève histoire des Canadiens français*, by the historian Yves Frenette, reads: "This book tells the story

12. On the transformation and fragmentation of French Canadian identity, see Thériault (1999); Langlois and Létourneau (2004). Acadians are an exception to this process of fragmentation, as their identity was already distinct from that of French Canadians because of their unique historical experience. Between 1755 and 1763, more than 10,000 Acadians were expelled by the British from the land they occupied in today's Nova Scotia and were deported to British American colonies or interned in British prisons. Many fled to New France and resettled in present-day Québec and New Brunswick. Some later returned to France; others migrated from New England to Louisiana, where they formed "Cajun" (from "Acadian") communities. Nearly half died en route in what has been termed the Great Expulsion. This traumatic history has shaped Acadian identity differently from that of the French who settled around the St. Lawrence valley and later freely migrated west and south. The Québécois redefinition therefore had no impact on Acadians' distinctive identity.

13. This is the average percentage of Francophones in provinces other than Québec. In New Brunswick, Francophones represent 32.7% of the province's population; in both Ontario and Manitoba, they represent 4%. In British Columbia and Newfoundland, the number is between 0.4% and 1.4%. With Québec included in the census, Francophones constitute 22% of Canada's population; without Québec, only 4.1%. See table 1.2, "Population according to mother tongue, Canada, provinces and territories," on the Government of Canada's website "Canadian Heritage" http://www.pch.gc.ca/eng/1358790862740/1358791051208#t12 (accessed June 22, 2015).

of a people that no longer exists. It traces the genesis and evolution of a group endowed with a strong national identity that nevertheless became irremediably fragmented in the 1960s" (1998, 9).

Contrary to what is often assumed outside Canada, the term *Québécois* does not of necessity correlate with political support for Québec's independence. When the term first circulated in the public sphere in the 1960s, its users were making a conscious statement. However, that statement was about the boundaries of their imagined community rather than a firm commitment to political sovereignty, a project that was as yet only embryonic. Since then, the term has been normalized to the extent that it is a descriptive rather than a normative political term: it refers, broadly speaking, to the population of Québec.

If the creation of the name Québécois implied a political, territorially based national community, ethnicity was surely not evacuated from the national project, as we shall see in subsequent chapters: the distinctions made in everyday speech between Anglo-Québécois, neo-Québécois, and *Québécois de souche* ("old-stock") or Québécois *pur laine* (pure wool), as well as the common slippage in everyday speech into "Anglophones," "immigrants," and "Québécois" (the last colloquially referring to descendants of French Canadians) are revealing. Recently some politicians, intellectuals, and activists have denounced that slippage and reemphasized the civic project of Québec by maintaining the primacy of the national-civic category *Québécois* while at the same time recognizing the necessity of hyphenation to distinguish among the various communities composing Québec (Bouchard and Taylor 2008a). They also explicitly rejected the appellation *Québécois de souche*, since the term implies a hierarchy of citizens based on origins and/or length of establishment. They proposed instead the adoption of "Québécois of French Canadian descent" to refer to the citizens of Québec from that ethno-national group. They consider that term more "egalitarian" than *Québécois de souche* because it does not imply the primacy, via temporality, of that group over others. This semantic strategy was harshly criticized by many who saw it as a backward step, when in fact the adjective actually emphasizes that the second term is an ethnic identity, a cultural-historic one, not a civic-*national* one. In this book, therefore, I use the terms *Canadiens* and *French Canadians* to denote the descendants of French settlers in Canada until the 1960s, and *Québécois* thereafter.

The French Canadian and the Québécois national visions are also markedly different. While the French language remains a core element of both, Catholicism was abandoned as an important or even a desirable marker of the nation in the Québécois project. Likewise, the Church was perceived no longer as a bulwark but rather as a barrier to the development of the nation. Whereas the French Canadian national vision was centered on the notion of ethno-religious survival, the Québécois project explicitly rejected that idea. Its aspiration and guiding trope was not to survive but rather to *develop*, and a key plank of the Quiet Revolution's platform was "catching up" (*rattrapage*) and "modernizing." The influence of the Church in Québec society—both institutionally and ideologically—was seen as an impediment to that effort. The instrument of that modernization was to be the provincial state, whose functions were radically expanded and empowered in order to better represent the interests of the "new" Québécois nation within Canadian federal structures.

In the 1970s, some political elites, followed by a significant portion of the Francophone population of Québec, pushed this project even further by arguing that far-reaching social, cultural, and economic development would come only through political emancipation from the Canadian federation. After its founding in 1968, René Lévesque's Parti Québécois won the 1976 provincial elections with the promise of a referendum on sovereignty.

Unintended Consequences

Like all complex historical processes, the Quiet Revolution unleashed both planned and unintended consequences. One of the latter was the fragmentation of all French Canadian identities throughout Canada; another was the decrease in birth rates, with its indirect correlate of increased Francophone immigration (including from predominantly Muslim parts of North and West Africa), which had significant effects on the perception of the place of religion in today's society. The plummeting of the birthrate in Québec during the Quiet Revolution did not stop in 1970. In 1986 it hit a record low of 1.37 children per woman, a rate that demographers call "low-low fertility." This created a wave of insecurity about the future of the nation, which was increasingly described in the media and political discourse as endangered (*en voie de disparition*). Three years later, in 1989, a documentary titled *Disappearing* was widely advertised and then broadcast on Radio-Canada (the French-language division of the Canadian Broadcasting Corporation), generating an intense discussion in the public sphere. Its official synopsis declared:

> Demographers predict that within 25 years at the most, the French Canadian nation will be moribund. *Then it will disappear*, unless [the

> nation] starts to produce more children and welcomes immigrants desiring to truly integrate—two eminently political options. By comparing experiences in other regions of the world with the situation prevailing in Québec, this vast analysis of the state of the nation gives warning by showing the mistakes to avoid, and proposes solutions that could, it seems, save the French people of America from extinction.[14]

The dire predictions of this much-viewed program suggest that the Quiet Revolution was not only about quantifiable demographic change but also about collective imagination and the practices of self-representation employed by Québécois of French Canadian descent. This anxiety about the demographic future of the nation persists to this day. A 2006 hit song called "Dégénérations" played on the decline of generational transmission and its "degenerative" aspects. The song nostalgically recounts the achievements of previous generations and critically assesses the moral void created by the baby boomers' Quiet Revolution:

> Your great-great grandmother had fourteen children
> Your great grandmother had almost as many
> And your grandmother had three, which was plenty
> Then your mother didn't want any—you were just an accident
> Now you, girl, change partners all the time
> When you screw up you save the day by aborting
> But some mornings you wake up crying
> After dreaming at night of children seated around a large table.
> (Mes Aïeux, "Dégénérations," 2006)

The insecurity about the future of the nation expressed in the public sphere must also be put in the context of the results of a referendum on the sovereignty of Québec held on May 20, 1980. In the referendum, 40.44% of Québec voters voted for and 59.56% against giving a mandate to the Québec government to negotiate the province's independence from the rest of Canada.[15] The 1980s were therefore marked not only by the

14. *Disparaître*, a film by Jean-François Mercier, produced by l'Office national du film du Canada, www.onf-nfb.gc.ca/fra/collection/film/?id=4665, accessed December 14, 2009. Emphasis in the original. Note the use of the term *French Canadian* to denote the ethnic basis of the "endangered" community.

15. Another referendum on sovereignty, in 1995, was much closer: 49.42% voted yes, and 50.58% voted no, with a 93.5% voter turnout, the highest in the history of provincial and federal elections in Canada.

realization of the demographic impact of the Quiet Revolution but also by the injuries left by an acrimonious battle between supporters of the "yes" and "no" camps, serious soul-searching by the "sovereignists,"[16] and complex and contested negotiations between Québec and the rest of Canada to constitutionally recognize Québec's distinctiveness within Canada.

It was to maintain the delicate linguistic balance in the province, and the political heft of Québec within Canadian federal structures, that Québec government agencies began actively encouraging the immigration of Francophone populations to Québec.[17] Since many of the new Francophone immigrants are non-Christian, their arrival has made religion once again a matter of public discourse. It has shifted the meaning of *Québécois* and pressed an older generation of Québécois to reflect on secularism and their historic rapport with Catholicism. Though many thought they had left Catholicism behind for good, they have discovered its influence even in the ostensibly secular responses to Islam, Sikhism, Orthodox Judaism, and other religions now complicating the public sphere. The debate over religion and secularism is moreover no longer only a debate among Québécois of French Canadian descent but one that involves a dialogue with the Other.

Theoretical Framework

Objectives

Beyond shedding light on the transformation of French Canadian identity into Québécois nationalism—a topic that has received little attention in the English-language literature—*Beheading the Saint* has three primary objectives.[18]

The first is theoretical and aims to interpret the role of religious and

16. Those who support the independence of Québec call themselves *souverainistes* or *indépendantistes*. They are referred to by their opponents as *séparatistes*, often contemptuously. Given that the latter term is often used as an insult in Québécois French, I adopt the more neutral *sovereignist*.

17. Québec has shared jurisdiction with Ottawa over immigration to its territory. Its Ministry of Immigration was created in 1968.

18. The Anglo-American literature on nationalism in Québec tends to focus on colonialism and separatist politics, often in comparative perspective with (e.g., O'Sullivan See 1986, Keating 1996, Hechter 2001, Stevenson 2006). To my knowledge, there is to date no extensive study of the transformation of national identity from French Canadian to Québécois in the English-language literature on nationalism. The most significant work in English is that of Handler (1988), which focuses on the politics of culture in Québec after the PQ's coming to power.

secular ideologies and practices in the making of national identity and its transformation. In my earlier work on nationalism and religion (Zubrzycki 2006, 18–22), I have shown the problematic causal assumptions made in nationalism studies between the decline of religion and the rise of nationalism. The argument, *grosso modo*, is not only that the secularization of society in the nineteenth century made room for the articulation of new identities and modes of political legitimacy but that national identities and nationalism emerged *because of* the void left by the retreat of religion. Nationalism, moreover, is often presented as having itself become the (or at least a) religion of modern times. That narrative is obviously problematic for the study of *religious* nationalism, since the latter phrase becomes tautological, to wit: nationalism as a quasi-religion emerges with the disappearance of religion. But it is also problematic for the study of *secular* nationalism because it fails to account for the persistence and diverse forms of religion, as well as the specific ways in which religion infiltrates the making of secular national identities. We therefore need a conceptual framework and theory of nationalism that explains different configurations of religious-secular national identities.

We know from a vast and rich literature that "secularization" is a much more complex phenomenon than the usual one-size-fits-all "decline of religion" proposition. José Casanova, in his classic study *Public Religions in the Modern World*, argues that secularization is composed of "three very different, uneven and unintegrated propositions: secularization as differentiation of the secular spheres from religious institutions and norms, secularization as decline of religious beliefs and practices, and secularization as marginalization of religion to a privatized sphere" (1994, 211). Philip S. Gorski (2000; see also Gorski and Altınordu 2008) also differentiated between types of secularization theories that address empirically different processes: the disappearance and the decline of religion on the one hand, and its privatization and transformation on the other. Mark Chaves referred to "secularization" as more specifically the declining *scope* of religious authority, a process rooted in concrete social struggles: "Secularization occurs, or not, as the result of social and political conflicts between those social actors who would enhance or maintain religion's social significance and those who would reduce it" (1994, 752). Bruce Lincoln (2003) called these "minimalist" versus "maximalist" articulations of religion. The tension is between privatizing and publicizing forces, between opposed views of the role of religion and of the Church in the public sphere. These were crucial interventions in the sociology of religion. In this work, however, I adopt the distinction proposed by Martin Riesebrodt, since it best allows me to disentangle processes too often lumped together: *secularization* (the separation of social and religious institutions), *disenchantment* (rationalization of consciousness), and *deinstitutionalization* (transformation of religious institutions, specifically shrinking membership and declining participation in religious practice) (2010, 174–81).

While crude secularization theories have been refined by these authors to be less ideologically driven, more empirically accurate, and theoretically more robust, in recent years, secularism, secularity, and "the secular" have supplanted secularization altogether (see Asad 2003; Taylor 2007; Warner, VanAntwerpen, and Calhoun 2010). Key terms in this work, therefore, also include *secularism* and *secularity*. I distinguish them as follows. Secularity is a principle, or, as for Charles Taylor, a condition of subjective experience, in which the religious and secular spheres are distinct. Religion is one option among many other ideational systems, identities, affiliations, and activities. Secularism, by contrast, is a political project that aims at instituting secularity, at upholding, enforcing, and politically and legally securing the separation of the religious and secular domains.

Building on these works but distinct from their respective aims, this book focuses on the process of *becoming secular*—on the aesthetic, bodily, social, and political practices of enacting secular identities. *Becoming secular* does not imply the total disappearance of religion in secular national societies: rather, it involves religious and secular configurations that are articulated and contested. Following Talal Asad's invitation to explore the "anthropology of the secular," I look at diverse spheres of social life where these processes occur. I draw much-needed attention to the aesthetic, embodied, performative processes involved in "becoming secular." This approach also has the methodological advantage of investigating secularity as a dynamic process rather than a static state or more or less a *fait accompli*. I attend to the fissures and frictions entailed in becoming secular, the debates and contestation between social and political actors as they seek to socially, aesthetically, and legally institute secularism. Importantly, in this model secularity is never fully achieved but always in process and always itself infiltrated by ghosts, as we will see in the emergence of rubrics like "national heritage" and "patrimony" as a novel version of sacrality now affixed to churches and monumentalized at other sites.

The second objective is empirical: it seeks to highlight the role of symbolic politics in shaping new identities and advancing institutional transformations. While a body of work has addressed the relationship between institutional transformations and change in collective identity in Québec (e.g., Breton 1988; Dumont 1993), the role of symbolic politics has been grossly neglected both in academic writings and more popular understandings of key features of the Quiet Revolution.[19] Here I demonstrate that a core feature of the Quiet Revolution was an aesthetic revolt whereby a new generation rejected the symbols of French Canada and its particular aesthetics, secularizing national identity in the process. Without proper attention to that aesthetic revolt and the role played by material symbols in that process, the picture of Québec's dramatic secularization and the reconfiguration of national identity during the Quiet Revolution remains at a level of bloodless ideals, and incomplete.

The third objective of *Beheading the Saint* is to provide a methodological blueprint for a visual and material sociology of identity transformation. Scholars of nationalism have felicitously moved away from the study of identity as a constructed yet static phenomenon to the study of identifications, the process through which identities are formed and transformed (e.g., Brubaker 1996; Glaeser 1999; Brubaker and Cooper 2000). A recent body of scholarship has shown how national identifications are constructed in everyday life through personal interactions and institutional practices (Brubaker et al. 2006; Fox and Miller-Idriss 2008) as well as through specific transformative events (Zubrzycki 2006). While we know from classical sociological texts, the anthropological literature, and cultural history that social solidarity is created through the manipulation of symbols during certain rituals and performances, and that these manipulations can sometimes generate new identifications (e.g., Durkheim [1912] 1995; Turner 1967; Hunt 1986; Ozouf 1988; Sewell 1996), we know much less about the role that symbols themselves play in that process. Can symbols produce change? If so, how? Why do certain symbols seem powerful and not others?

While there have been repeated calls to pay attention to the visual and the material in historical change, identity transformation, and nationalism, few studies actually do the kind of empirical work required to demonstrate the role of visuality and materiality in those processes, rather than merely posit or suggest it. To meet these objectives I turn to a varied set of theoretical and methodological tools.

19. For example, an educational website prepared by the Government of Québec in 2010 to commemorate the fiftieth anniversary of the Quiet Revolution's beginning proposed five great themes of transformation: the role of the state, the modernization of education, the development of (secular) welfare, the promotion of culture and language, and the creation of a modern economy. Symbolic politics is conspicuously absent from this list. See "La Révolution tranquille," www.RevolutionTranquille.gouv.pc.ca, accessed June 5, 2013.

A Visual and Material Sociology of Nationalism

Appropriately dubbed the "iconic" or "pictorial" turn, the attention to the visual has slowly left the confines of art history, cultural studies, and communications to enter the social sciences. In sociology, it has had the greatest impact in historical and cultural sociology, through the work of scholars like Victoria Bonnell (1997) on the power of the visual in Soviets citizens' political indoctrination and Robin Wagner-Pacifici (2005) in showing the significance of iconographic depictions of rituals of military surrender in legitimating transfers of political authority. To be sure, visual culture and vision are intrinsically sociological phenomena: vision is not constituted solely through the physiology of sight but rather is a cultural process that is learned and cultivated, and refined in the social relationships between viewers as well as between the viewers and the object viewed. Jacques Lacan and Michel Foucault called the relationship forged in the social act of looking *le regard*, the gaze. While the gaze has received the most attention from scholars interested in race and gender, the religious studies scholar David Morgan recently turned to the study of the "sacred gaze," defining it as "the manner in which a way of seeing invests an image, a viewer or an act of viewing with spiritual significance" (Morgan 2005, 3). What Morgan regards as "spiritual significance" is rather hazy, however, and it is sociologically more productive to restate his definition of the sacred gaze as the process through which a given way of seeing *sacralizes* an image, a viewer, or an act of viewing. I thus study vision as a cultural act potentially imbued with sacredness under certain social conditions.

Visual culture is also important for sociologists because it delineates imagined communities. It provides a shared repertoire of images and objects that shape memory and identity (Morgan 1999, 8). Because images and objects act as concrete substitutes for abstract ideas (Agulhon 1981), they are powerful agents of socialization, marketing, and propaganda (Barthes 1957; Bonnell 1997; Cushing and Tomkins 2007; Hall, Stimson, and Becker 2006). Deciphering the various components of what the French historian Maurice Agulhon (1981) has called "pictorial discourses" set forth by institutions and social actors allows us to analyze the stories people tell about themselves. But precisely because visual symbols, complex pictorial discourses, and material culture can be used as means of socialization or tools of propaganda in the hands of elites—what Chandra Mukerji (2012) calls "political pedagogy"—they can also become the object of struggles between groups promoting different ideologies, identities, or political agendas. That iconomachy in turn sometimes leads to iconoclasm, the discrediting and displacing of rivals through the destruction of their symbols (Morgan 2005). Dwelling on visual and material culture allows us to track conflicts about, and changes in, political visions of the nation (Zubrzycki 2011).

Analyzing images in relation to their various uses and contests about their meanings and deployments is also productive because images have a special ability to mediate imaginary, linguistic, intellectual, and material domains (Nora 1997; Mitchell 1986, 1998; Rogoff 1998; Freedberg 1991). As W. J. T. Mitchell (1998) has pointed out, attention to the visual pushes us to attend to all the senses, since every "visual object" is in fact perceived through multiple senses. The sight of a painting of Monet's haystacks, for example, can cue tactile and olfactory sensations. Studying images, pictorial discourses, and visual culture more broadly is thus necessarily an intertextual enterprise, one in which "images, sounds, and spatial delineations are read onto and through one another" (Rogoff 1998, 24).

The study of visual culture and visuality is thus closely related to that of *materiality*, another interdisciplinary field that has expanded rapidly over the last decade, above all in anthropology and science and technology studies (e.g., Appadurai 1986; Keane 2003, 2006; Woodward 2007; Miller 2005, 1–50; Tilley et al. 2006; Fehérváry 2013). Materiality studies is concerned with understanding objects, things, and the ways people interact with them; it sees the material world not only as an embodiment of values and ideational systems (e.g., Durkheim [1912] 1995, 2010), or as congealed social relationships (as a Marxist materialist approach would), but as giving shape and meaning to social relationships. From this perspective, things may even exert a form of agency, as extensions of personhood that impinge on and call forth responses from social actors (Gell 1998). Works in materiality studies seek to transcend the dualism between subjects and objects to show how social relations are built through and around the consumption of material culture (rather than merely in its production, as Marx had it). These concerns have been taken up primarily by scholars in neighboring social sciences; yet even within sociology proper, several authors have demonstrated the value of this approach (Mukerji 1994, 1997, 2012; Latour 2007; Alexander 2008; Bartmanski and Alexander 2012; McDonnell 2010; Zubrzycki 2011).

Chandra Mukerji (2012), for instance, has developed a model of political pedagogy that takes into account the role of material culture in creating and shaping a shared consciousness and collective identity. She convincingly shows why the gardens of Versailles, precisely because they were not discursive but rather "materially exemplary," did not generate opposition to the political project they embodied but instead shaped subjects' political allegiances (5). In a different but related line of inquiry, I have shown (2011) that the visual depiction and embodiment of historical narratives and national myths—in myriad cultural forms, the built environment and the landscape—which are *experienced* by individuals in a variety of practices and settings, is what rendered those distant and abstract discourses close and concrete. It is through what I call the "national sensorium" that social actors sensorially experience national narratives and myths, and that political projects articulated by elites generate sentiments of national belonging and emotional attachment to what is necessarily a distant imagined community.

In a similar vein, Jeffrey Alexander (2008) analyzed the intersection between aesthetics and materiality in his theory of "iconic consciousness," the process by which an aesthetically shaped materiality comes to signify social value. He defines icons as symbolic condensations that anchor social meanings in a particular material form. Meaning is thus made visible and tangible; it can be seen, felt, touched—in other words, "experienced." As the signifier is made into a material thing, the content becomes form.[20] Agulhon was concerned with a similar process, namely that through which imagery comes to stand for a concept or ideological content, as the French revolutionary figure of Marianne comes to represent the French Republic. These icons are not empty things: rather, they are "meaning" embodied. While this view is partly consistent with Wendy Griswold's definition of "cultural objects," which are "shared significance embodied in form i.e. . . . an expression of meanings that is tangible or can be put into words" (1987, 4–5), here meaning is necessarily material, not merely discursive or aural.[21] Meaning is transmitted through contact with the material object—the icon—which imparts its power through the senses (Zubrzycki 2011; Bartmanski and Alexander 2012).

Moving Ahead

In the study of materiality and meaning-making, one aspect that remains relatively unexplored is how the aesthetic and material forms of an icon

20. Mabel Berezin, in her study of Fascist theater in Italy (1994), convincingly demonstrates that meaning can also be found in artistic form alone, regardless of its narrative content.

21. Materiality studies scholars would reject that distinction, seeing all discourse as material: a text is printed onto a page, which is bound into a book that can be carried, opened, shelved, torn, or burned. Even oral tradition is embodied and material, as it is spoken, sung, or performed by bodies in specific material contexts.

can in turn alter its "inner" content, its meaning. The works of Tia DeNora (2000) and the anthropologist Webb Keane (2003, 2006) provide useful leads. Inspired by the work of the psychologist J. J. Gibsons, DeNora expands the concept of *affordance* to the sociological study of culture. The idea is that material objects have certain properties that can be lent to some uses more easily than to others: they "afford" actors the possibility of performing certain actions with the object. The weight, size, and form of an artifact, for example, may "afford" actors the option of carrying it, rolling it, or breaking it—or proscribe those same possibilities.

In a related but different vein, Keane's theory of "bundling" proposes that an object's very materiality—that is, the specific aspects of its form (its weight and color, the materials of its composition, its relative malleability, permeability, mobility, and so on)—endows it with a life of its own and potentially allows it to acquire significations different from the abstract ones that social actors initially ascribed to it. Material things, he argues, "always combine an indefinite number of physical properties and qualities, whose particular juxtapositions may be mere happenstance. In any given practical or interpretative context, only some of those properties are relevant and come into play. But other properties persist, available for promotion as circumstances change" (Keane 2006, 200). The emphasis here is on the semiotic *potential* of an object at a given moment. While Durkheim and his intellectual descendants understood the totem, idol, or icon as sacred and powerful because it embodied and materialized collective representations, they neglected the materials that give shape to abstract collective ideals, viewing them as "nothing but a block of stone or a piece of wood, things which in themselves have no value."[22] In this volume, I consider icons in their multiple dimensions: as collective representations, as embodiments of ideals and narratives to which the icon gives material form, and as clusters of materials with their own manifold attributes, each of which affords (or constrains) social actors' repertories of potential actions, such that every act changes the icon's meaning, however slightly.

My sociological analysis of icons, then, takes into account semiotic, historical, and social dimensions of the relation between subject and object. It sees pictorial discourses as not merely descriptive or reflective of

22. Durkheim writes that "collective ideals can only be manifested and *become aware of themselves* by being concretely realized in material objects that can be seen by all, understood by all, and represented to all minds" (2010, 49–50, my emphasis). Society therefore projects ideals of its own creation onto an object—a totem, an idol, an icon—thereby becoming conscious of those very ideals made materially explicit.

national visions deployed by elites and consumed by the masses but as inscriptive, ultimately *productive*, of those very visions. It understands that icons have a life of their own and a material logic that potentially enables them to shape identities and transform society independently of the meaning initially attributed to them by actors, and independently even from the stated intentions (or lack thereof) of the actors using them (Keane 2003, 2006). As Robin Wagner-Pacifici (2010) insists, "It is only by gaining access to the operations and logics of the inner workings of cultural objects that any cultural sociology can begin to track the meanings and resonance of these objects in the social contexts in which they appear," arguing further that "such knowledge of aesthetic objects actually provides insight into the ways that these objects *model* social reality in their own turn" (109, emphasis mine). Wagner-Pacifici, like Alfred Gell and many proponents of the visual-material turn in the study of religion (cf. Promey 2014), focuses primarily on art objects. In this book, I extend the argument to symbols and icons deployed in social action. To that end I develop the concept of *aesthetic revolt*.

By *aesthetic revolt* I mean a dual process whereby social actors contest and rework iconic symbols in the public sphere. Through those material manipulations, symbols acquire significations that lead to the articulation of new identities and provide momentum for institutional reforms. One contribution of this work, then, is to provide a detailed empirical demonstration that symbols and icons are not merely derivative but themselves participate in the creation of the social, acting as catalysts for what Piotr Sztompka (1993) has called moments of "social becoming." It does not suffice to claim that context, content, form, and performance all "matter." The challenge is precisely to show the specific ways in which they are interrelated and interdependent, and to identify the fine chains of significations through which meaning is constituted and disseminated—chains that, once engaged, turn the wheels of change.

While the study of material religion is by now well established (e.g., McDannell 1995; Morgan 2005; Keane 2008; Stolow 2010; Promey 2014), moving the study of religious practice from the analysis of elites and ideals toward the study of everyday life, this important scholarly turn has not been reflected in the study of the politics of religion, which has remained infelicitously wedded to institutions, ideals, social movement theories, and statistical calculi of active membership. With few exceptions (e.g., Kertzer 1988), it is as though the politics of religion has remained in a separate realm. Another contribution of this book is therefore methodological, demonstrating how semiotic questions about materials are simultaneously social and political questions. Toward this end, I explore the politics of national identity in Québec through marches, parade floats, *tableaux vivants*, and the material construction and destruction of the images of saints. Such an approach attunes the reader to the oft-unnoticed role of aesthetics in the articulation of politics, nationalism, and religion.

Methods, Data, and Organization

This book is a cultural sociology of historical events. It seeks to interpret how political identities are transformed. It is organized in two parts. The first (chapters 1–3) focuses on the making and unmaking of French Canadianness; the second (chapters 4–6) investigates the making and debating of Québécois identity.[23]

National Icons, Performances, and Debates

In chapter 2, I discuss the construction of Catholic French Canadian identity in the mid-nineteenth century and its narrative elaboration, centering on the figure of St. John the Baptist. I then analyze the narrative's iconic embodiment in the saint by looking at his representations in popular iconography, and I examine the narrative's pictorial materialization and performance in nineteenth-century processions and twentieth-century parades.

Parades are a rich source of data because of their liminal character: these cyclical rites are at once ordinary and extraordinary, traditional and innovative, highly scripted and liable to improvisation. Parades are used both to enforce the existing political order—the military parade, for example—and to subvert it, as in the case of gay pride or Carnival parades. They are at once expressive and socially constructive. As I show in chapter 3, even parades devoted to the reinforcement of the status quo may be slowly taken over from within and without. They are thus not only collective representations but also shifters of collective representations. Moreover, as Susan Davis has noted, parades are both familiar and spectacular. This dualism made them an especially significant mode of expression in nineteenth-century American cities (1986, 3).

23. I draw here the broad outline of the book. A detailed discussion of methodology, specific sources, and different types of data used for individual chapters appears in appendix C.

Because of their aesthetic expressiveness and collective performance in public space, moreover, parades may evoke an emotional power that the simple literary formulation of ideas or values often lacks (see Durkheim [1912] 1995; Orsi [1985] 2010; Ryan 1989; Zubrzycki 2011). Finally, parades typically constitute an organized body taking up public space to "spell out a common identity" (Ryan 1989, 133). They served as important vectors and builders of collective identity in mid-twentieth century Yankee City (Warner 1959), just as gay pride parades in the 1970s institutionalized the collective memory of the 1969 Stonewall riots in New York City and gave a public face to groups which until then lived "underground" (Armstrong and Crage 2006). This performative cohesion does not mean, of course, that participants share a single common identity, but it does suggest a certain amount of consensus over what an ideal identity or way of life should be. As public performances, parades tend to be highly orchestrated, involving a large number of participants (sponsors, organizers, creators, choreographers, coordinators, actors, and marchers)—as well as a mass audience watching in the streets or listening at home to radio or television broadcasts that overlay the visual images and soundscape with commentaries that instruct the audience as to the narratives presented and the proper emotional responses to them. As such, the historian Mary Ryan claims, they "can tell us something of the historical process whereby cultural meaning is created" (1989, 133).

While a certain level of consensus is required to produce a parade, the very performance of that normative project is precisely what makes the parade the perfect platform for articulating protests. Davis (1986), Ryan (1989), Glassberg (1990), and Newman (1999) all show that by taking part in parades and street festivals, ordinary men and women have played a significant role in forging the political culture of the United States.[24] Parades (like protests), because they occur in the public sphere and occupy public places, serve as sites for contests over legitimacy. Geertz (1985) demonstrates that processions and parades, as displays of power, produce charisma and legitimate authority, while Hunt (1986) and Davis (1986) show that the opposite is also true: namely that such ritual events, when even slightly distorted, may be disruptive of political authority, that "they could

24. The literature on parades is especially rich regarding the Irish case because of the continued relevance of parades to the affirmation of national identity in Northern Ireland and the violent conflicts that those events both commemorate and often create (see Kenney 1991; Jarman 1997; Kirkland 2002; Ross 2007; Smithey 2011).

be political actions and rhetorical means by which performers attempted to accomplish practical and symbolic goals" (Davis 1986, 5).[25]

Parades are particularly significant in my analysis because they serve as the sites of both the performance and the subversion of an established national narrative embodied in the saint, providing the stage for the spectacular articulation of new secular national identity in the 1960s. Because St. John the Baptist embodied the dominant national vision, and the celebrations on his name day pictorially narrated that vision in elaborate allegorical floats and *tableaux vivants* moving through public space, the saint became the object of protests through which social actors and political contenders performed and ultimately transformed their national identity in the 1960s. The vehicle of these protests was the parade itself. The material form of the saint and of his core attributes fomented a debate about national identity and religion in the public sphere, and the altering of the physical aspect of the icon—its iconoclastic unmaking—was a turning point in the articulation of a new, secular national identity in Québec.

Thus national identity is fashioned and refashioned not only in and through official ideologies and institutional rearrangements, but also through aesthetic revolts. The first part of the book is based on a wide variety of archival data, including texts such as political speeches, religious sermons, hymns and songs, editorials, correspondence; and visual evidence such as designs for floats, photographs and amateur films of parades, ceremonial portraits, and photo reportage.

In the second part of *Beheading the Saint*, I tackle the aftermath of the dramatic end to the parade and the institutionalization of the new Québécois identity, still very much a work in progress. In chapter 4 I examine the making of the new Québécois nation through a reconfiguration of the St-Jean-Baptiste holiday as la Fête nationale. This analysis draws on a range of archival sources as well as on participant observation. Having grown up in Québec gives me a lived sense of the celebrations—both those that were exalted and those that fell flat.

In chapter 5 I turn my attention to the relationship between religious symbols, cultural patrimony, and secularism in an analysis of the debates over "reasonable accommodation" and the Charter of Values/Charter of

25. Abner Cohen (1993) refers to this type of politics, articulated in nonpolitical cultural forms, as "masquerade politics." Carnivals and parades fall under that category. Although I agree with Cohen that this cultural form is utterly political, I am uncomfortable with his formulation, as *masquerade* implies not only play and carnival but also deception.

Secularism proposed in 2013. I show the ghostly presence of Catholicism in Québec society.

A Word on Key Tropes

As this is a work of cultural and visual sociology, the reader will notice the importance of visual materials in the analysis. Few are merely illustrative; most are presented as evidence for the arguments I put forward. While the story I am telling unfolds historically, inserted between chapters are transtemporal essays around key tropes of French Canadian/Québécois national identity: anticolonialism and language, the family, the soil, the sheep, and the flag. These essays are based on exemplars found in visual arts, commercial and political ads, commemorative posters, parade floats, and newspaper caricatures as well as in poetry, theater, and popular songs. These key tropes provide analyses not only of fundamental elements of Québec society, but also of such elements that are considered by members of the national community to be "typical," "important," and "representative." Such tropes are recurrent motifs in public debates, political discourse, and cultural life. It is important to show how recurring—even canonical—stories about French Canadianness and Québécois-ness remain, evolve, are transformed, or are subverted. These examinations of key tropes, then, are more than interludes punctuating the book; they are part and parcel of my analysis of the formation and transformation of nationalism in Québec.

KEY TROPE *Anticolonialism and Language*

TROPE 1.1 Now or Never! Masters in our own House (Les Classiques des sciences sociales).

THE QUIET REVOLUTION WAS A DECADE OF INTENSE TRANSFORMATIONS often narrated within the framework of emancipation and development. A Parti libéral du Québec poster widely used during the 1962 provincial electoral campaign proclaimed that nationalizing the eleven private electrical companies was "the key to the kingdom." Nationalizing hydroelectric power was the way to strengthen Québec by making its population "masters in [their] own house." The takeover of hydroelectric power was a resounding victory for the Lesage government and the minister of national resources, René Lévesque, its much-admired engineer.

The clenched fist used on the poster was a common nationalist symbol, also used by leftist and radical Marxist groups, who envisioned the emancipation of Québec coming about through a takeover of capital from the hands of Anglo-Americans. *White Niggers of North America*, a book-length essay published by Pierre Vallières in 1968 and followed the same year by the powerful poem "Speak White," by Michèle Lalonde ([1970] 1974), linked the French Canadian plight to class struggles and colonial oppression: "From Saint-Henri to Santo Domingo . . . We know that liberty is a Black word / as misery is Black / as blood is muddied with the dust of Algiers or of Little Rock / . . . / We know now / that we are not alone."

Speak white[1]
it is so lovely to listen to you
speaking of *Paradise Lost*
or the anonymous, graceful profile trembling in the sonnets of
Shakespeare

We are a rude and stammering people
but we are not deaf to the genius of a language
speak with the accent of Milton and Byron and Shelley and Keats
speak white
and please excuse us if in return
we've only our rough ancestral songs
and the chagrin of Nelligan[2]

speak white
speak of places, this and that
speak to us of the Magna Carta
of the Lincoln Monument
of the cloudy charm of the Thames
or blossom-time on the Potomac
speak to us of your traditions
We are a people who are none too bright
but we are quick to sense
the great significance of *crumpets*
or the *Boston Tea Party*

1. Translated by D. G. Jones. Italics denote terms in English in the French-language original.

2. Émile Nelligan (1879–1941) is Québec's most admired Romantic poet. At the age of twenty he was confined to the Saint-Benoît asylum in Montréal, where he remained until his death in 1941.

But when you *really speak white*
when you *get down to brass tacks*
to speak of Better Homes and Gardens
and the high standard of living
and the Great Society
a little louder then *speak white*

raise your foremen's voices
we are a little hard of hearing
we live too close to the machines
and only hear our heavy breathing over the tools

speak white and loud
So we can hear you clearly
from Saint-Henri to Santo Domingo[3]
yes, what a marvelous language
for hiring and firing
for giving the orders
for fixing the hour to be worked to death
and that pause that refreshes
and bucks up the dollar

Speak white
tell us that God is a great big shot
and that we're paid to trust him
speak white
speak to us of production, profits and percentages
speak white
it's a rich language
for buying
but for selling oneself
but for selling one's soul
but for selling oneself

Ah
speak white

3. Saint-Henri was a poor working-class neighborhood of Montréal, inhabited by French Canadians, Irish, and Blacks.

big deal
but for telling about
the eternity of a day on strike
for telling the whole
life-story of a nation of caretakers
for coming back home in the evening
at the hour when the sun's gone bust in the alleys
for telling you yes the sun does set yes
every day of our lives to the east of your empires[4]
Nothing's as good as a language of oaths
our mode of expression none too clean
dirtied with oil and with axlegrease

Speak white
feel at home with your words
we are a bitter people
but we'd never reproach a soul
for having a monopoly
on how to improve one's speech

In the sweet tongue of Shakespeare
with the accent of Longfellow
speak a French purely and atrociously white
as in Viet Nam, in the Congo
speak impeccable German
a yellow star between your teeth
speak Russian speak of the right to rule speak of repression
speak white
it's a universal language
we were born to understand it
with its tear-gas phrases
with its billy-club words

speak white
Tell us again about freedom and democracy

4. "In the east of your empires" most likely refers to the ethnic divisions of Montréal: French Canadians lived in poor working-class neighborhoods on the east side, whereas the richer, English-speaking business elites lived on the west side.

We know that liberty is a Black word
as misery is Black
as blood is muddied with the dust of Algiers or of Little Rock

Speak white
from Westminster to Washington take turns
speak white as on Wall Street
white as in Watts
Be civilized
and understand our conventional answer
when you ask us politely
how do you do
and we mean to reply
we're doing all right
we're doing fine
we
are not alone

We know now
that we are not alone

As Lalonde writes, speaking white meant not merely speaking English—the language of business and power—but also speaking "correct" French:

We are a bitter people
but we'd never reproach a soul
for having a monopoly
on how to improve one's speech
. . .
speak a French purely and atrociously white
speak white
it's a universal language
we were born to understand it
with its tear-gas phrases
with its billy-club words.

Part of the overall emancipation of the Québécois, then, was also "linguistic liberation"—from English in the workplace and from tight symbolic violence against the French spoken in Québec. In 1968, Michel Tremblay's

TROPE 1.2 Bill 101. The bilingual stop sign became the symbol of the fight over Bill 101's clause on signage. Supporters of the bill routinely painted over part of the word "Stop" to transform the English word into "101" (photo: Agence Québec Presse, Pierre Roussel).

play *Les belles-soeurs* was presented in Montréal. It was the first time that *joual*—the working-class dialect of Montréal—was spoken in public, breaking an unspoken taboo and creating an uproar. Many artists soon followed suit.

Bill 101 (*Charte de la langue française*), passed in 1977, is perhaps the last attempt at linguistically decolonizing Québec. The centerpiece of Québec's language policy, it declares French the official language of Québec and guarantees "fundamental language rights," such as speaking French in the workplace and receiving services in French. Its two most controversial items concern education and signage. All children are to be educated in French, unless one parent was educated in English in Canada: children of immigrants, including English-speaking ones, must therefore send their children to French-language schools. Signage must also include French; on bilingual signs, the French version must be predominant.[5]

5. See *Charter of the French Language*, Éditeur officiel du Québec, http://www2.publicationsduquebec.gouv.qc.ca/dynamicSearch/telecharge.php?type=2&file=/C_11/C11_A.html, accessed June 23, 2015.

PART ONE *Making and Unmaking French Canadianness*

2 The Iconic Making of French Canadianness

A people, like a child, learns through its eyes.

—Father Alexandre Dugré

THE NATIONAL NARRATIVE IN QUÉBEC IS BUILT AROUND TRAUMAS, chief among them "the Conquest" (1759–63), when New France was lost to England. But it is also composed of stories of resilience: of survival against all odds, and of rebellion against authorities, from the English to the Catholic Church. This chapter aims to plot key narratives and core symbols as they are related to political, cultural, and structural factors in order to provide an overview of French Canadian nationalism before its transfiguration into Québécois, as well as to map out a set of historic landmarks with which to follow the story. It furnishes a context in which a specific vision of national identity, the ethno-religious vision of French Canadianness, was discursively articulated and visually represented. We will see why and how it flourished, becoming the dominant version of national identity from the mid-nineteenth century until the Quiet Revolution.

The first part of the chapter provides a broad outline of the colonial situation in the eighteenth and nineteenth centuries, and specifically analyzes the emergence of liberal nationalism in the Patriots' political project in the 1830s. The crushing of that movement and subsequent institutional rearrangements gave free rein to the Catholic Church to articulate a new vision of the nation, which I present in the second part of the chapter. That new national vision was given tangible form in the figure of St. John the Baptist. I analyze the rich discursive, visual, and material fields of representation, and the process of its becoming iconic in the third part of the chapter.

The Rise and Fall of Liberalism and Republican Nationalism

Before diving into the development of different forms of nationalism in what is now Québec, a few words on early colonial history will be helpful. Canada was "discovered" by Jacques Cartier in 1534. Québec City was founded in 1608 and Montréal in 1642. By the 1710s, the territories of New France extended from Newfoundland in the east to the Prairies in the west, and from Hudson Bay in the north to the Gulf of Mexico in the south. That vast territory was divided into four colonies with separate administrations: Canada, Acadia, Newfoundland, and Louisiana. Unlike the British colonies, Canada was sparsely populated by settlers and severely neglected by France.[1] Voltaire notoriously claimed in 1758 that Canada was merely "a few acres of snow," lacking the economic value that would make it worth investing in and defending against other colonial powers.[2] When the colony was lost to England as a result of the Seven Years' War (commonly referred to as the Conquest in Québec and Canadian historiography), the population established around the St. Lawrence Valley numbered approximately 70,000 (60,000 settlers and 10,000 Aboriginals).

After New France was officially ceded to Great Britain in the Treaty of Paris of 1763, the colony was renamed the Province of Québec. The French seigneurial system of land tenure was not recognized; neither was Catholicism or the ecclesiastic hierarchy. The introduction of the Test Oath, which required pledging allegiance to the British monarch, the head of the Anglican Church, effectively eliminated French Canadians from public office, since they were Catholic. The Quebec Act of 1774 reversed some of these restrictions in order to appease French Canadians and ensure the loyalty of the clergy and seigneurs when there were troubles in the thirteen American colonies. It confirmed the ownership rights of seig-

1. France devoted most of its colonial attention in the Americas to the Caribbean, which generated enormous wealth compared to Québec or Louisiana. As Paul Christopher Johnson summarizes, writing of Louisiana, the North American possession "was not itself particularly lucrative or productive, compared with the massively profitable sugar colonies of Guadaloupe, Martinique and above all Saint-Domingue, 'the pearl of the Antilles'" (2008, 152–53). This observation is equally true of Québec.

2. In French, "Vous savez que ces deux nations sont en guerre pour quelques arpents de neige vers le Canada, et qu'elles dépensent pour cette belle guerre beaucoup plus que tout le Canada ne vaut." The sentence appears in chapter 23 of Voltaire's novel *Candide* ([1758] 1957).

neurs, abolished the Test Oath and confirmed the use of French civil law (*code civil*) while maintaining English criminal law. In 1791, with the proclamation of the Act of Constitution, two separate provinces were created from the conquered territory: Lower Canada (roughly corresponding to the territory of modern Québec), overwhelmingly inhabited by the descendants of French settlers, and Upper Canada (modern Ontario), inhabited by descendants of French settlers, English colonizers, and newly arrived "Loyalists" who fled the United States after the Declaration of Independence in 1776.

The Civic Nationalism of *Les Patriotes*

The Conquest was felt as a humiliation and the British colonial rule experienced as unjust and exploitative. By the beginning of the 1800s, liberal middle-class elites, influenced by republican ideas from France and the United States, formed the Parti Canadien and then the Parti Patriote. Although most of the Patriotes and their leaders were French speakers, the movement was not constituted on a linguistic, cultural, or ethnic basis. There were prominent Scots and Englishmen among the Patriots' leadership. Instead, the arguments made for sovereignty were political, inspired by the ideals of the American Revolution and influenced by other national independence movements, such as those of Ireland and Poland, which the Patriots frequently referred to in speeches, pamphlets, and ceremonial toasts at meetings and banquets.

During the Patriots' first ceremonial gathering in 1834, on the occasion of the traditional St-Jean-Baptiste feast, twenty-five toasts were made. The first rendered homage "to the people, at the source of all legitimate authority," and the second to the legislative assembly. These were followed by toasts to leading Patriots; to Daniel O'Connell, the Irish insurrectionist; to victims of repressions; to David Hume and the liberals of the British Parliament; to the reformists of the English colonies; to the government of the United States; to General Lafayette (who was toasted in silence, since he had recently passed away); and to the freedom of the press and the newspaper *Le Canadien*, Québec City's Patriot daily (Sulte 1929, 40–41).[3]

3. This event, a banquet, was held on the feast day of St. Jean-Baptiste because that holiday had been a significant one since the beginning of the colony, as we shall soon see. It was the first banquet of many and is now retrospectively claimed to be the founding moment of the Société Saint-Jean-Baptiste, a nationalist organization officially created in Québec City in 1842, but with chapters all over North America, wherever French Canadians lived in sufficient numbers. Today's Montréal chapter of the Société Saint-Jean-Baptiste (SSJBM), a sovereignist organization, traces its his-

The Patriots called themselves *fils de la liberté*, a literal translation of the American Sons of Liberty, and they designed a flag for the republic they fought to establish. It was inspired by the French tricolor, with green, white, and red horizontal lines, and often also adorned with indigenous Canadian symbols like the beaver, the maple leaf, and, less often, the muskellunge fish (see figure 2.1).

In 1834, the Patriots presented a list of grievances and demands, known as the 92 Resolutions, to the colonial authorities. The 92 Resolutions consisted of a series of demands for political reforms, including the application of the elective principle to the political institutions of the province and the requirement that the budget be controlled by the assembly. The requests were ignored for three years and then, in 1837, dismissed by the British colonial secretary. Increased immigration, a cholera epidemic, economic insecurity, and general anticolonial feelings fueled the movement and widened its appeal among liberal laypeople and peasants alike.[4] By 1837, the Patriots were able to mobilize local populations and organized a series of armed insurrections that were violently suppressed by the British. Villages and harvests were burned in retribution, more than 1,500 rebels were imprisoned, hundreds were condemned to death, and many more were deported and later executed.

Several liberals, including the Patriot leaders Louis-Joseph Papineau and Robert Nelson, fled to the United States. It was in Vermont that Nelson drafted, in French, the declaration of independence of Lower Canada in February 1838. It declared the people of Lower Canada absolved from all allegiance to Great Britain and dissolved the political bonds between the two entities. It proclaimed Lower Canada as a republic in which "all persons shall enjoy the same rights," including "the Indians [who] shall no longer be under any civil disqualification." It abolished the seigniorial sys-

---

tory directly back to the republican and secessionist movement of the Patriots and to that initial 1834 gathering, even though the organization actually became very close to the Catholic Church after the crushing of the rebellions, remaining so until the end of the Quiet Revolution.

4. By peasants I mean small farmers, known in French as *habitants* (and later as *agriculteurs*), farming the land along the St. Lawrence River. The term also referred to the people more generally. It is estimated that in 1851, 70% of the population of Québec were small farmers, overwhelmingly engaged in subsistence farming (Greer 1993). For a history of the rebellion, see Bernard (1983) and Greer (1993); for an analysis of the movement and its ideology within the context of rising national movements of emancipation in the Americas and Europe, see Bellavance (2000, 2004) and Harvey (2005). On liberalism, nationalism, and anticlericalism more broadly, see Bernard (1971).

FIGURE 2.1 Charles Alexander, *L'assemblée des six comtés à Saint-Charles-sur-Richelieu, en 1837*, 1891, Oil on canvas, 300 cm x 690 cm. Collection Musée National des Beaux-Arts du Québec, Acc. no. 1937.54. Photo: MNBAQ, Jean-Guy Kérouac.

This painting depicts a key assembly of the Patriote movement, held on October 23–24, 1837, in defiance of a government ban on public assemblies. Leaders protested British colonial rule: some called for the boycott of British products, while others called for an armed insurrection. The assembly adopted important resolutions—it proclaimed human rights, refused to recognize the new Executive Council of Lower Canada, and approved the Société des Fils de la Liberté. The Catholic Church condemned the assembly, and the authorities issued warrants for the leaders' arrest three weeks later. The rebellions started shortly thereafter. In the painting, the figure addressing the crowd from the stage is Louis-Joseph Papineau, leader of the Patriotes. The Patriot flag is flown by members of the crowd. Influenced by the French tricolor, it is said to represent the Irish (green), French (white), and English (red) of Lower Canada. The French and American flags, representing two revolutionary movements that greatly influenced the Patriots, appear in the lower right corner.

tem of land tenure, "as if such tenure had never existed in Canada," and declared all Crown lands as well as so-called Clergy Reserves (land used for the support of Church of England clergy as stipulated in the Constitutional Act of 1791), to be the property of the state of Lower Canada. It further specified that both the "French and English languages shall be used in all public affairs." The *nation canadienne*, as it was ideally conceived and presented, was thus constituted by all citizens of Lower Canada, regardless of faith, language, ethnicity, or race, explicitly including Aboriginals.

The Patriots and the rebellions they led constitute what comes closest, in Canada, to what Benedict Anderson ([1983] 1991) has called "creole nationalism," a movement for the emancipation of a colony from a European empire.[5] What distinguishes the case of Canada from anticolonial rebellions of the United States or Latin America—besides the failure to achieve independence—is that the Patriots sought the emancipation of Lower Canada not from its former metropole, France, but from its new imperial ruler, Great Britain. With the crushing of the rebellions, the republican agenda soon receded in the background, and a different national ideology was articulated and given flesh to.

Political Marginalization and Cultural Survival

The Patriots' declaration of independence had no political traction, and even its symbolic significance is only marginal to the narrative of Québécois nationalism. What *did* remain in the historical consciousness was the humiliation caused by the so-called Durham Report, named after the British envoy sent to investigate the causes of the rebellions and issue recommendations. In his infamous 1839 report to the British authorities, John George Lambton, the first Earl of Durham,[6] recommended the decisive assimilation of French Canadians, a process that he believed could

5. What Anderson called Creoles were American-born Europeans, who, simply by reason of their place of birth, had fewer rights and opportunities than their European-born counterparts. They typically came from the middle classes and small bourgeoisie and were educated professionals such as lawyers, doctors, and small merchants whose professional and economic advancement was stalled by the colonial situation. This description fits the profiles of many Patriot leaders and supporters.

6. John George Lambton (1792–1840), commonly referred to in Canadian historiography by his noble title, was a Whig statesman, colonial administrator, governor general, and high commissioner of British North America. He is lauded in English Canadian history for his recommendation to introduce responsible government but denounced in French Canadian and Québécois historiography for claiming that "there can hardly be conceived a nationality more destitute of all that can invigorate and elevate a people than that which is exhibited by the descendants of the French in

best be achieved through their political marginalization.[7] To achieve this, Durham proposed merging Upper Canada and Lower Canada. According to his calculations, "If the [English] population of Upper Canada is rightly estimated at 400,000, the English inhabitants of Lower Canada at 150,000, and the French at 450,000, the union of the two Provinces would not only give a clear English majority, but one which would be increased every year by the influence of English emigration; and I have little doubt that the French, when once placed, by the legitimate course of events and the working of natural causes, in a minority, would abandon their vain hope of nationality" (Durham 1839, 307).

Turning French speakers into a minority of the new polity offered a pragmatic solution to the impasse in which the colony found itself. In the wake of the rebellions and their brutal suppression, Durham observed, "Never again will the present generation of French Canadians yield a loyal submission to a British government; never again will the English population tolerate the authority of a House of Assembly in which the French shall possess or even approximate to a majority" (53). According to Durham, the numerical marginalization of the Canadiens would provide a strong incentive for them to willingly assimilate linguistically and culturally to the new majority group. For Durham, and from the British perspective more broadly, this strategy would benefit not only the colony but also the French Canadians themselves. Following the principles of social Darwinism (see Hobsbawm [1992] 1995, 24–45), Durham saw the French Canadians' situation as one of "hopeless inferiority." Only assimilation into the English could raise them up: "It is to elevate them from that inferiority that I desire to give to the [French] Canadians our English character. . . . [T]he great mass of the French Canadians are doomed, in some measure, to occupy an inferior position, and to be dependent on the English for employment. The evils of poverty and dependence would merely be aggravated in a ten-fold degree, by a spirit of jealous and resentful nationality, which should separate the working class of the community from the possessors of wealth and employers of labour" (292–93). Assimilation would also protect against the risk of further rebellions, a risk that would be increased if ethno-national feelings were exacerbated by socioeconomic inferiority.

Lower Canada, owing to their retaining their peculiar language and manners. They are a people with no history, and no literature" (Durham 1839, 294).

7. Durham also recommended that freedoms accorded to French Canadians in the Quebec Act (1774) and the Constitutional Act (1791) be abolished to discourage future insurrections. That specific recommendation was ignored.

As a result, in 1840–41, the Act of Union joined Upper and Lower Canada into a single polity—the United Province of Canada, also known as "the Canadas." As a numerical minority in the new polity, French Canadians were thus rendered politically impotent. Their numerical inferiority did not, however, have the effects expected by Lord Durham. Rather than assimilate in order to "elevate" themselves and improve their lot, the Canadiens instead resisted assimilation by reorienting their national vision away from political independence and toward a project of cultural survival. Assimilation was to be resisted through the preservation of French language and Catholicism, aided by population growth through French Canadians' high fertility rates and the glorification of large families, the so-called revenge of the cradle.[8]

Seen in hindsight and from afar, it is now clear that the repression of the Patriots' rebellions stifled an emergent civic definition of the Canadian nation and led to the development of an ethno-religious vision of the *French* Canadian nation instead. Indeed, it was during that period that the adjective *français* was added to the noun *Canadiens*. It is generally accepted that this addition was not only the result of a desire to distinguish their society from that of the British, who following the 1840 Act of Union began to call themselves Canadians: it was also an explicit ideological ethnicization of the nation, promoted by the same Catholic Church that had fiercely opposed the liberal project of the Patriots (see Gagné 2007). The Church vehemently opposed the civic vision of the nation advanced by the Patriots and even considered the latter as "enemies of the Church." After the Patriots' defeat, the Church promoted the term *Canadien français* to neutralize what it perceived as a subversive political identity and to reorient national identity along *cultural* lines instead.

The failure of the rebellions was a pivotal event in the history of Québec and Canada. The most obvious and direct consequences were that the colony remained within the British Empire. But it also had significant consequences for the structure of dominance in Canada and in the insti-

8. See the section "Key Trope: The Family" for examples of the emphasis on large families as the salvation of the nation. The synthetic fertility index shows that in 1871, married French Canadian women in Québec had on average 9.7 children each (Gauvreau and Gossage 2000, 44). As Linteau et al. note (1983, 22), to reach such high averages, families with fifteen and even twenty children had to be commonplace. Anecdotal evidence as well as memoirs and novels suggest as much. The synthetic fertility index remained very high into the 1920s, at about 8.2 children per woman. As a result of the depression, however, the rate in 1931 dropped to 6.6, still surprisingly high. With the Quiet Revolution of the 1960s, fertility dropped drastically.

tutional support (or lack of it) for specific ideologies, as the following section discusses.

Clerical Nationalism and National Mythology

One important consequence of the failure of the Patriots' rebellions in 1837–38 was the successful establishment of the Catholic discourse of the French Canadian nation. The post-rebellion political landscape was especially beneficial to the Church, as the Catholic hierarchy in Lower Canada had vehemently condemned the Patriots' liberalism and revolutionary impulses. With bounties on their heads, the surviving rebellion leaders went into hiding or escaped to the United States, and the republican project faded from the political agenda and the public sphere.

The crushing of the rebellions not only purged the country of "dangerous elements" but also effectively placed the Church at the center of civil society. The Church now had ample room and an array of institutional tools to disseminate its own program and vision of society. Still, the Church could not hold power on its own, any more than the British could. The two therefore slowly forged a marriage of convenience. The defeat of the governing liberal bourgeoisie thus resulted in an ideological and institutional vacuum which the clergy, aided by British authorities, energetically filled. Education, health, and welfare were slowly but solidly confessionalized, turning the Church in French Canada into a "crypto-state" until the creation of the provincial welfare state in the 1960s (Ferretti 1999).

The Catholic Church was now positioned as the institution best able to create, sustain, and disseminate a national project. Unlike that of the Patriots, the Church's project was devoid of overtly political content; instead it was defined in ethno-religious terms centered on the idea of *survivance*, or cultural survival (see Dumont 1971; Lamonde 2000; Mann 1988).

The Discursive and Visual Construction of French Canadianness

To sustain its national vision, the Church built a retrospective messianic narrative of French Canadians' historical destiny in North America. That messianic narrative gradually elevated St. John the Baptist to be its figurehead, drawing parallels between biblical accounts of his life and French Canadian history. According to the Christian Bible, John the Baptist was Jesus's cousin, born roughly six months before him to Mary's previously barren cousin, Elizabeth. John's special bond with Jesus was evident even prenatally: he is said in Luke 1:39–56 to have "leapt for joy" in his mother's

FIGURE 2.2 Leonardo da Vinci, *Saint John the Baptist* (1513–16). In what is believed to be da Vinci's last painting, John has long, curly hair, is dressed in pelts, and holds a reed cross in his left hand while his right index points toward the heavens (and toward the apparent source of light in the painting). Several other painters imitated da Vinci's depiction, and the pointing gesture has become one of the defining features in representations of the saint (Musée du Louvre).

womb on hearing Mary's greeting. His miraculous conception foretold that of Jesus, whom John later baptized in the Jordan River. His mission was to herald the New Age and announce the coming of the Messiah. As told in John 1:23, the saint, called the precursor in the Catholic tradition, proclaimed: "I am the voice of one crying out in the wilderness, 'Make

FIGURE 2.3 Titian, *Saint John the Baptist* (ca.1540). A slightly older saint, fully bearded, points toward the heavens with his right hand, holding a cross-shaped staff in his left. A lamb is at his feet, and a creek flows nearby, a common symbol of his role as the Baptist (Gallerie dell'Accademia, Venice, Italy).

straight the way of the Lord.'" He is also said to have declared: "Behold the Lamb of God, who takes away the sin of the world!" Thus St. John is often depicted with a lamb at his side.[9]

9. The Christian use of the lamb as a symbol originates from the Hebrew tradition. To protect Jews from the tenth plague visited by God on the Egyptians—the

As recounted in Matthew 14, John was beheaded by King Herod when Herod's stepdaughter, Salomé, asked him to "give [her] the head of John the Baptist here on a platter." The saint's decollation is the most vivid image from his life, but devotional iconography also depicts him in a dramatic pose with right arm lifted, index finger pointed at the heavens, in the declarative gesture announcing the coming of Christ (figures 2.2 and 2.3). This pose was popular in French Canadian depictions of the saint (figures 2.4–2.6).

In nineteenth-century discourses of Catholic clergy in Lower Canada, St. John the Baptist's mission was equated with that of the French in the New World. Just as the precursor heralded the coming of Christ and baptized him, setting him on his way to redeem a corrupted world, in the Church's narrative the French had discovered Canada and brought civilization and Christianity to the pagan Natives they evangelized, creating a providential country in a New World. Like the precursor, they prepared the way, clearing dense forests to create fields where the new truth would be planted and thrive. Like the saint, the French Canadian people claimed a privileged relationship with Christ; they were a chosen people (see Smith 2003).

The original, French-language version of what much later became the national anthem "O Canada" was initially composed as a religious-patriotic hymn for the 1880 North American Congrès national des Canadiens-Français on St-Jean-Baptiste Day (Chouinard 1881). It is a powerful expression of the French-Catholic mission in the Americas:

> O Canada! Land of our forefathers
> Thy brow is wreathed with a glorious garland of flowers
> As in thy arm ready to wield the sword
> So also is it ready to carry the cross
> Thy history is an epic of the most brilliant exploits
> Thy valor steeped in faith
> Will protect our homes and our rights

---

death of their firstborn sons—Moses instructed the Jews to sacrifice lambs and mark their doors with the animals' blood so that the Angel of Death would pass over their houses. This event was commemorated with the feast of Passover. The Last Supper that Jesus celebrated with his disciples was on Passover. His crucifixion positioned him as the sacrifice, *agnus Dei*, the lamb of God. In the French Canadian narrative, the symbol of the lamb further signified civilization through the progress of the Christian missions.

Under the gaze of God, next to the giant river
The Canadien grows up hopeful
He is born of a proud race[10]
Blessed was his cradle
His mission in this new world
Was written in the Heavens
Always guided by His light
He shall keep the honor of his flag

From his patron, Precursor of the true God
He wears the aura of fire
Enemy of tyranny
But full of loyalty
He desires to remain in harmony
His proud liberty
By the effort of his genius
On our land he establishes truth

Sacred love for the throne and the altar
Fill our heart with Your immortal breath
Among the foreign races
Our faith guides us
Let us be a people of brothers
Under the yoke of law
And let us repeat like our fathers
The cry of victory, "For Christ and for King."[11]

10. In the nineteenth century, the term *race* in French and English denotes what today we would call ethno-nationality.

11. The first verse is the official translation of the French original; the translation of the remaining three verses is my own. The lyrics are by Judge Adolphe-Basile Routhier and the music by Calixa Lavallée, a popular composer of the period. The hymn was proclaimed Canada's national anthem on July 1, 1980—100 years after its creation. (Until then, Canada's official anthem was "God Save the Queen.") There have been some twenty English versions of "O Canada" since its popularization in English Canada in the twentieth century. The contemporary official English lyrics are based on a version written in 1908 by Mr. Justice Robert Stanley Weir on the occasion of Québec City's 300th anniversary, which was only slightly altered in 1968. The original French lyrics have been retained. French- and English-speaking Canadians therefore learn and sing very different national anthems. For a history of the anthem, see Canadian Heritage, "National Anthem: O Canada," http://pch.gc.ca/eng/1359402373291/1359402467746, accessed January 20, 2016.

FIGURE 2.4 Prayer card, ca. 1921. St. Jean-Baptiste, a lamb at his feet, is shown holding a tall cross and in his traditional pose, pointing his index finger to the sky as a sign of Christ's coming. The conspicuous Sacred Heart flag, the predecessor of Québec's current flag, the wreath of maple leaves on the ground, and the wide St. Lawrence River in the background make the representation uniquely French Canadian. The inscription reads: "Saint Jean-Baptiste, Precursor of the Messiah, Patron of the French Canadians, pray for us!"

Prayer cards were important devotional objects in daily life. They were given, like today's greeting cards, to mark first communions, graduations, weddings, entry into holy orders, retirement, and other significant life events. They were often offered as get-well wishes, with specific saints invoked to remedy different ills or problems. Prayer cards were also obtained by individuals to signal their personal devotion to the saint for whom they were named, to invoke specific kinds of divine help, and as souvenirs from pilgrimage sites. They were small enough to be carried in a missal, wallet, or purse, and were sometimes signed by the giver. On the import of visual and material culture in Christianity, see Miles (1985) and McDannell (1995) (Archives de folklore de l'Université Laval, Fonds Larouche-Villeneuve, F716 [HF 143–5], Université Laval, Division de la Gestion des Documents Administratifs et des Archives).

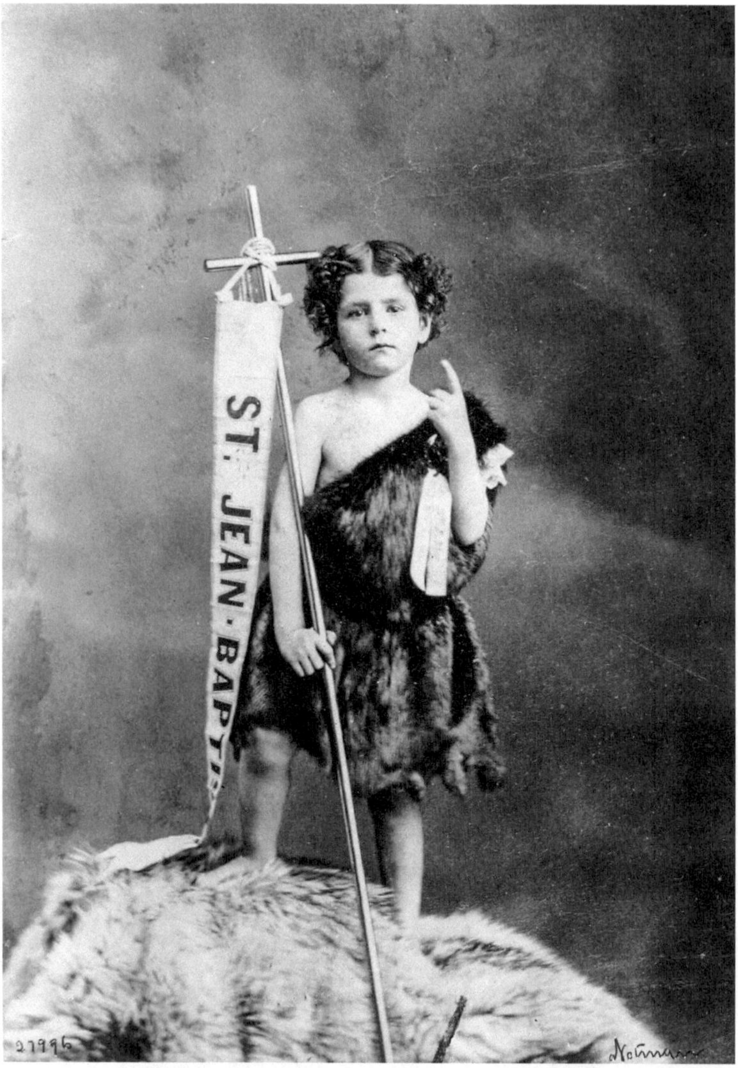

FIGURE 2.5 Religious iconography often depicts Saint John the Baptist as a child, especially in French Canada. The selection of the boy who would represent the saint during the Montréal parade was always a grand affair, and in the late 1800s, the lucky one was photographed in his costume by the famous William Notman. Note that the child in this photograph is lifting his left finger instead of the right. This seems to be due to Notman's desire for a better composition with this specific model. Other archival photos from the same session show the child holding the staff and pointing toward the heavens with the right hand, crowding the left side of the image. Instead of asking the child to move the staff to his left hand to free the right hand, the artist depicted the child gesturing with the left. As a Protestant, Notman is unlikely to have been aware of specific details of Catholic imagery (I-27996.1, Photograph, Saint Jean-Baptiste, Montréal, QC, 1867. © Musée McCord.).

FIGURE 2.6 In this nineteenth-century engraving by John Henry Walker, Saint John the Baptist is definitively linked with French Canada by the key symbols of the beaver and the maple leaf. When English Canadians adopted these as their own emblems, French Canadians increasingly substituted the *fleur de lys*, which highlighted the cultural connection to France and retreated from an initial "creole" or indigenous national identity (see Bizier and Paulette 1997). Note here that the saint is again depicted with the left index finger pointed toward the sky (instead of the right). Walker often produced engravings from Notman's photographs and is likely to have been inspired by the image shown in figure 2.5 (M930.51.1.83.1. Engraving, Saint Jean-Baptiste, © Musée McCord.).

"O Canada" was thus initially a hymn defining the identity of the Canadiens in ethnic and religious terms. It extols a proud "race" blessed and guided by its faith, whose divine mission is accomplished by the sword and the cross.

The hymn also emphatically recognized the (British) secular power and rejoiced in the political status quo: the Canadiens are "enem[ies] of tyranny but full of loyalty" who share a "sacred love for the throne and the altar" and are loyal to both "Christ and King." The new colonial regime shielded the Church from the dangers threatened by the French Revolution and, closer to home, repressed the Patriots' rebellions. In exchange, the British expected the Canadiens' loyalty to the Crown, which the Church labored diligently to foster. Much later, during the Quiet Revolution, the Church would be fiercely criticized for this quid pro quo.

Clerical Nationalism

The long nineteenth century (1837–1959) was the apex of ultramontanism in French Canada. Ultramontanism is a religious doctrine that claims the superiority of papal authority over local temporal and spiritual hierarchies. It rejects the separation of church and state and argues for the primacy of religion over politics. (The name comes from the Latin *ultra montes*, "beyond the mountains," which in France—where the movement originated—meant beyond the Alps, alluding to the pope in Rome.) Many French ultramontane clerics found refuge in Québec during and shortly after the French Revolution, as well as after the revolutions of 1830 and 1848. Many conservative clerics also came to Québec after the establishment of state secularism in France in 1905. In Québec, ultramontanism manifested itself primarily as an insistence on church control over education and its dominance in social and political life. Ultramontane (or clerical) nationalism was a vision promoting a church-dominated nation.

The French Canadian people, in the Church's narrative, were an "apostolic people," chosen and entrusted with a providential mission supported by the "twin pillars of faith and language," according to Jules-Paul Tardivel, a leading ultramontane nationalist.[12] Those twin pillars were the par-

12. Tardivel 1881, in Jewsiewicki (1995, 233). Tardivel extolled the virtue of a rural, agricultural, hierarchical society controlled by the Roman Catholic Church. On ultramontanism in Québec, see Eid (1978). Although the nineteenth century was dominated by that type of nationalism, other ideological currents and political movements existed as well, most notably the Rouges, heirs of the Patriots. For a discussion of liberalism, nationalism, and anticlericalism after the Patriots' defeat, and the various tendencies and factions within that liberal left, see Bernard (1971).

allel supports of the national mission. The French language and Catholicism distinguished and ultimately protected French Canadians from "foreign races" on the continent. The proscription against marrying outside the Catholic faith helped guard against linguistic assimilation.[13] Religion, language, and ethnicity became increasingly fused and mutually reinforcing, resulting in the creation of a national identity. This was articulated in a coherent messianic narrative and represented in the evocative figure of St. John the Baptist (figure 2.7).

The French Canadian mission was also articulated in opposition to Anglo-Saxon Protestantism and its corrosive values of materialism and individualism. In the words of the influential Mgr. Louis-Adolphe Pâquet, the archconservative founding member of the daily *L'Action Catholique*, on the occasion of the St-Jean-Baptiste celebrations:

> Our religious and civilizing mission is the special vocation of the French race in [North] America. We are not merely a civilized race, we are pioneers of civilization; we are not merely a religious people, we are messengers of the religious idea; we are not merely the submissive sons of the Church, we are among its zealots, its defenders, its apostles. Our mission is not to manipulate capital, but rather to assemble ideas; it consists not in lighting the fires of industries but in feeding and radiating the luminous fire of religion and thought. Let us leave to other nations, less idealistic, this feverish mercantilism and this vulgar naturalism that attach them to matter. We strive for doctrinal and evangelical honor.[14]

The same sentiments were succinctly captured in a popular proverb: "Church steeples will always be higher than factory chimneys." The archbishop of Québec City, Mgr. Bégin, made a similar argument in a pastoral letter penned on the occasion of Québec City's 300th anniversary, opposing ambition to virtue and defining French Canadians' national character in religious terms. He used Samuel de Champlain, who founded Québec City in 1608, as exemplar: "It is not to some adventurer, to a business man seeking fortune nor to a warrior or a fine diplomat that Providence

13. The enforcement of that religious rule actually promoted the assimilation of some non-French-speaking Catholics into the French Canadian community, notably the Irish.

14. *La vocation de la race française en Amérique: Sermon prononcé le 23 juin 1902 à Québec*. Bibliothèque électronique du Québec, http://beq.ebooksgratuits.com/pdf/Paquet-vocation.pdf, accessed June 15, 2015.

FIGURE 2.7 "Thinking of the Divine Mission." Prayer card, date unknown. Saint John the Baptist is represented here as a prepubescent boy. The card's verso carries the traditional prayer addressed to the saint:

O Saint John the Baptist, illustrious precursor of the Messiah, whom the Savior has proclaimed the greatest among the children of men, and whom our Holy Father Pope Pius X has named patron saint of the French Canadians, you have wonderfully prepared, through your austere life, penitent and angelic, the way for the reign of the Sacrificial Lamb. We beseech you, obtain for us the grace of walking in your glorious footsteps, to conserve our forefathers' faith, to zealously defend the interests of the Holy Catholic Church, and to realize Divine Providence's designs for each of us so that after the exile of this life we can dwell in the celestial homeland to sing the praises of all peoples' eternal King, century after century. Amen. Imprimatur: 29 April 1921. L.-N. card. Bégin, arch. de Québec ("La Pensée de la mission divine. Saint Jean-Baptiste, patron des Canadiens français," Archives de folklore de l'Université Laval, Fonds Larouche-Villeneuve, F716 [HFL/04.01–5], Université Laval, Division de la gestion des documents administratifs et des archives).

gave the mission to build . . . the foundations of New France's first city, but to a citizen of irreproachable mores, profoundly Christian in his spirit and lifestyle, for whom to be French was to be Catholic and to be Catholic was to be a better Frenchman" (Mgr. Bégin 1908, 221).

The French Canadians' mission was not only to be disseminated through ideas but also yoked to arduous yet noble agricultural labor—both the image and the practice of it. Canadiens, like their patron saint, were to renounce the luxuries of city life and the lure of industry for a simple but enlightened life on the land. According to a pamphlet popular at the turn of the century, "The instruments of French Canadian destiny" were "the cross, the sword, and the plow" (Thibault [1884] 1905).[15]

Locating heavenly virtue in the simple act of tilling the soil had obvious consequences for French Canadian Catholics. In practical terms, it meant that industrial and economic development were left to Anglo-Protestants. At the turn of the century, the population of Québec was still primarily rural (Linteau 1999, 97), and data from the 1931 census show the long-term effects of that way of life.[16] Among those who owned large enterprises, only 10.6% were French Canadians, although they constituted 75% of the active population at the time. Of the small proportion (8.9%) of French Canadians involved in commerce, more than two-thirds were involved in retail, as small grocers and shopkeepers, whereas just over one in ten "English" engaged in commercial activity focused on retail; the rest concentrated on wholesale. In addition, the English, who represented 17.4% of the active working population over 10 years of age, owned, managed, or directed almost two-thirds of enterprises involved in storage and wholesale (63.5%), as well as half of those in insurance (50.2%), electrical power (55.2%), and finance (45.5%). Finally, only 4.2% of the French Canadian workforce were office clerks, whereas 16.2% of Anglo-Protestants and 11.4% of Jews occupied clerical positions. To quote Everett C. Hughes' Chicago School classic study of a mid-size town in Québec in the early 1940s: "The French constitute a large majority of all persons employed in industry. In the ranks of labor they predominate most strongly. They thin out as

15. Charles Thibault, a lawyer, was speaking at the 1884 St-Jean-Baptiste celebrations. The allocution became canonical and was widely disseminated in pamphlet form as well as in school textbooks in the first half of the twentieth century. On ultramontanism and clerical nationalism in Québec, see Eid (1978).

16. Data in this section were compiled from the 1931 census by the economist François-Albert Angers and published in 1939 in the now-classic study *La position économique des Canadiens français dans le Québec* (Montréal: École des Hautes Études Commerciales, Université de Montréal).

one goes from the shop to the office, and eventually disappear as one goes up the authority scale" ([1943] 2009, 46).

This last fact is certainly the result of French Canadians' lower levels of education, a situation that prevailed until the Quiet Revolution and the creation of the Ministry of Education.[17] In its messianic vision of history and nation, the Church did not explicitly seek to justify poverty. Nevertheless, by recognizing only certain forms of productive labor as consistent with Catholic virtue, and by promoting a life outlook focused on humility and acceptance of one's fate, it effectively endorsed the relatively poor status of its constituents.

The new nationalists of the 1960s would later hold the Church accountable for its insistence on agriculture as the only legitimate work, and for keeping French Canadians from dreaming big. They denounced the Church as both the past cause of and the present hindrance to the project of *rattrapage*, the "catching up" or modernization that was so urgently needed. Their criticism was not unfounded.

St-Jean-Baptiste Day as Ethno-National Holiday

In agrarian societies, seasonal festivals typically occupy an important place. The feast of St. John the Baptist is one such festival. In the Catholic calendar, the feast day of St. John the Baptist is June 24. It coincides with the summer solstice, long celebrated by pagans as the feast of light. The syncretic fusion of the two celebrations of light and enlightenment has proved both resilient and compelling. From Europe to Latin America, predominantly Catholic societies celebrate St. John the Baptist's feast day with bonfires and fireworks. The feast is especially popular in agrarian societies and rural communities as the day officially signals the beginning of summer, and because it also marks the onset of the season of hard labor, providing the last occasion for collective celebration until harvest.[18]

In French Canada, bonfires occupied a central place in the celebration as early as the seventeenth century. On the eve of the holiday, a large bon-

17. In 1958, for example, only 13% of Francophones completed 11th grade, while almost three times as many Anglophones did (Corbo 2002, 16).

18. Vloberg 1942; Vaultier 1946; Van Gennep 1949; Guss 2000; Provencher 1982, 194–98; Desdouits 1987; Boisvert 1990. David M. Guss (2000) points out that the meanings attached to St. John the Baptist and the feasts associated with his birthday made the saint easily transportable to the New World. Throughout Latin America, San Juan Bautista and his festivals were adapted to specific populations, including indigenous peoples.

fire (*feu de joie*) was blessed by the parish priest and lit by the local official.[19] The night was spent dancing around the fire. According to tradition, girls who managed to jump over the fire would be married within the year. The feast day also celebrated the special powers of water. The morning dew was carefully collected, as it was considered to have healing power, and June 24th was the first day of summer when immersion in rivers and lakes was allowed and deemed safe.[20] Entire families would swim that day, sometimes leading their domestic animals and cattle to the water as well, an activity followed by large picnics (Desdouits 1987, 151). These celebrations were not widely politicized until the early 1840s, when the feast was invested with the Church's new religious-national ideology. Thereafter, it was built up not only as a seasonal and Catholic event but also as the feast of the French Canadians, an ethno-national holiday.

Among the many public functions orchestrated by the Catholic Church, the festivals of St. John the Baptist were among the most popular. From the mid-nineteenth century on, they provided occasions for sermons, political speeches, nationalist manifestos, and popular assemblies promoting a distinct vision of French Canadianness. The days surrounding June 24th provided opportunities for heightened and condensed national(ist) activity.[21] In addition to bonfires, the observations on the eve of the festival included the ringing of the Jean-Baptiste bell, one of the largest church bells in North America.[22] In the second half of the nineteenth century, the saint's day was marked by the celebration of a high mass at the Notre Dame Cathedral in Montréal. The mass was preceded by a large procession and followed by picnics for the crowds and elaborate banquets for the elites. Streets and houses were decorated with religious banners and

19. The earliest mention of bonfires is made in 1646 in *Les relations des Jésuites*. Here is an account of that year's celebrations: "The bonfire was set at 8:30 pm on the 23rd. The Governor lit it was while I was singing *Ut queant laxis* . . . 5 cannonballs were shot, along with 2–3 shots of musket."

20. To this day, June 24th is the traditional opening day for outdoor municipal swimming pools in Québec.

21. This section is based on ephemera such as commemorative programs, as well as secondary sources such as master's and doctoral theses (Boisvert 1990; Guay 1973). Published primary sources include Chouinard (1881, 1890), Lemay (1898), Dugré (1923), Morin (1924), Société Saint-Jean-Baptiste (1926), Sulte (1929), Asselin (2002 [1913]). For analyses of the St-Jean-Baptiste celebrations and the SSJBM, see Blain (1964), Mathieu (1969), Giguère (1975), Rumilly (1975), Reid (1980), Turcotte (1987).

22. The Jean-Baptiste bell, or *Gros Bourdon*, was installed in the western bell tower of Notre-Dame Cathedral in 1843. It weighs twelve tons and requires twelve men to pull on its ropes.

FIGURE 2.8 Illustration of the St-Jean-Baptiste procession in Montréal, *L'Opinion publique*, 1874. "La grande fête nationale des 24–25 juin 1874 à Montréal. La procession passant dans la Rue St-Jacques." Note the presence of the American flag, carried by a representative of French Canadians living in the United States (M979.87.15A. © Musée McCord.).

flags, and sermons and political speeches inevitably touched on patriotic and messianic themes.

In certain years the St-Jean-Baptiste celebrations were the occasions for special congresses organized and sponsored by local chapters of the Société Saint-Jean-Baptiste, gathering representatives and members from across the entire French Canadian diaspora of North America (figure 2.8). In addition to solidifying bonds with the mother country through commemorations and feasts, the congresses served as forums where leaders discussed current issues and problems faced by various communities of French Canadians. They also provided occasions for fund-raising for a variety of French Canadian causes, such as support to French-language schools outside Québec or financial assistance to those in need and later also for blood collection for French Canadian hospitals.

Although Montréal and Québec City were the centers of these St-Jean-Baptiste festivities, parades also took place in small towns and villages throughout Québec, Ontario, and Manitoba—and, indeed, wherever French Canadians settled in sufficient numbers to create and sustain French Canadian associations (Sociétés Saint-Jean-Baptiste). In the United States, large French Canadian communities were established in the nineteenth century in East Coast towns such as Lowell, Massachusetts, and Lewiston, Maine, to work in mines as well as textile and leather factories. Similar small communities were established throughout the American Midwest (Frenette 1998).

St. Jean-Baptiste became the constituting figure of the diaspora, such that diasporic belonging was marked, and even constituted, by the June 24 celebrations. It came as little surprise, then, that the precursor was officially recognized in 1908 as the patron saint of French Canadians in North America by Pope Pius IX.[23]

Pictorial performances

St. Jean-Baptiste was rendered visible and present to the population mainly through parades and processions. As important public rituals forcefully linking religion with collective identity and history, these annual events created a sacred community of destiny (Wuthnow 1994; Taylor 2007). This made them valuable resources for social and political actors, and it makes them important sources for understanding the cultural construction of Québec's national identity.

In the mid-nineteenth century, the small St-Jean-Baptiste bonfires

23. Until 1908, Saint Joseph was Canada's official patron saint. As Boisvert (1990) has noted, St. Jean-Baptiste in French Canada is not as important as the Virgin of Guadalupe is for Mexicans, Our Lady of Częstochowa for Poles, or Saint Patrick for the Irish: no cult was associated with him, nor any form of personal devotion. Jean-Baptiste was, however, a very common name for French Canadian men, as Patrick is for the Irish, to the extent that Jean-Baptiste became a nickname used by Anglo-Canadians and Americans to speak of French Canadians (often derogatorily, like "Paddy" for Irishmen).

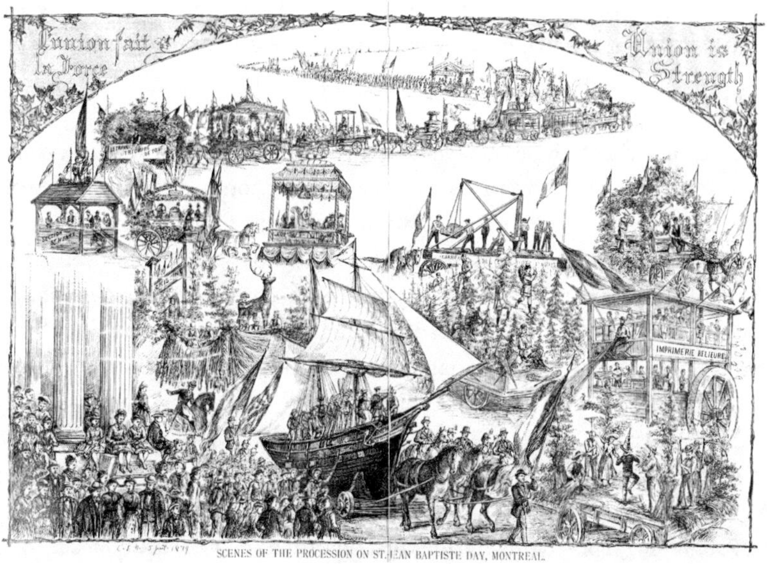

FIGURE 2.9 Illustration depicting the St-Jean-Baptiste procession in Montréal in 1879. By then, the ceremony had evolved into a parade with elaborate floats. This illustration includes the political motto at the top left and right, in both French and English: "L'union fait la force/Union Is Strength" (Bibliothèque et Archives Nationales du Québec, BAnQ Vieux Montréal, Collection Edouard-Zotique Massicotte, P750, Album de rue B-109-a).

blessed by village priests were replaced by elaborate processions in the streets of Montréal and Québec City on the saint's name day (figure 2.9). They were modeled on the processions of Corpus Christi, a moveable feast celebrated on the Thursday after Trinity Sunday. In years when Corpus Christi fell sufficiently close to June 24, street decorations and gigantic floral arches of triumph were left in place for the St-Jean-Baptiste procession. These religious processions over time developed into expansive parades combining religious and secular imagery (Guay 1973). Unlike most American parades, which resemble marches involving a succession of relevant social groups and organizations and are relatively democratic (although the range of participants depends on the occasion),[24] the French Canadian parades were more akin to pageants, highly orchestrated events telling a distinct story through spectacle (Nelles 1999). Although anyone

24. Susan Davis (1986) describes an 1832 parade as a "colorful spectacle present[ing] a ceremonious image of the city's social makeup," divided into distinct divisions: city leaders, military, masters and employees of several trades, etc. She sees parades as an important, varied, and popular mode of communication in nineteenth-century American cities.

could watch, participation was restricted to groups that properly expressed the desired narrative according to the annual theme chosen by the SSJBM.

The religious-patriotic narrative had to be represented in material form in order to gain persuasive force. Father Alexandre Dugré, a prominent Jesuit priest in the 1920s, argued that "a people, like a child, learns through its eyes; . . . the illustration is superior to the printed word; . . . the poster is superior to the book, which often remains unread; and the *tableau-vivant* and the heroic parade are far superior to the history library."[25] St-Jean-Baptiste parades became the primary visual and material expression of the national narrative, presenting tangible, vivid, dynamic displays of what French Canadianness was or should be about. They were, to borrow Chandra Mukerji's apt formulation, "a social technology of experiential learning" (2012). Aesthetics were used as heuristics and as a pedagogical tool. As the narrator of Fernand Dansereau's documentary *La Parade* (1973) poetically intones just before the camera rolls across rows of figures in historical costumes and a steady flow of *tableaux vivants*, "The Saint-Jean-Baptiste Day parade is a way to remember" inviting the viewer to "now silently watch ourselves [in the parade] as we remember."

The Montréal parades had yearly themes to structure the pictorial discourse, illustrated by a series of impressive floats. Some were historical, such as "Four Centuries of History" (1927) and "Birth of a French and Catholic City in the 18th Century" (1942). Others were ethnographic, such as "Homage to the French Canadian Peasant Family" (1941) and "Homage to the French Canadian Woman" (1961). Still others celebrated French culture and French Canadian folklore, such as "Folktales and Legends of French Canada" (1929) and "Her Majesty the French Language" (1957), or showcased the geography of French Canada, as with "The St. Lawrence River and the Great Lakes" (1935) and "The St. Lawrence Seaway" (1959). Religion was a recurring leitmotif, and the yearly theme was explicitly religious on several occasions, as with "Radiant Faithfulness" in 1954.[26]

25. The 1923 original quote opens with "Le peuple," which can mean both the nation and the populace (i.e., both *a* people and *the* people). Dugré, advocating national indoctrination, is playing on both significations here, but his argument focuses on the appropriate form of communication for a mostly illiterate populace (quoted from Guay (1973, 11), and from Fernand Dansereau's 1973 documentary *La Parade*).

26. See the full list of yearly themes in appendix A. From 1924 to 1966, the annual parades had themes related to French Canada and North America more broadly. The last three parades explicitly and self-consciously shifted the reference to Qué-

FIGURE 2.10 "Jesus's friendships," prayer card (Archives de folklore de l'Université Laval, Fonds Larouche-Villeneuve, F716 [HFL/03.02], Université Laval, Division de la gestion des documents administratifs et des archives).

Hundreds of thousands of spectators gathered along the streets to admire dozens of floats amid regiments of Canadian papal soldiers (*Zouaves*) and religious banners and flags adorned with images of the patron saint and

bec: "Québec's International Vocation" (1967); "Québec '68" (1968); "Québec, My Love" (1969) (Fonds P81, Archives nationales du Québec à Montréal). This referential shift presents another measure of the transformation in identity that took place during the Quiet Revolution and of the role of the parades in that shift.

FIGURE 2.11 Commemorative medal for the 1878 St-Jean-Baptiste holiday (No. 1991 .3357, Musées de la civilisation, collection du Séminaire de Québec. Photo: Jessy Bernier).

decorated with the maple leaf and the beaver, other important symbols of the French Canadian nation.

While the themes varied and the floats were redesigned every year, the last float in the parade was always dedicated to St. John the Baptist. In religious paintings and the ubiquitous prayer cards, commemorative medals, folk sculptures, and nationalist memorabilia, he was usually represented as a golden-haired child in the company of a lamb, emulating popular European paintings of the Holy Family showing Jesus and John playing together (see figures 2.10–2.13).

Inspired by these popular depictions, from 1851 until 1963 the saint's float always featured a carefully chosen, curly-haired boy holding a pet lamb (Guay 1973) (figures 2.14–2.15). The boy chosen to play the "petit Saint

FIGURES 2.12 (ABOVE) AND 2.13 (OVERLEAF) Illustrations on the cover of a popular magazine, representing St. Jean-Baptiste as a young child. The saint's curls are a defining element in the depiction of the French Canadians' patron saint. Figure 2.12, from 1903, is a good example of religious-national iconographic collage: holding the shepherd's staff/cross in one hand and caressing the lamb with the other, St. Jean-Baptiste sits pensively at the foot of a maple tree, another key symbol of the Canadiens. Figure 2.13, from 1904, is noteworthy for the wreath of flowers surrounding the image of the saint, composed mainly of roses and white lilies. The rose is the symbol of England, the lily that of France. The French Canadians, according to a common saying, were "born under the lily, but raised under the rose" (*Album Universel*, June 24, 1903; June 24, 1904).

LE MONDE ILLUSTRE

ALBUM UNIVERSEL

21e ANNÉE — No 1053 | MONTRÉAL, 25 JUIN 1904 | 40 PAGES, 5c le Numéro

SAINT JEAN-BAPTISTE

FIGURE 2.14 For almost a century, the French Canadian nation was represented in processional and parade *tableaux-vivants* as "a little Saint Jean-Baptiste." That representation survived until 1963, when the boy was replaced by an adult statue. Girls were sometimes chosen to represent the saint, as their hair could better be coiffed to resemble his iconic curls. In 1895, the saint's float was a horse-drawn carriage, adorned with branches of maple (Bibliothèque et Archives nationales du Québec, BAnQ Québec, Fonds Philippe Gingras/P585 / P127).

Jean-Baptiste" was treated like a king, bringing honor and fame to his neighborhood, and followed by photographers and crowds of the curious. This iconic representation—constant in its general features yet shifting in important ways—would take center stage in the debates of the Quiet Revolution of the 1960s, creating turmoil and inspiring violence in the public sphere. The next chapter examines the representation of the child St. Jean-Baptiste more closely.

FIGURE 2.15 St. Jean-Baptiste with his lamb (tied to a rope) on a parade float. Ottawa, June 24, 1953 (Bibliothèque et Archives nationales du Québec, BAnQ Gatineau, Fonds Champlain Marcil, 07H P174 S6 D4739 P08).

KEY TROPE *The Family*

EVERYWHERE THE FAMILY IS USED AS A METAPHOR FOR THE NATION. Family metaphors are used to describe the bonds between individuals (such as *fraternité*, brotherhood) and the relationship between individuals and the nation-state (*enfants de la patrie* are implicitly bonded to the fatherland or motherland). The family is also seen as the foundation for the national edifice, and biological and cultural reproduction are key themes in nationalizing discourses. In French Canada, that theme became especially important after the Conquest (1759–63) and the Durham Report (1839). With immigration from France stopped and the French Canadians increasingly marginalized, resistance to assimilation would be possible only through an increase in fertility rates and a vigorous promotion of French Canadian values. The Catholic Church and the Société Saint-Jean-Baptiste deftly promoted these strategies of resistance, called *survivance*,

TROPE 2.1 "La mère canadienne." Cover of commemorative program of the 1943 St-Jean-Baptiste holiday (Bibliothèque et Archives nationales du Québec, BAnQ Vieux Montréal, Fonds Société Saint-Jean-Baptiste de Montréal, P82).

TROPE 2.2 "The Cradle." Float part of the 1943 St-Jean-Baptiste parade in Québec City (Bibliothèque et Archives nationales du Québec, BAnQ Québec, Fonds Ministère de la Culture et des Communications et de la Condition feminine-Office du film du Québec/ E6,S7,SS1,P12168. Fête de la Saint-Jean-Baptiste à Québec: Le berceau, char alléorique de la Cie F.X. Drolet/Herménégilde Lavoie).

TROPE 2.3 "La maison paternelle," 1931 (Bibliothèque et Archives nationales du Québec, BAnQ Vieux Montréal, Fonds Société Saint-Jean-Baptiste de Montréal, P82/698).

TROPE 2.4 St-Jean-Baptiste float in 1954 parade in St. Basile (Bibliothèque et Archives nationales du Québec, BAnQ Québec, Fonds Paul-Émile Duplain, 03Q P322 S3 D01-08 P001).

year-round. The glorification of the French Canadian mother and her large, happy family was further promoted at the St-Jean-Baptiste festival.

As Mgr. Louis-Nazaire Bégin, archbishop of Québec City, wrote in a 1908 pastoral letter: "The entire world admires and glorifies the fertility of our families. God indeed gave us the blessing He once promised to his chosen people: healthy and numerous generations. The Canadian woman is indeed a fruitful vine that constitutes the true wealth of families and our fatherland; and it is indeed to the Canadian faithful to the teachings of his Church and to his forefathers' traditions, who invests all his glory and wealth in a crown of vigorous sons, that the poet of Israel was comparing the young shoots surrounding the paternal Olive tree (psalm 127)" (225).

In 1943, the St-Jean-Baptiste parade was dedicated to the (French) Canadian mother whose grown sons were at war in Europe (trope 2.1). The poster for this event shows a noble and proud woman, regal in posture and modest in dress, holding her infant. Behind her are generations of women pioneers who nursed children and took care of the home and the land. The land, the poster reminds the viewer, was protected by the Catholic Church, depicted in the background.

Parade floats often represented and performed the ideal of the French Canadian family. In the first example shown here (trope 2.2), the theme is "The Cradle" (*le berceau*), "the glory and the salvation of the nation." This is an explicit reference to the so-called revenge of the cradle, through which French Canadians were to resist the threat of national extinction after the Conquest (and after Lord Durham's recommendation to assimilate them) by "outbreeding" the English. The second, labeled "The Paternal Home," depicts a modest country house with trees and grass (trope 2.3). The parents on the front porch are chaperoning a young courting couple. The third float depicts a large family, comprising nine children, their parents and grandmother, in their "living room," most likely representing the nightly ritual of reciting the rosary (*le chapelet en famille*) (trope 2.4). From 1950 until 1970, every night at 7 p.m. the radio station CKAC broadcast Cardinal Léger, archbishop of Montréal, saying the rosary. Families throughout the province would gather around the radio to recite the prayers "live" with the cardinal.

While the most important parades were in Montréal and Québec City, many smaller localities and villages staged their own parades in Québec and French Canadian communities throughout Canada and the United States. Two of the floats shown here, *tableaux vivants*, were from small villages.

3 Iconoclastic Unmaking

The Quiet Revolution's Aesthetic Revolt (1959–69)

> Let us kill St. John the Baptist! Let us burn the *papier-mâché* traditions with which they have tried to build a myth around our slavery.
>
> —Pierre Vallières, "White Niggers of America"

> The days of *papier mâché* are over.
>
> —Pierre Perrault, June 29, 1969

FROM THE VERY BEGINNING OF THE 1960S, WHEN THE QUIET Revolution was not yet quite revolutionary, the St-Jean-Baptiste holiday provided a key opportunity to voice criticisms of the Catholic vision of the nation, its symbols and its forms of expression, and to articulate, at first quite tentatively, an alternative definition of national identity. An essential yet overlooked component of the Quiet Revolution was an aesthetic revolt against religious-national symbols of the nation, through which a new definition of the nation emerged.

Opposition to the religious vision of the nation and to clerical power did not emerge *ex nihilo* during the 1960s. It had a long history, with its roots in the Patriots' liberal movement and running through the twentieth century (Lamonde 2000). In 1948, for example, a group of artists, under the leadership of Paul-Émile Borduas, released *Le Refus global* (*Total Refusal*), an anti-establishment and anti-religious manifesto that advocated the total rejection of all conventions and promoted freethinking without fear, "in the joyful pursuit of the untamed need for liberation." The manifesto incited "resplendent anarchy" and repeatedly used the term *petit peuple*—which refers both to the nation's small size and to the fact that it was modest in its aspirations and riddled by fear. This state of affairs was perceived to be the result of the double colonization of French Canadians by the English and by the Catholic Church:

> A little people closely tied to the cassocks that have remained the sole repositories of faith, knowledge, truth, and national wealth. . . .
>
> A little people born from a Jansenist colony, isolated, vanquished, defenseless against the horde of clerics from France and Navarre out to perpetuate in this fear-ridden place . . . the prestige and advantages of a Catholicism despised in Europe. . . .
>
> A little people that, in spite of everything, multiplies in the generosity of the flesh instead of spirit, in the north of this immense America. (Borduas [1948] 1974, 9–10; my translation)

The *Refus global* can therefore be seen as a direct ancestor of the Quiet Revolution. Another close relative was *Cité libre*, an anti-clerical, pro-union periodical cofounded in 1950 by Pierre Elliott Trudeau, with frequent contributions from René Lévesque, Pierre Vallières, and other prominent intellectuals and activists.

This type of opposition to the Church became more meaningful during the 1960s as it coincided with, and was bolstered by, political developments. With the death of Premier Maurice Duplessis and the subsequent opening and reshuffling of the political field, a wide variety of new political groups, loosely connected political formations, and politically engaged intellectual and artistic circles emerged on the provincial scene, often splitting and merging with others.

While it is beyond the scope of this chapter to paint the political landscape of Québec at that time, it is critical to distinguish among the various actors involved in the promotion of a secular social order and the making of the modern state. Three main categories of political actors can be delineated: 1) mainstream political actors, involved in the formation of the welfare state and the definition of a new national project during the Quiet Revolution, including Jean Lesage's Parti libéral du Québec and its bright star, René Lévesque, a future premier of Québec; 2) groups such as Pierre Bourgault's Rassemblement pour l'indépendance nationale (RIN) (1960–68), which were not directly involved in state affairs or the official opposition but were influential outside regular political channels by shaping public debate and organizing protests and strikes; and 3) marginal but vocal groups like the Marxist Front de libération populaire (FLP) and the Front de libération du Québec (FLQ), which rocked the 1960s and early 1970s with violent protests, iconoclastic actions, and even terrorist acts.[1]

1. These last two groups should not be confused. The FLQ, created in 1963 from the radical elements of the RIN, advocated—and resorted to—violence as a means to

FIGURE 3.1 St. Jean-Baptiste Lesage. Caricature of Jean Lesage, the Québec Premier who initiated the Quiet Revolution, with René Lévesque, his minister of natural resources, a future sovereignist leader and premier (1976–85). Lesage is here represented as the national saint, the "new protector of French Canadians" (*La Patrie*, June 20, 1963).

Reworking National Icons

The St-Jean-Baptiste holidays of the 1960s were not always turbulent, but they were always ebullient. They provided the stage on which two primary sets of national actors, the Church hierarchy and a new wave of secular nationalists, debated the future of the nation. On June 24, 1961, for example, Cardinal Léger, archbishop of Montréal, declared in his sermon during the traditional St-Jean-Baptiste Day mass that "the French Canadian people must be a faithful witness, enlightened, and courageous" (*Le Devoir*, June 27, 1961). Meanwhile, René Lévesque, the popular television news reporter turned minister of national resources, told a Montréal crowd that "a people has no need for robots and sheep that follow with

promote Québec's sovereignty. It disintegrated with the arrest of several members following the so-called October Crisis of 1970, when the group's kidnapping of Québec's vice premier and a British diplomat led to the death of the former and the institution of the War Measures Act in Québec. The FLP was constituted by the remaining left wing of the RIN in 1968, when the RIN was dissolved. The remainder of members of the RIN joined René Lévesque's newly created Parti Québécois in 1968.

zealous conformity everything that has been done in the past. A people needs its outsiders and its violent ones; it needs its malcontents and its visionaries, and sometimes [it also needs] its rebels" (*Le Devoir*, June 27, 1961). While the cardinal explained to the faithful that "the mission of a people like ours, born in faith, is to bear witness in the world" (*La Presse*, June 27, 1961), Lévesque called on French Canada to stop harping on "the Providential mission of this little people in the North American land and to look forward and ask 'where are we going?'" (*Gazette*, June 25, 1961). Of note here is Lévesque's use of the expression *petit peuple*, echoing the *Refus global* of a dozen years before.

In a few evocative words, Lévesque articulated an attack on the Church's conservative vision of the nation, which he characterized as focused on survival instead of on expansion and development. In his view, this vision had been internalized to such an extent that it shaped what members of the nation deemed plausible or even desirable for themselves—economically, professionally, or politically. Lévesque was urging them instead to become architects of their own destiny. Social and political actors during the Quiet Revolution arduously worked to reverse what they saw as public passivity. The so-called *grands projets* of the 1960s—such as the constitution of Hydro-Québec, the building of the Montréal Metro, and the hosting of the 1967 International and Universal Exposition (Expo 67)—should be seen in this broader ideological context. The new nationalists' goal for Québec was to enable it to emerge from the Church's constraining shell and catch up with the world.

Protesting the Iconic Tableau's Meaning

The growing opposition to the religious narrative of the nation gained ground, in the 1960s, through attacks on St. John the Baptist and his lamb. The new wave of nationalists objected to this iconic form on two principal grounds. First, they rejected its religious-national narrative as retrograde; second, they found the depiction of the nation as a *child* infantilizing, underscoring the nation's dependence (figure 3.2). Their objections, and the responses to them, set off a series of symbolic transformations, culminating in the beheading of the St-Jean-Baptiste statue in 1969 and contributing to the demise of French Canadianness and the crystallization of a new Québécois identity.

The lamb was a problematic component of the saint's iconography. While theological interpretation highlights the salvific nature of the lamb, critics emphasized a secular and more insidious interpretation. In their

La Patrie DU DIMANCHE 15¢

19 juin 1960

Présence française au Canada

• Le char qui clora le défilé historique de la Saint-Jean-Baptiste, le 24 juin, portera cette année le petit François Cantin, 8 ans, fils de M. Gaston Cantin, de 2285, Sauriol Est, un petit Saint-Jean-Baptiste prédestiné, physique de l'emploi, comme on peut s'en rendre compte par la photo couleur ci-dessus: tête de chérubin aux cheveux bouclés, choisi entre une foule de candidats. Ce cousin de l'Enfant-Jésus fréquente l'école des Saints-Martyrs, rue Parthenais.

Le petit Saint-Jean Baptiste, chez lui, à l'église, à l'école et dans la parade. p. 2.3.4.5.

•

Mesdames, Elaine Bédard vous confie un de ses secrets. p. 6.7.

•

Tournons la bobine. p. 8.

•

Lorsque l'enfant parait. p. 10.

FIGURE 3.2 Petit St. Jean-Baptiste 1960. The boy chosen to represent the national saint was a minor celebrity in the weeks leading up to the holiday. His picture was published in newspapers (even in Montréal's Anglophone *Gazette*), along with details about his home life. In 1960, St. Jean-Baptiste was portrayed by 8-year-old François Cantin, the son of Gaston Cantin, a butcher. The article in *La Patrie* described the child at home with his family, at church, at school, and in the parade (*La Patrie*, June 19, 1960).

view, if John the Baptist was the nation's patron and protector, the lamb was the nation itself, exploited and ultimately sacrificed. In a strategic semantic shift, the new critics began to speak of a *sheep* instead of a lamb, emphasizing passivity and submissiveness rather than divine innocence.

Webb Keane notes that material things "always combine an indefinite number of physical properties and qualities, whose particular juxtapositions may be mere happenstance. In any given practical or interpretative context, only some of those properties are relevant and come into play. But other properties persist, available for promotion as circumstances change" (Keane 2006, 200). In this case, the physical characteristics of sheep and lambs, in particular the wool, acquired new significance. The critics referred to the nation as a sheep allowing wolves to "eat the wool off its back," casting the problematic economic situation of French Canadians as largely due to their acceptance of exploitation by others.

Keane further observes that because "things always contain properties in excess of those which have been interpreted and made use of under any given circumstance, [they] retain an unpredictable range of latent possibilities. [As such], [t]hey do not *only* express past acts, intentions and interpretations. They also invite unexpected responses" (Keane 2006, 201). The "sheep" became the symbolic foil against which a new political elite defined their national vision of progress, economic development, and political self-reliance.

Lévesque's use of the sheep as a negative metaphor for the nation in 1961 was not accidental. A day before his speech, Québec's first sovereignist group, the RIN, had criticized the lamb and jokingly suggested that Québec's animal emblem should be a lion (the *Gazette*, June 24, 1961). A few months later other physical attributes of the sheep came into the discourse. The RIN chose as its official logo a ram's head with gigantic horns (figure 3.3). A founding member explained in his memoir that "the ram opposes the traditional Saint-Jean-Baptiste sheep, an unflattering representation of French Canada. In the Zodiac, Aries is a sign of spring. It is a symbol of strength and renewal" (D'Allemagne 1974, 62). The ram's head was drawn in profile to emphasize the horns as a sign of virility and maturity.

In contrast to this new symbol, with its connotations of power, the St-Jean-Baptiste lamb or sheep became an object of ridicule. The noted socialist sovereignist Raoul Roy ran a café-salon called the Hanged Sheep (Palmer 2009). And in 1962, in a visual commentary on an ongoing strike, the daily Montréal newspaper *La Presse* published on its first page a cartoon depicting a herd of sheep jumping through a hoop and off a cliff, with the caption "Happy Saint-Jean-Baptiste Day *Regardless*!" (June 23, 1962). This mockery of the sheep was sometimes also voiced: the RIN organized assemblies against "colonial" institutions during which protesters bleated loudly, a symbolic performance criticizing both the colonial regime and the French Canadians supporting it.

On St-Jean-Baptiste Day in 1962, the parade was delayed when the lamb was kidnapped by "separatist militants." Marcel Chaput, the RIN presi-

FIGURE 3.3 André D'Allemagne, co-founder of the Rassemblement pour l'Indépendance Nationale (RIN). The RIN's logo, a ram, was chosen in 1962 in explicit rejection of the St-Jean-Baptiste lamb (Bibliothèque et Archives nationales du Québec, BAnQ Vieux Montréal, Fonds Antoine Desilets, P697,S1,SS1,SSS16,032_009).

dent, declared the parade as a "shameful display" whose star attraction was "a young Saint Jean-Baptiste of indefinite gender, accompanied by his damned sheep [*maudit mouton*]." Chaput thus not only disparaged the masculinity of the saint but also profaned a sacred symbol, the *agnus Dei*. According to him, the Société Saint-Jean-Baptiste was "perpetuating a state of inferiority it claims to be combating" by representing the nation in that specific form (*La Presse*, June 28, 1962). The next year, breaking with a long tradition, the animal was omitted from the traditional *tableau vivant*, never to return (figure 3.4). The SSJBM Board announced in its

FIGURE 3.4 In this cartoon, titled "End of an Era in Quebec," the sheep is turning its back on a long list of Canadian Prime Ministers. On the upper right corner, the author notes that "there isn't a little sheep at the St-Jean Parade any longer." The cartoon explicitly links the removal of the symbol from the parade with Québec's growing assertiveness and articulation of its own national project (Normand Hudon, 1963. M997.63.410. © McCord Museum).

April 1963 newsletter that "This year there [will] be no little lamb—either white or black—in the parade because of its growing unpopularity. 'New times, new ways,' the wiser ones will say" (*Le Bulletin national*, April 1963, p. 5). Note here the playful recognition that the white lamb had become a black sheep.

This was not the first time the iconography of the child saint and lamb had been criticized. Olivar Asselin, president of the SSJBM in 1913–14, referred to it as "a sad and clownish spectacle" and argued for the removal of the lamb from the parade:

> Some may want to maintain Christian traditions in our national societies . . . [but] the lamb here is less a religious symbol than the emblem of the passive and stupid submission to tyrannies.

> Let's assume that, with regard to patriotism, we must take into consideration the traditional signification of symbols; that Saint Jean-Baptiste and his lamb, supposedly representing the role faith played in America among the French Canadian people, must for that reason stay in the June 24th processions. Does that mean that the mode of figuration cannot be discussed? . . . A child and a lamb can make a pretty heraldic effect . . . but . . . when a pretty child is exhibited for half a day under a burning sun at the risk of making him dumb for life, . . . and when at his side is a lamb that couldn't care less about its role, lifts its tail, relieves itself and bleats, I want to be able to exclaim, without disrespect to religion or the fatherland, that this kid who nervously stuffs his finger up his nose and only wants to go back home is not Jean [the Baptist], but the son of [some] grocer! (Asselin [1913] 2002, 86–92)

Note how Asselin's critiques were articulated against both the signified—the lamb as a symbol of French Canadian divine mission—and the material signifier—the bleating, urinating animal. Asselin's arguments against the lamb anticipated those of the critics during the Quiet Revolution, but they could not overcome the power of clerical nationalism in 1913. The lamb (and the saint) thus remained in place for another fifty years.

It was surely easier to remove the lamb from the tableau than to remove the saint himself. Yet the child saint too had often been the target of verbal attacks. Chaput's derisive comment points to another aspect of the saint's representation that became problematic at a moment of nationalist awakening: his gender and sexuality. The representation of the saint as a child made him appear not only weak but also effeminate. Great emphasis was placed on his curls—hair was a key criterion in the process of selecting a child to represent the saint in the Montréal parade. In smaller communities, when a boy with suitably lavish curls could not be found, a girl was sometimes chosen.[2] The representation of the saint as a child thus underlined not only the infantilization of the nation but also its emasculation. The RIN's choice of a ram for its logo was a deliberate attempt to oppose this representation. (Later, in the mid-1960s, the Catholic Church launched an effort to virilize the saint in sermons and new iconic depictions.)

The growing reaction against the child saint was strong enough to

2. "Le Défilé de la St-Jean-Baptiste à Ste-Anne-de-Beaupré," unpublished manuscript, 8 December 1975, Collection Guy Giguère, AFEUL.

drive the Société Saint-Jean-Baptiste to publicly justify the image, as in this press release published in several newspapers in 1962:

> Why a Child in the June 24th Parade?
>
> Every year, some find our choice to represent our patron as a child in the historic parade scandalous. One should take into account that among the 800,000 people who line Sherbrooke Street every year, there are some 400,000 children under the age of ten. The Société Saint-Jean-Baptiste sees no reason to deprive them of this graceful and poetic *tableau*, much closer to their heart than the other historic and necessarily more austere floats. All the education experts agree with us on this point. Let us leave to the small children, on this national holiday—which is also theirs—this naïve representation. Besides, Saint-Jean-Baptiste Day is the "Christmas of Summer," and on this day the Baptist has an irresistible appeal, like the Baby Jesus in the Christmas crèche. (*L'Information nationale*, June-July 1962, p. 4, released and reprinted in *Le Devoir*, June 23, 1962, p. 20)

Here the SSJBM justifies the childish representation of the saint by invoking its appeal to children and the importance of their visual and ludic socialization. It also attempts to affirm the sacredness of the saint by reminding the readers of the saint's special connection to Jesus via its reference to the holiday as summertime Christmas.

Reshaping the Icon

When attempts to justify the childish representation of the saint failed to silence the critics, in 1962 the Société Saint-Jean-Baptiste de Montréal tried a new approach by changing the material form of the representation. They presented two St. Jean-Baptistes. The first, which led the parade, paying "official homage to the Patron of the French Canadians," was a majestic bronze statue of the saint as an adult. The other, which closed the parade, depicted him as a little boy on a float called "Christmas in Summer" (*Le Bulletin national*, May 1962, p. 7).

This strategy created a regressive pictorial narrative. A more intuitive choice would have been to place the two representations in chronological order, leading the parade with the child and closing with the adult statue, thus visually representing the saint, and by implication the nation, coming of age instead of regressing from adulthood to childhood. (This in fact was the editorial choice of the paper *La Patrie* in its coverage of the parade, as seen in figure 3.5.) For the SSJBM, apparently, tradition

FIGURE 3.5 One Parade, Two Saints. In 1962, the Société Saint-Jean-Baptiste de Montréal decided to include two saints in its annual parade: a float with the traditional "petit Saint Jean-Baptiste" would close the parade as it had always done, but a majestic bronze statue of an adult saint would lead it. The two were juxtaposed on the first page of the weekly *La Patrie* on June 24, 1962.

prevailed over narrative logic and potentially negative interpretations by spectators.

By introducing this dual representation of the saint, the SSJBM opened the door to further transformations. In the following year, the parade reverted to presenting a single, traditional representation of the saint as a child. But it departed dramatically from tradition in omitting the lamb and surrounding the child saint with "an honor guard waving the torch of a reinvigorated nationalism" (*La Presse*, June 25, 1963). In 1964, in yet another departure, the live "petit Saint Jean-Baptiste" was permanently replaced by an adult statue. The removal of the live character and its replacement by a statue was partly prompted by the potential danger to the child impersonating the saint as opposition to the parades increased. In 1963, the "honor guard" around the saint served not only as a virile demonstration of national authority but also as protection for the child.

While these shifts in the annual parade were sudden and quite dramatic, the transition in the representation of the saint was often more gradual in other visual venues. In magazines, for example, St. John was often portrayed as an adolescent.

An editorial in Montréal's main English-language daily, the *Gazette*, clarified the transformation of the icon to its Anglo-Canadian readership, who were often unaware of the debates that occupied the French Canadian community:

> Gone is the little boy with the golden hair, with the small lamb clutched at his side. This symbolizes an overall change of character and meaning. The day of the arcadian and rustic ceremony is finished. In today's parade, Saint Jean-Baptiste will appear as a statue 11 feet high, modern in every respect, a symbol, as sculptor Gaétan Therrien says, of that which is "strong, powerful, dynamic." This change in the character of the ceremony is an authentic reflection of the changes that recent years have brought to French Canada. Just as French Canadians have put aside the arcadian theme in their national celebrations, they have been striving to put aside the arcadian theme in their national character. The change of image marks a change of substance, a change in the reality of things. The vigor of French Canada today is the vigor of a society seeking a new and progressive identity. And if this vigor sometimes seems to have about it a great hunger, this is not surprising. For there is an urge to experiment, to explore, to test, a desire to take nothing for granted, but to search out things as far as they extend, to look not for the horizons of yesterday but for the horizons of tomorrow.[3]

3. *Gazette*, editorial, June 24, 1964. The term *arcadian* originally referred to a mountainous region of Greece sparsely populated by shepherds, and it developed into a poetic metaphor for idyllic wilderness. It is here used to refer to the idealized vision of rural French Canada and to the representation of the patron saint with his little lamb.

The new saint was mature, strong and modern, the opposite of his traditional representation. The Catholic Church supported these transformations. It reasoned that to be relevant and resonant—and indeed to survive—the symbol needed to change. Mgr. Paul Gosselin, archbishop of Montréal in the 1960s, sought to demonstrate that relevance by emphasizing that the saint himself was a transitional symbol and thus reflective of Québec's own transition:

> Saint John the Baptist is a transitional character. He closes the Old Testament and announces the New Testament. With him ends the era of prophets, the course toward truth, and the wait for the Messiah. After him will come the awaited Messiah, He who is the way, the truth and the life. The Baptist could be a man of our disrupted and changing times. After two thousand years of Christianity, humanity still seeks its way. There is no lack of false prophets, even here at home, to engage humanity in the tortuous paths St. John talked about. . . .
>
> What is [his] message? Is it a call to rebellion against authority, an invitation to remove God from one's conscience and from human society, a desire for emancipation from all constraint, all rules, in order to think anything and act as one wishes? On the contrary. . . .
>
> John is a true prophet . . . . False prophets engender hatred, revolt, contempt and ultimately chaos. The real ones, like the Baptist, prepare the way to truth and love. May God deliver us from those trafficking in error and safeguard the message of the precursor, our national patron. (*L'Action Catholique*, June 25, 1961)

In this sermon, Mgr. Gosselin equates the Church with John the Baptist and secular reformists with false prophets urging "rebellion against authority," "inviting the removal of God from one's conscience and society," and ultimately plainly "trafficking in error." By the mid-1960s, as the Québec Church itself was undergoing radical transformation following the Second Vatican Council (1962–65), it muted its resistance to the secularization of Québec society (Routhier 1997; Seljak 1996). But it still attempted to rescue St. Jean-Baptiste as the national symbol by discursively emphasizing the saint's virility and strength of character:

> Saint Jean-Baptiste, our patron, was not this pale figure a certain tradition may have complacently presented. He was on the contrary a man of direct and dense words, a demanding man, a man of sweeping horizon,

> audacious, robust and severe. . . . He stood straight, yet knew how to disappear behind the One arriving after him and Whom he had announced the coming; he had the build of great men.[4]

The SSJBM and the Church demonstrated a keen understanding of the critiques formulated against the cherubic representation of the Saint and responded to them with creative discursive and material reworkings of the symbol.

Sacrality Forfeited

The meaning of St. John the Baptist as the patron saint of French Canadians and the symbol of the nation was determined by the messianic national narrative articulated by the Catholic Church. That meaning was materialized in the form of the cherubic, curly-haired boy with a docile white lamb at his side. While this choice of symbol and its specific aesthetic form were driven by religious-national ideology, the material properties of the form itself were also freighted with their own meanings. Opposition to, and changes in, the aesthetic form of the symbol therefore acted recursively to shape its meaning.

The removal of the lamb from the tableau, in response to critics who saw it as a symbol of passivity and weakness, set off the series of transformations that led to the dethroning and beheading of St. John the Baptist. Along with the lamb, connoting Christ, religion was removed from the pictorial discourse, and French Canadianness was visually stripped of its providential mission. The saint was thereby secularized. Without the lamb, moreover, the child could no longer be clearly identified as St. John the Baptist, precursor of the Messiah and national patron saint: all that was left was an insignificant little boy. The spectators' gaze, too, was therefore desacralized.

Until this time, two interwoven threads of sacrality had surrounded the patron saint: the first, perhaps most obvious, was the religious signification of the symbol, as a Catholic saint animated by a host of beliefs and practices; the other, woven by the Catholic Church in the mid-nineteenth century to give flesh to the religious vision of the nation, was the sacralization of the saint not as religious figure but as *national* icon. St. John the Baptist was a *sacred religio-national symbol*. It was sacred because of both

4. Mgr. Gosselin, homily preached during the St-Jean-Baptiste Day mass, reproduced in *L'Information nationale*, July-August 1969, p. 4. In French, the last phrase reads, "Il avait la carrure des grands hommes," specifically referring to broad, square shoulders.

its religious signification and its secular, national ones. With the removal of the lamb, the sanctity of the saint was doubly forfeited: the saint qua religious symbol was secularized, and the saint qua national icon was desacralized. Thus materially altered, the icon became both secular and profane.

Once the saint's meaning was altered by the removal of the lamb, his representation as a child quickly disappeared, since the child saint and the lamb had constituted a single visual and semiotic configuration. These two symbolic transformations occurred in quick succession: the lamb was removed from the *tableau vivant* in 1963, and a year later, in 1964, the child was replaced by an adult statue. This transformation was in part pragmatic, related to the SSJBM's feelings of insecurity and fears for the safety of the child representing the saint. Yet these concerns did not absolutely mandate the removal of a child figure: the living child could, for example, have been replaced by a child statue of the saint.

St. John's sudden maturation was significant not only because it reflected Québec's own coming of age but also because it demonstrated that no sacred symbol was untouchable or beyond critical reach. Paradoxically, by altering the symbol in an effort to save it, the Church and the SSJBM participated in its desacralization and ultimate demise. The icon no longer represented a divine nation but rather a secularized one; and it was no longer a sacred representation of the nation but rather a profane one.

That the derision directed at the sheep and the child saint and their resulting transformations occurred in the very first years of the Quiet Revolution suggests that they were not merely *expressive* of institutional transformations in progress but *constitutive* of them (see figure 3.6). They acted as catalysts for transformations, a point I return to in the conclusion of this book.

Parades and the Public Reconfigurations of National Identity

Not only the iconic figure of St. Jean-Baptiste, but also the parade itself became a matter of controversy. It was criticized for its kitsch and bad taste, for its *dépassé* aesthetics, and for its increasingly commercialized character. In the words of the RIN chairman Marcel Chaput, the sponsorship of floats by businesses, many of them foreign companies "that could not care less about the French Canadian nation and [rather] only think of how great the return on their investment will be," constituted "an indecent display of servility" (*La Presse*, 28 June 1962). Even the choice of a parade as the nation's preeminent collective celebration became contro-

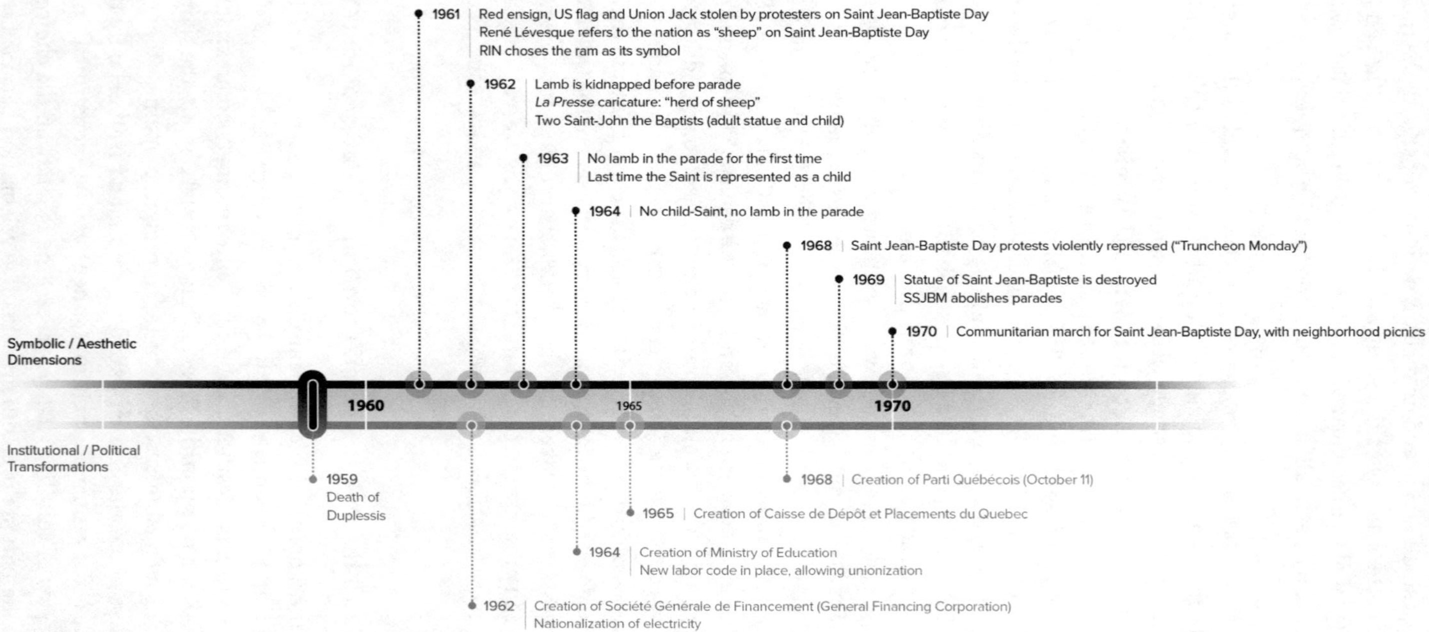

FIGURE 3.6 Aesthetic Revolt and Quiet Revolution Timelines, 1959–1970.

versial. It came to be seen as emblematic of the French Canadian nation's herdlike passivity, with the populace watching from the sidelines while a select few paraded before them.

Beginning in 1961, the parade became a prime target of protests and a venue where political outsiders—those who were not directly involved in the reform and restructuring of the provincial state—could make their voices heard. The St-Jean-Baptiste Day parade was always attended by dignitaries, journalists, and television crews, along with hundreds of thousands of spectators watching from Montréal's sidewalks. Another two million watched at home on television or listened to the radio coverage of the event. It thus afforded an ideal platform for small political groups and protesters.

Despite an increased police presence, the parades were constantly disrupted. Protesters tugged at the multiple strings of the cat's cradle created between the onlookers—spectators, television crews, dignitaries, and journalists—and the objects of their gaze—the floats, actors, marching bands, and majorettes. At first the disruptions were relatively superficial. Activists stole the Union Jack, the Red Ensign, and U.S. flags flying on various Montréal buildings in 1961 because, they explained, "the Union Jack is a foreign flag [and] the Red Ensign is not the Canadian flag." They added, "We're not a colony of the United States *either*" (my emphasis), revealing their view of Québec as being colonized by Anglo-Canadians (*La Presse*, 27 June 1961). They vociferously booed the singing of "O Canada" in 1966 because they rejected its religious vision of the nation and because the hymn was increasingly becoming associated with Canada, whereas they were redrawing the symbolic boundaries of their own imagined community around Québec. The anthem was also criticized because its lyrics linking throne and altar, Christ and king, emphasized the alliances between the Crown and the Church, perceived in the 1960s as two conspiring colonial powers.[5]

By the mid-1960s, the idea of an independent Québec, while not fully articulated, was on the table among various left-wing political groups. The visit of the president of France, General Charles de Gaulle, to Québec in July 1967 and his famous "Vive le Québec libre" address spectacularly launched the idea into popular consciousness. A year later, in 1968, the Parti Québécois was born.

5. Booing "O Canada" became a common form of nationalist protest in Québec from the 1960s until the mid-1970s, not only because the hymn was perceived as federalist but also because it expressed a national vision that was defunct by the end of the 1960s.

"Vive le Québec libre!": Crystallizing the Idea of an Independent Québec

The 1967 St-Jean-Baptiste parade was overshadowed by other events, including the Expo 67 in Montréal and the celebrations of Canada's centennial. The exposition is often described as a key moment in the shaping of Québécois national consciousness. It opened Québec to the world and brought prestige to the city and the province. Québécois went en masse to Expo 67 that summer, just as the world was coming to Montréal and discovering Québec.

The centennial celebrations were also the occasion of a dramatic boost for the sovereignist cause. In midsummer, the president of France, Charles de Gaulle, was invited by the Canadian government to attend the celebrations. De Gaulle's visit to Québec and his famous "balcony speech" (*discours du balcon*) in Montréal, which ended with a deliberate and vociferous "Vive le Québec libre!" that was met with thunderous cheers, gave momentum to the emerging independence movement and made those aspirations known to the entire world.[6] Those four words, because they were uttered by de Gaulle, put Québec on the global map. The following day, places as remote as China had, for the first time, heard of Québec.

Although de Gaulle visited Canada at the invitation of the federal government, he planned his visit in consultation with the government of Québec. He broke protocol by arriving by boat in Québec City instead of flying directly to Ottawa. He also chose to travel the two hundred miles to Montréal in an open car to greet the people lined along the sides of the road and waiting for him in town squares. The Québec government had declared Monday, July 25, a public holiday, and, despite pouring rain, an estimated 500,000 people gathered to see de Gaulle. Some, seized by the collective effervescence, decided to follow him all the way to Montréal.

His choice of route was significant: the King's Way (*Chemin du Roy*) is the oldest route linking Québec and Montréal, dating from the French

6. This section is primarily based on archival footage and documentary films on de Gaulle's visit, as well as my attendance at a special event at the Société Saint-Jean-Baptiste de Montréal on July 25, 2007, to commemorate the fortieth anniversary of his "Vive le Québec libre." The event included the screening of *Le Chemin du Roy*, a documentary of de Gaulle's visit (Cyr and Leblanc 2005b) and testimonies of several people involved in it. At the conclusion of de Gaulle's balcony speech, the live audience broke into warm applause. See also *La visite du Général de Gaulle au Québec*, by Jean-Claude Labrecque (1967), available at http://vimeo.com/25725959, accessed May 15, 2015.

regime. Eighteen thousand Québec and French flags lined the *Chemin du Roy*, and twenty-one large "Arcs de Triomphe" made of fir branches adorned the road. With de Gaulle wearing his military uniform and famous kepi instead of his habitual dark presidential suit, every time his car drove under an arch, it evoked images of the liberation of Paris from Nazi occupation. Admiring onlookers held conspicuous placards with slogans such as "Québec libre" and "France-Libération-Québec," linking the hoped-for liberation of Québec to that of France in 1945.

As the day progressed, many people listening to the radio broadcasts of the procession were inspired to join the crowds. As a result, the closer de Gaulle got to Montréal, the larger and more fervent the crowds grew. Concomitantly, de Gaulle's speeches became more stridently supportive of French Canada and Québec. Adopting the language of the Quiet Revolution, he spoke of the natural inclination and legitimate right to be "masters in one's house" and to "hold the reins of national destiny." He praised the endurance of the "French of Canada" and admired the enormous economic and technological progress of recent years.

By the time de Gaulle arrived at Montréal's City Hall, the entire area was overflowing with crowds of supporters and political militants. The moment was ripe for the general to say what he had come to say:

> It is a great emotion that fills my heart seeing before me the French city of Montréal! In the name of the old country, in the name of France, I salute you! I salute you with all my heart!
>
> I will confide a secret that you will not repeat [crowd laughs]. Here, this evening, and during today's entire journey, I found the atmosphere to be similar to that of the Liberation! [Crowd roars.] And along the way, . . . I have noticed what immense effort of progress, of development, and consequently of emancipation that you are accomplishing. And it is in Montréal that I must say that, because if there is a city in the world that is exemplary of modern success, it is yours! I say it is yours, [but] I allow myself to say, it is ours!
>
> If you knew what trust France, reawakened after immense ordeals, now has in you; if you knew what affection she has started to feel again for the French of Canada! And if you knew the extent to which she feels compelled to assist you in your march forward, in your progress. That is why [France] has finalized agreements with the Government of Québec . . . so that the French on this side and the other of the Atlantic will work together towards the same French undertaking. Besides, France knows well that the aid she will bring here, each day a little more, will

> be reciprocated because you are in the process of creating elites, factories, enterprises and laboratories that will amaze everyone and that will allow you one day, I am certain, to help France! [Bravas.]
>
> That is what I have come to tell you this evening, adding that this incredible Montréal reunion will stay with me as an unforgettable memory! All of France knows, sees, hears what is happening here, and I can tell you, she is better for it!
>
> Long live Montréal! Long live Québec! [Roars]
>
> [Pause]
>
> Long live *free* Québec! [Roars.]
>
> Long live, long live . . . long live French Canada!
>
> (And long live France!)

Participants in the events describe that day as a crescendo slowly building to the climactic line of the Montréal balcony speech. It was de Gaulle the liberator, not de Gaulle the president, who was visiting: and he was visiting Québec, not Canada.

His use of the word *free* created a serious diplomatic incident. The prime minister of Canada, Lester B. Pearson, criticized de Gaulle in a televised address the following day. In response, de Gaulle flew back to France before his planned visit to Ottawa. Yet the speech did not please all nationalists either: some felt de Gaulle's visit and speech smacked of colonialism, this time French. Even so, the speech inspired new Québécois militants, who understood it to communicate France's support of the nascent independence movement.

The Coup de Grâce for the Saint

A year after de Gaulle's visit, in 1968, the St-Jean-Baptiste parade provoked more violent demonstrations. The presence of Pierre Elliott Trudeau on the dignitaries' dais was vigorously opposed because of his public hostility to the idea of an independent Québec. The event degenerated into a riot, leading to 290 arrests and leaving 125 injured, a day remembered as "Truncheon Monday" (*lundi de la matraque*) (Rose 1968; Cyr and Leblanc 2005a). The television broadcast of the 1968 parade completely omitted any reference to the confrontations taking place just a few feet from the dignitaries' podium, across the street in Parc Lafontaine. Radio-Canada filmed the parade as if nothing else was happening, creating a surreally purified event: people watching on their television sets saw elaborate floats and happy majorettes parading in front of dignitaries, while a few steps away protesters were breaking the safety cordon, throwing rocks at Trudeau, and being clubbed by policemen.[7]

Although Truncheon Monday is the most-remembered St-Jean-Baptiste Day of the 1960s in narratives of the Quiet Revolution because of its violence, the parade and protest of the following year were arguably more consequential. In 1969, an apparently accidental occurrence turned out to be a transformative historical event (Sewell 1996).

The theme of the 1969 parade was "Québec, My Love." Its twenty-six floats celebrated all the glories of Québec: its natural beauty, cultural attractions, special events and holidays, folktales and legends, and not least its patron saint. Given the previous year's ungainly turn of events, for this year's parade, one thousand uniformed police officers lined the streets of Montréal, on alert to intervene at the smallest sign of disruption. Initially, however, the subversion of the parade was subtle and immune to police intervention. It took place on Radio-Canada's televised broadcast, as the two commentators hired to narrate the event, the noted documentary filmmakers Pierre Perrault and Bernard Gosselin, mocked the spectacle they were supposed to dignify.

PERRAULT: Let's say that the parade gets 500,000 spectators in Montréal. That means at least 1,000,000 Montrealers are *not* coming! How do you think they're celebrating Saint-Jean-Baptiste Day, if they celebrate it at all? . . .

GOSSELIN: They're watching the parade at home on the television, I suppose.

PERRAULT: I've got another explanation: I think that the best way to celebrate the parade—and if I were not here commenting today, that's where I'd be—is to go trout fishing.

GOSSELIN: But Pierre, it's only because you can't play the drums that you say that.

PERRAULT: . . . The parade is on *East Sherbrooke Street* [in English] . . . Who's that, Sherbrooke? Do you know?

GOSSELIN: Sherbrooke, no idea.

PERRAULT: You don't know? Me neither! We're not at home! Thankfully there's Lafontaine Park just behind. There, some great things happened, I think.

7. On the disjuncture between the events and their "live" television broadcast, see the documentary *Les feux de la Saint-Jean* (Cyr and Leblanc 2005a).

The commentators opened their remarks, then, by highlighting public apathy toward the national celebration (with one million staying home) and suggesting that there were better things to do that day. They mocked the colonial legacy by suggesting that Montréal's most important and longest street—nineteen miles long—is named after someone completely forgettable. (Sir John Coape Sherbrooke [1764–1830], whom the commentators claimed not to have heard of, was a British officer and administrator who was appointed lieutenant governor of Nova Scotia in 1811 and served as governor in chief of British North America from 1816 to 1818.) They also cynically referred to Truncheon Monday with their reference to Lafontaine Park, where "great things" happened.

They persisted in their commentary with increasingly bold political statements, including questions about the role of religion in defining national identity:

PERRAULT: "Québec, My Love"?! No! This is not what I want to hear. I'd like to hear: "Québec, *my country*" [*mon pays*]! I think it's much more intense, and we really need to hear that we have a country. . . . That's what the parade is for! . . . Whichever way we choose to signify it . . . , what all those people have in common is the search for an identity through a geography. [Pause] And a country. We agreed to come here, Bernard and I, because we wanted to see whether we could recognize ourselves in that parade. What is a Catholic French Canadian? Is that the [proper] image of ourselves?

Finally, they criticized the commodification of the parade and mocked French Canadians' lack of pride:

PERRAULT: Well, it's starting. "Québec knows how"—Government of Québec. It's on gastronomy, apparently; I saw the ads for the float: "Breton crêpes," "St-Tropez restaurant," "Chez Théo, Belgian restaurant" . . . What does Québec know how to do??

GOSSELIN: Québec, it seems to me, knows how to imitate others. It seems that's what we're most proud of! . . .

PERRAULT: We don't see anything that resembles Québec on the float; there are no [long list of Québec dishes]. . . . We don't have the courage . . . to put those on the market, we don't have the required pride to share those [dishes]. That's what's important; what's important is to be oneself at all levels. There are thousands of French Canadians who own all kinds of restaurants and they sell us hot dogs, hamburgers . . . and club sandwiches. Incredible! So we have to say—What Québec could do and does *not* do.

GOSSELIN: Agreed. . . .

PERRAULT: I'm beginning to wonder if French Canada exists other than in folklore, and to be honest folklore bores me; we cannot live folklore. There are beautiful things, but . . .

GOSSELIN: Pierre, don't you think it's urgent to create a Ministry of Bragging in Québec, then?

PERRAULT: . . . Two new ministries: The Ministry of Bragging, because we have to know our heritage . . .

GOSSELIN: . . . and the Ministry of Kvetching, because people have to complain when things are not right.[8]

In that last comment, they mockingly referred to the mushrooming of new ministries created in the 1960s (Ministry of Youth, Ministry of Cultural Affairs, Ministry of Natural Resources, Ministry of Education, Ministry of Health, Ministry of Revenue, Ministry of Provincial-Federal Relations, and so forth), but by the same token underlined the absence of ministries, agencies, or institutions that actively promoted an emergent Québécois identity.

The commentators not only criticized the parade and the problems of Québec it emblematized but also openly expressed their support for the sovereignty of Québec by affirming Québec to be their *country*. Because of their apparently good-natured tone and humor, it took a full 31 minutes for the producers to realize the ongoing sabotage and four more to take the commentators off the air.[9] The televised parade then proceeded more or less as planned, but without commentators.

Soon after the last float was paraded in front of the television crews and the dignitaries' podium, however, a group of protesters breached the barricades confining the spectators to the sidewalks and took over the street. Thousands of protesters marched just behind the last float, which that year bore a papier-mâché statue of St. Jean-Baptiste in a futuristic setting. Television announcers referred to this unofficial sequel to the official

8. "Le défilé de la Saint-Jean-Baptiste, 'Québec, mon amour,'" June 24, 1969, archival footage of televised broadcast obtained from Radio-Canada. My transcripts and translation.

9. The commentators were replaced by the host who had introduced them. He only read the names of floats. After the parade was officially over, he was joined by another radio announcer. Together, they described the "parallel parade" as it followed the last float.

parade as the "parallel parade." The following day, the Montréal newspaper *La Presse* juxtaposed images of the "two parades" under the heading: "For Saint-Jean-Baptiste Day: Two Parades, Two Mindsets." The two events presented contradictory visions of the nation, the first articulating the values and vision of French Canada and the second explicitly opposing those values and vision and violently protesting them by attacking the core symbol of French Canadianness, St. Jean-Baptiste.

Much consideration had gone into this representation of the saint. A few months earlier, on January 20, 1969, members of the section of the SSJBM responsible for the parade (the Commission des Fêtes du Canada français) had met with the artists commissioned to design that year's floats. The meeting minutes indicate consensus about representing the saint in adult form: one member of the commission insisted that the saint should be "virile, in the prime of life," and another chimed in that he should be "an adult, from his times, a biblical character." An additional suggestion to represent St. John "in the desert, surrounded by locusts" (in keeping with Gospel descriptions) was not adopted. The final design for the float represented the adult saint in a long robe crossing a dense forest, marching with resolve toward a futuristic city (figure 3.7). The official internal script of the parade described the saint "stepping over forests and rivers, leading us toward the Québec of the future" (P82/321).

Though St. John's was the only float with a police motorcycle escort, the police could not protect the saint from agitated crowds. The protesters carried placards that declared them to be "fed up with Saint-Jean [celebrations] on the sidewalk," a powerful double-entendre referring not only to the parades but also to the economic situation of French Canadians: in French, to be "on the sidewalk" (*sur le trottoir*) signifies destitution. They also incited the Québécois to "take to the street" (*Québécois, dans la rue*!). Proclaiming their solidarity with anticolonial movements in Vietnam and Latin America, they argued that Québec's situation should be understood in the same terms (figure 3.8).

Identical slogans and arguments had been forcefully presented by Pierre Vallières, a journalist, writer, and intellectual leader of the FLQ, in his book-length essay *White Niggers of America*, written in prison and published a year earlier, in 1968:

> Workers of Québec are fed up with speeches, flags, hymns, and parades. They want to have their own industries, control over the sale and consumption of their products, political power and economic security, the privilege of studying and sharing in the discoveries of science, etc. They

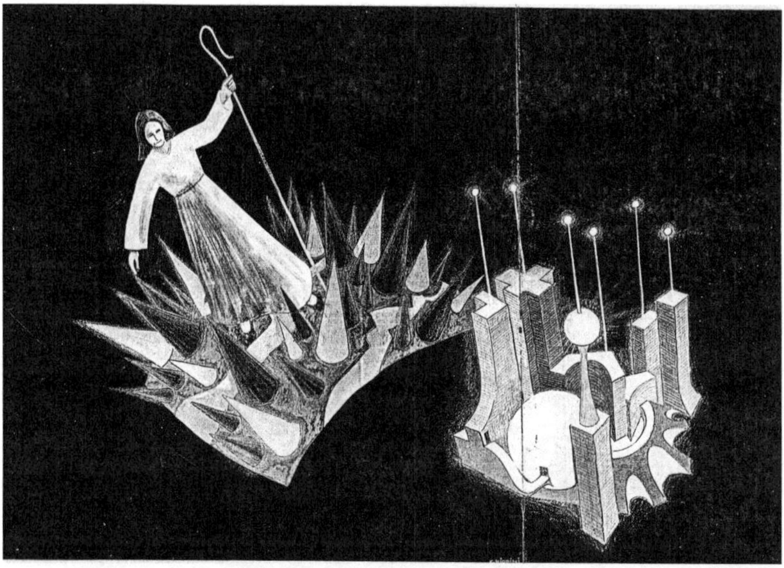

FIGURE 3.7 In this preliminary design for the saint's float in the 1969 parade, the saint is represented in adult form and holds a curled shepherd's crook instead of his traditional cross-shaped staff. On the actual float, the papier-mâché statue of the saint carried the traditional form of his staff (see figures 3.9 and 3.10) (Bibliothèque et Archives nationales du Québec à Montréal, Fonds P82/328 [Société Saint-Jean-Baptiste de Montréal]).

> no longer want to sit like beggars on either side of Sherbrooke Street every June 24 to behold, with joy befitting the occasion, the allegorical floats of an artificial "national pride" bought on credit at Household or Niagara Finance. The people are going to rise to their feet, parade in the streets themselves, and make of this country something other than a medieval masquerade organized by grocers who can scarcely see beyond the borders of their own parish. (1968, 33)

Vallières explains the historical conditions of French Canadians/Québécois in Marxist terms and characterizes traditional French Canadian nationalism as a pernicious form of false consciousness:

> The true reason for the insecurity of the workers is not that their wages are inadequate, that jobs are scarce, or that they are ignorant; it is essentially that they have no control over economic and social policy. That is what the workers of Québec have to get through their heads, as the saying goes. Because otherwise they will continue to remain for generations the white niggers of America, the cheap labor that the preda-

FIGURE 3.8 Protesters followed the 1969 parade, their placards proclaiming them to be "fed up with Saint-Jean [celebrations] on the sidewalk." In the eyes of young, progressive, politically active Québécois, watching the St-Jean-Baptiste parades from the sidelines was emblematic of French Canadians' passivity. Other placards proclaim the population to be "fed up with constitutional dead-ends" (*On est tanné des avortements constitutionnels*), referring to the fact that Canada's constitution could be amended only by the British Parliament (this was the case until 1982) (Bibliothèque et Archives nationales du Québec, BAnQ Québec, Division des archives photographiques, Fonds E-10, 69-147).

tors of industry, commerce, and high finance are so fond of, the way wolves are fond of sheep. Let us kill St. John the Baptist! Let us burn the papier-mâché traditions with which they have tried to build a myth around our slavery.

The Front de libération populaire, which organized the parallel parade or "People's March," distributed pamphlets in which they linked French Canadians' economic situation and discrimination in the labor market to the St-Jean-Baptiste celebrations:

> We have the lowest salaries in Canada;
> We represent 45% of the unemployed in Canada;
> We are thrown out of work like garbage . . . ;
> We, first arrived in America, are the last to be allowed to speak our language to earn a living;
> . . .
> We have our natural resources stolen by Americans;
> THAT'S WHAT WE, WHITE NIGGERS OF AMERICA, CELEBRATE ON JUNE 24!
>
> (Pamphlet distributed by the Front de libération populaire, quoted in *Journal de Montréal*, June 24, 1969, emphasis in original)

The small Marxist FLP and other leftist organizations considered it essential to abolish French Canadian's "servile mentality," symbolized by St. Jean-Baptiste and embodied by the parade. They organized the "People's March" to protest the parade and to campaign for the active participation of the people in national affairs. As it progressed, increasing numbers of spectators joined in. By the time it reached the west side of Montréal, it had swelled to between 10,000 and 15,000 protesters. The crowd was dense and excited, especially around and behind the St-Jean-Baptiste float. One subgroup in particular trailed the float closely for several miles. Suddenly several of its members seized the saint's float and overturned it. As the statue of the saint crashed onto the street, its head broke off (figure 3.9).

The float was overturned in front of the Ritz Carlton Hotel on Montréal's west side, the richer and predominantly Anglophone side of town.[10]

10. Until relatively recently, Montréal was said to be inhabited by "two solitudes," French and English. The expression originated in a novel of that title by Hugh MacLennan, published in English in 1945 and translated into French in 1963. The "solitudes" were separated not only by linguistic, cultural, and psychological barriers

FIGURE 3.9 When the saint's float was overturned, the head broke off from the body and was never found. Riot police can be seen in the background. The photo's caption reads: "As the parade was passing the Ritz Carlton Hotel, demonstrators surged forward and overturned the key float, a figure of St. Jean-Baptiste" (*Montreal Star*, June 25, 1969).

Here were two symbols sharing space for a brief instant: one associated in the 1960s with French Canadian servility and economic backwardness, the other signifying Anglophone wealth. Although it is impossible to divine the feelings of protesters at that moment—the historical record makes no mention of their declarations—it seems plausible that this juxtaposition of symbols caused a surge of anger in the protesters, whether by coincidence or by the design of the organizers. In that moment they lunged forward to destroy the icon that they saw as legitimating and even participating in the exploitation of those the Church claimed to represent.

Murder by Iconoclash

In the various sources I have consulted, I have found no indication that the saint was deliberately ritually beheaded. The journalistic descriptions,

but also by geographic and socioeconomic boundaries. Montréal is an island, with streets running east-west and south-north. The east side of town is primarily French-speaking, and the west side English-speaking. Between the two "solitudes" runs the north-south Boulevard Saint-Laurent. This is the "zero" street: the streets on either side bear the designations "East" and "West." It is also the neutral street, the immigrant street that originates in the city's port and provided a neutral meeting point for the so-called two solitudes. The St-Jean-Baptiste parades were held on Rue Sherbrooke, the city's main east-west artery. Starting on Montréal's east side the parade ended at the edge of the west side of town.

FIGURE 3.10 The headless papier-mâché statue of St. Jean-Baptiste is surrounded by protesters: men, women, and children. One protester proudly poses on the vanquished symbol. The caption in *La Patrie* reads: "Youth dismembered the symbol of French Canadians. The statue's head rolled away and probably constitutes today a trophy for some young rebel. The remains of the corpse were torn apart and scattered" (*La Patrie*, June 29, 1969).

however, were exceedingly thin, even those incorporating eyewitness accounts. The *Montreal Star*, for example, could only report what an American businessman saw from his room window on the 7th floor of the Ritz: "First I saw them put a placard in the hand of the St-Jean-Baptiste statue. Someone quickly replaced it with a fleur-de-lys flag. All of a sudden, they overturned the float. Then police moved in and there was fighting. Everyone was shouting" (June 25, 1969).

Regardless of the protesters' intent, the fact that it was the head that was ruptured from the body—rather than, for example, an arm or the saint's staff—endowed the incident with powerful significance, evoking the beheading of John the Baptist in the Bible. The biblical account provided both the interpretation of the event and the language for its description. The protesters were referred to as "headsmen" (*bourreaux*) (*Le Journal de Montréal*, June 26, 1969), and their action was described as the national Saint's "decapitation" (*Le Journal de Montréal*, June 24, 1969; *Le Devoir*, June 25, 1969). "The Saint's head rolled," one newspaper announced, "serving as a trophy" for Herod-like political elites (*La Patrie*, June 29, 1969) (figure 3.10). The parade as a whole was described in the press as a "massacre" (*La Presse*, June 25, 1969). In short order, the decapitation of the St-Jean-Baptiste statue came to be presented as its inescapable destiny instead of the accidental result of vandalism by overenthusiastic youth.

The incident can be described as what Bruno Latour has called *iconoclash* (Latour 2002). Unlike iconoclasm, in which the motivation and intentionality of the destruction are clear, iconoclash is characterized by an ambiguity in the intent of the actors, their action, and its reception. In this case, it is unclear whether the youths who attacked and overturned the saint's float actually meant to behead the statue or merely intended to disrupt the parade by desecrating it. The biblical precedent, however, seemed to remove any ambiguity from the act, and this interpretation was cemented by the visual reproduction of the headless body in the press during the days that followed.[11] The murder of the saint took place not (or not solely) during the violent act of protest itself but rather in the discursive wake of the events—in the media's narration and interpretation of the act.

The concept of iconoclash highlights the crucial link between materiality (the broken, headless papier-mâché statue), visuality (widely disseminated media photos of the headless statue), and narrative (the accounts of the "beheading" of the statue, following the biblical script). It also suggests that the beheading of the statue was different from other symbolic beheadings and dismemberments, such as the deliberate and highly ritualized decapitation of figures of saints in Revolutionary France, which were by definition iconoclastic.

The decapitation of the patron saint was also widely interpreted as another blow inflicted by left-leaning nationalists on the Catholic Church and the ethno-religious vision of national identity. A letter to the editor of the populist *Journal de Montréal*, from a self-defined "French Canadian who's had enough," shows how debates about St. John the Baptist went hand in hand with institutional transformations and pushed forward a new vision of the Québec nation. The writer of this commentary, rendered in the form of a prayer, clearly rejects that vision:

> O Jean-Baptiste, twice beheaded, the first time for Herod's pleasure,
> the second for René Lévesque and company,
> Have mercy on our misery and cowardice.
> Have mercy on our society, like you, beheaded . . .
> Have mercy on our hysterical, vandal, fanatic youth, completely led

11. The statue's head was never found, but according to rumor, it was passed from one group to another as a trophy (*La Patrie*, June 29, 1969).

astray by the breakdown of the family, immigration, and our great Ministry of Education.[12]
Have mercy on our race, which thinks that to grow up it is absolutely necessary to become atheist.
Have mercy on those energumens who are at the root of our destitution and de-Christianization.[13]
Have mercy on our race, ashamed of its past and throwing everything overboard.
Have mercy on our people, [which is] not evolving, but rather [involved] in a scandalous revolution against itself.
Remain our patron saint, O Beheaded Saint Jean-Baptiste.
Assist those on the Right, disgusted.
And vomit on the others a well-deserved fundamentalist communism, so that we all may repent.

(*Le Journal de Montréal*, July 10, 1969)

For the author of this prayer, the society created through the Quiet Revolution was a maimed one; the secularization of Québec is described as itself a form of beheading, and the removal of the Catholic Church from its traditional domains, such as education, is felt as the amputation of a limb from the nation's body.

While some deplored the torture and execution of the saint and the vision of society it represented, others applauded it. In an interview shortly after the event, the filmmaker Pierre Perrault, one of the hastily silenced commentators of the parade, explained the motivations for his satirical comments: "The days of papier-mâché are over. For too long, people were given drums and trumpets to keep silent. That's not how one builds a country. As far as I'm concerned, the real parade happened when we had already been taken off the air. The real parade was the young people who arrived en masse after the last floats to overturn the statue of St. Jean-Baptiste. We have a country to build. It's no time to make speeches and line up majorettes. That is just another way to distract people and keep them silent" (*Le Petit Journal*, June 29, 1969). Perrault's rhetoric in this ad-libbed interview is brilliant. He invokes both the symbolic mean-

12. The Ministry of Education was created in 1964. Its foundation was controversial because it took control of public education out of the hands of the Catholic Church (though education remained confessional).

13. The theological term *energumen* originally denoted a person possessed by an evil spirit. It has come to mean *fanatic* in both French and English. While rarely used in English, it is quite common in French.

ing of the saint's statue and the fragile material of its construction to criticize the French Canadian national project, or the lack thereof. In claiming that "the days of papier-mâché are over," he suggests the need to build a nation from sturdier materials than those that the statue represents. That nation, however, should be not merely a cultural construct, like French Canada, but political: a *country*. Perrault further equates the noisy diversions of "drums and trumpets" with the silencing of the nation, and the parade's artifice with the distraction of the masses. He thus builds an eloquent argument for abolishing the parade to allow true nation building, to make Québec a country.

On the other side of town, perhaps strolling on Rue Sherbrooke, Anglophone readers picking up a copy of the *Montreal Star* the day after the parade read the headline "Violence Mars SSJB Extravaganza: Parade in Danger of Being Banned." They saw a large, innocent-looking photograph of five uniformed members of a marching band, with the caption "The parade started off with lively airs by a cadet's band, but ended up with demonstrators overturning a float, stoning police and looting." Sharing top billing on the front page was a story about a bomb found in Wales in a bag "near a monument commemorating the occasion in 1958 when [Prince] Charles first set foot in Wales." The article went on to discuss various Welsh nationalist groups and the potential danger to Prince Charles, scheduled to board a yacht at that site after being invested as Prince of Wales. This editorial juxtaposition served as a warning to the *Star*'s English-speaking readership that no nationalist event could be seen as entirely innocent or harmless.[14]

The *Montreal Star* article on the St-Jean-Baptiste holiday announced that "a decapitated effigy of St. Jean-Baptiste sits on a battered float in a city junk yard today, possibly summing up the fate of parades marking French Canada's biggest holiday." The journalist was dead right: the traditional parade never returned, and the rupture effectively closed a chapter in Québec history. The verbal attacks and material reworkings of St. Jean-Baptiste throughout the 1960s until its final iconoclash-istic destruction in 1969—what I have called aesthetic revolt—killed Catholic French Canadianness and left its head rolling in the street. But from another perspective, the beheaded saint augured future redemption: emptying the

14. The main story claimed that "the real target" of the June 24 protest was Anglophone McGill University but that "poor planning coupled with an inadvertent police action" derailed those plans. *Montreal Star*, June 25, 1969.

street of St-Jean-Baptiste parades left room for a whole new form of secular Québécois identity.

Institutional Abolition of the Parades

In the days following the parade, François-Albert Angers, the president of the SSJBM, received several letters from discontented members such as Louis-Henri Bonneville, a pharmacist, who lamented that the St-Jean-Baptiste holiday had become "a nest and a pretext for revolution, contempt for authority, disorder and anarchy" (June 25, 1969, Archives du centre de recherche Lionel-Groulx, P63/A3.2). Another member of the SSJBM, though, resigned from the society because it was too conservative and detached from the ongoing national struggle. He explained that even though "there no longer is a sheep chained to the saint, the people still has a chain around its neck" (Maurice Chaput to F.-A. Angers, July 18, 1969, and Sept. 28, 1969, P63/A3.2).

Angers responded to these criticisms in a statement issued after an SSJBM meeting, which was published in major Francophone newspapers:

> The celebration of *la [fête] Saint-Jean* is one of our oldest popular traditions, and a significant part of our people is still attached to it. It is in recognition of this solidly anchored tradition for a people that was still 99.99% Catholic, that in 1908 [Pope] Pius X consecrated Saint John the Baptist as official patron saint to the French Canadian people. In so doing, the Church was showing much greater concern [then] to popular sentiments than certain anarchists [today]. By giving us Saint John the Baptist for our patron, the Church was putting her seal on the traditional conviction that the French Canadians understood themselves as precursors on American soil. The Church was supporting our presence [here] with a symbol of strength, and not of weakness, as misinformed mockers assert. In every country of the world, ancient symbols change signification as beliefs change. Yet they are preserved and respected as a sign of the permanence and continuity of national life. Even for those who no longer have religious faith, Jean-Baptiste remains a historical man who announced the greatest cultural revolution ever produced in the history of the world. For open-minded people, he shouldn't be prevented from remaining the symbol of an ideal, and of a French Canadian future.... Those who no longer know how to respect and uphold such traditional values are wrong in their belief that they can truly represent the people's soul. For the people's soul is not petty; and the vandalism in-

> volved in the destruction of the saint's float under the pretense that he no longer means anything to us is only the sign of ideological pettiness that the people does not endorse. (SSJBM press release, July 19, Archives du Centre de Recherche Lionel-Groulx, P63/A3.4, pp. 4–5)

Angers also received disturbing letters of a different kind. The disruptions of the parade meant that sponsored floats had not received the promised television exposure (Petrofina Canada, Letter to the Commission des Fêtes du Canada Français, Archives nationales du Québec, P82 1995-01-002/321). Sponsors withdrew their financial support and refused to pay their outstanding obligations to the SSJBM.

The parades were ultimately abolished as much for lack of funds and willing sponsors as for reasons of vocal and physical opposition to their message and vision. Obviously, these economic and cultural reasons were thoroughly intertwined; together they wove the cords that choked support for the parades.

Blinks, Winks, and Historical Transformations

Certain moments in the transformation of the symbolic structure of the St-Jean-Baptiste tableau highlight the interactions among agency, unintentional actions, and consequential historical change. The removal of the lamb from the *tableau vivant* had significant but unforeseen consequences: it altered the meaning of the child and hastened his replacement with an adult statue a year later. The unintentional decapitation of St. John the Baptist, by contrast, had all-too-predictable consequences. Although it was accidental, it was easily seen as a deliberate and symbolically loaded decapitation because of the parallel with the biblical story. In other words, in Clifford Geertz's famed expression (1973), the blink was interpreted as a wink. Thus the consequences of the material manipulations were more evident and immediately legible in the case of St. John the Baptist than in the case of the lamb because the biblical story of the saint's life constrained how it could be read (or, more accurately, seen). Consider the following alternative scenarios: the float is overturned without damage to the statue; another part of the statue, such as its left foot, is broken; or the statue is defaced with paint. None of these outcomes would be likely to have had the same impact as the breaking off of its head.

That this wink was most likely a blink was not relevant. Photographs of the beheaded statue in the press during the days that followed affirmed the interpretation of the event as a deliberately iconoclastic gesture. Its subsequent presentation in the media as the willful murder of the saint constituted what William H. Sewell Jr. describes as an "act of signification." As Sewell points out, the symbolic interpretation of events on the part of social actors themselves "is part and parcel of the historical event" (Sewell 1996, 861). This act of signification, of interpreting the headless statue of St. Jean-Baptiste lying in the street as a beheaded corpse, left no alternative but to dispose of the saint and abolish the parade in his honor. The biblical script rendered the repair of the symbol inconceivable: St. John, unlike Jesus, was not resurrected. With the demise of the patron saint, a novel articulation of national identity, that of secular Québécois, became possible. The beheading, therefore, marked the death of French Canada as a viable national vision. That transformation was institutionalized through the abolition of the annual parade and the creation of new modes of celebration for the new nation. While at first glance appearing anecdotal, upon closer investigation the "happening" is revealed to have been in fact a historic "event" (Sewell 1996).

The effects of these symbolic manipulations are embedded both in the material logic and discursive penumbra of the symbols themselves and in the broader historical conjuncture and specific performative context of the parade. The orbits of meaning of both lamb and saint depend on the material features of their representations. The omission of the lamb from the saint's day celebrations stemmed from criticisms of its vulnerable, fleecy, and pastoral characteristics. Likewise, the representation of the saint at different ages, and using different materials, was affected by its public reception, and in turn it influenced the events and the interpretations that followed.

The removal of the lamb arguably precipitated the events that followed. The lamb was removed because some of its material characteristics, including its wool, became newly significant in the context of the Quiet Revolution's emphasis on *rattrapage* and economic reforms. Without the lamb, the child St. Jean-Baptiste was rendered incomprehensible and had to be replaced by a mature figure. The overturning of the float and the removal and decapitation of the saint, in turn, could be read according to the biblical script only because the saint was now represented as an adult. That entire chain of events, finally, had impact because it was forged in the public sphere, in the context of parades dedicated to the saint.

These events show that the properties of symbols intersect with, but are not strictly limited to, human intentionality. They take part, *act*, in the causation of events—in this case, the transformation and secularization of national identity.

KEY TROPE *The Soil*

THIS ILLUSTRATION (trope 3.1) IS FROM THE 1932 ST-JEAN-BAPTISTE Day commemorative program. The theme of that year's parade was "Glory to the Soil," and it exalted the virtue and importance of agriculture as a way of life. It shows a grandfather and grandson sitting on the porch of their stone farmhouse, looking pensively at the rural landscape. The juxtaposition of the generations implies the importance of continuity with the past, and the caption, "La terre de chez-nous," can be translated as "our land," or "the soil of our land." By 1931, 59.5% of Québec's population was urban (Linteau et al. 1991, 31). Most French Canadian city dwellers were working in low-paying manual labor, with large families living in cramped rentals. The agricultural way of life was therefore somewhat

TROPE 3.1 Bibliothèque et Archives nationales du Québec, BAnQ Vieux Montréal, Fonds Société Saint-Jean-Baptiste de Montréal, P82.

romanticized by the working classes: the farmer was seen as his own boss, living modestly but in dignity.

Throughout the nineteenth century, the Church and many intellectuals also idealized and forcefully promoted the agricultural way of life, which they saw as more noble and presenting fewer moral dangers than life in the city. For Esdras Minville, a prominent conservative economist and sociologist in the 1920s and 1930s, the countryside was the "reservoir of the nation" (*le réservoir de la race*), since the countryside had a higher birthrate and offered more sanitary living conditions (more sun, fresh air, and less risk of disease epidemics). In addition, it functioned as a better guardian of traditional French Canadian culture because it was more resistant to American cultural influences (Foisy-Geoffroy 2004, 38–39). The Church encouraged the colonization of Abitibi in Northern Québec in the 1910s and during the Depression to save urban workers from dramatic poverty and depravity. The "Glory to the Soil" theme can be seen as part of that endeavor and of the broader ruralist movement.

The quaint ad (trope 3.2) for the Steinberg grocery chain was published in *Le Devoir* on June 25, 1964. It was customary, until the late 1960s, for large corporations and smaller businesses (as well as political groups and parties) to publish ads in the form of good wishes to French Canadians on their patronal/national holiday. These ads extolled the virtues of French Canadians while reminding them of the business's role in employing and serving them. This specific ad celebrates the *cultivateur* (the word used in Québec to refer to a small farmer). The *cultivateur* is depicted carrying on his shoulder a basket of potatoes, pipe in mouth, knee-deep in a row of vegetables, with his farm in the background. On the far right, Steinberg advertises that week's specials, with Québec produce prominently advertised at the top of the list. The text extols the role of agriculture in Québec:

> Long Live the *Cultivateur*!
>
> The *cultivateur* has always occupied a paramount place in French Canada's long and colorful history, from the beginning of colonization. His multiple virtues have all been praised: the man of the land with legendary patience, the man imbued with tradition, whose sense of humor and probity give our province its truly unique character.
>
> Even if, since the industrial era, Québec has been transformed almost beyond recognition, "La Belle Province" remains tied to the land. From its fertile soil comes almost everything we need for our subsistence. A well-fed people is a happy people.
>
> For us at Steinberg's, the farmer is not merely a supplier but also a

TROPE 3.2 *Le Devoir*, June 25, 1964.

friend. Working with him, we have learned to value his judgment and respect his integrity. In our constant and continued effort to bring to our customers the freshest fruits and vegetables of the highest quality, he remains our closest collaborator and our most reliable guide.

Today, before his cultivated fields, on the eve of a summer of labor, we offer him this rich homage. Long live the *Cultivateur*!

Steinberg, a Montréal-based, Jewish-owned supermarket chain, was advertising in Québec's elite and traditionally nationalist French-language newspaper *Le Devoir*, where the romanticized view of the Canadien-*agriculteur* was unlikely to resonate with readers in 1964. In fact, the ad highlights the very economic inequality that the Quiet Revolution program of *rattrapage* and development sought to redress, with capital and large businesses held by English-speaking Protestants and Jews while French Canadians were busy working the land or toiling in factories. While the agricultural way of life was romanticized by members of the urban working classes in the first half of the century because farmers at least owned their land, by the 1960s that romance had faded. The ad therefore also highlights the extent to which big business was disconnected from the important changes in *mentalité* that occurred in 1960s Québec.

This attitudinal change, these new values, and the mores of the Quiet

Revolution's baby-boomers were harshly criticized in the first verse of the song "Dégénérations" by popular folk band Mes Aïeux, some forty years later:

> Your great-great grandfather was the one who cleared the land
> Your great-grandfather was the one who worked the soil
> Your grandfather turned a profit from the land
> Then your father sold it to become a government employee
> Now you, boy, you don't know what to do
> In your one-bedroom apartment; too expensive yet cold in winter
> Sometimes a vague desire comes upon you to own something of your own
> And you dream at night of owning an acre of land.

PART TWO *Making and Debating Québécois-ness*

4 Iconographic Remaking and the Politics of Identity

The Ambiguous Reinvention of the Fête

When destroying monuments, spare the pedestals. They can always be useful.[1]

—Stanisław Jerzy Lec

The Beginning of a New Era

The beheading of the St-Jean-Baptiste statue in the 1969 parade closed one chapter in Québec history and opened another. As a contested symbol within Québec's fraught political terrain, the eradication of the saint and his parade left a gap. Some of the very actors involved in the discursive destruction of the religious-national icon were subsequently invited to "rethink" the St-Jean-Baptiste celebrations. They included Pierre Perrault, one of the Radio-Canada commentators who had mocked the 1969 parade he was supposed to praise on the air. In 1970, he replaced the parade with a "popular march" through Montréal's historic neighborhoods and large communitarian picnics. In the mid-1970s, June 24th became the occasion of impressive and hugely popular concerts and parties in the Parc Mont-Royal, a large park on the hill in the heart of Montréal, some of which continued for days. Traditional religious observances gave way to festivities that had no religious tenor and little political content.

1. From *Myśli nieuczesane* (Unkempt thoughts), my translation. The Polish original reads, "Burząc pomniki, oszczędzajcie cokoły. Zawsze mogą się przydać." It does not claim that pedestals will always be used for new monuments, as the common translation implies; it merely suggests that they *can* be useful in that regard. What is significant is to identify when and how certain monuments, icons, and symbols are replaced with new ones, *which* ones, and why.

FIGURE 4.1 Promotional poster for the 1971 St-Jean-Baptiste celebrations. The holiday was still known as "La St-Jean," but its Catholic dimension had already been replaced by the day's association with the summer's solstice (Bibliothèque et Archives nationales du Québec à Montréal, Fonds P82).

Yet St. Jean-Baptiste remained visible in an abstract and secular form. When the sovereignist (and secularist) Parti Québécois came to power on November 15, 1976, it established June 24 as Québec's legal *national* holiday.[2] "La Fête nationale," as the holiday has since then been officially designated, is celebrated with rock concerts, fireworks, and public bonfires, events at which the nation's bards and political figures affirm their alle-

2. St-Jean-Baptiste Day was often referred to as the French Canadian national holiday in the first half of the twentieth century, but it was not legally instituted as such: it was "national" in the ethnocultural sense, as St. Patrick's Day is the Irish national holiday. In 1977, it became a state-sanctioned holiday: that is, national in the civic sense. Although St-Jean-Baptiste Day was observed as a day free of work before 1977, its "nationalization" made it a paid holiday (Decree no. 1600–77, May 18, 1977).

FIGURE 4.2 The celebration of the Fête nationale in Québec City in 2005 reflects the new national aesthetic that developed in the 1970s (THE CANADIAN PRESS/Jacques Boissinot).

giance to Québec amid a sea of blue and white *Fleurdelisé* flags. The aesthetics of this spectacle could not be more different from those of the traditional parades (see figure 4.2).

Although la Fête nationale is celebrated on the saint's name day, its Catholic heritage has been officially purged. Government publications and websites describe the pre-Christian origins of the summer solstice celebrations and the traditions inherited from the early days of the colony's festivities. Québec's official tourism website, Bonjour Québec, explains that the Fête nationale "originates in the tradition, practiced in several countries, of celebrating the summer solstice with bonfires and popular dances."[3] The website of the Movement national des Québécoises et Québécois, the organization responsible for the coordination of the holiday since 1984, declares that the celebration dates from "time immemorial" and is related to the summer solstice.

To underline the pagan origins of the holiday, in 1981 the color yellow,

3. Government of Québec, Bonjour Québec, www.bonjourQuébec.com/qc-fr/repertoire-evenements/fête-festival-evenement/fête-nationale-du-Québec_1413304.html, accessed July 15, 2013. Similar narratives are found in de Carufel and Ayotte (1980) and Paulette (1980). While the Catholic history is no longer completely repressed, the holiday does not figure prominently.

symbolizing the sun, was added to the blue and white of the *Fleurdelisé* as an official color of the Fête nationale (Chartier and Vaudry 2007, 100, 236). Although in recent years perfunctory references to the saint have been reintroduced to official histories of the holiday, the emphasis remains heavily on the pre-Christian and political origins of the celebration. Indeed, it is now increasingly linked to the 1834 Patriots' banquet and the ideals that that event embodied.[4]

In sum, a century of celebrations is now almost wholly disregarded, excising the ethno-religious genesis of the French Canadian nation prior to its Québécois redefinition. While the holiday is still commonly referred to as "La Saint-Jean" (and rarely, if ever, colloquially called by its official name), few people under the age of forty-five can explain why it is celebrated on June 24 or referred to by that name.[5] How did this happen in the decades since the Quiet Revolution? I assess this broad transformation through two much more specific questions. First, why did the Parti Québécois choose the saint's name day for the national holiday at the very moment when the nation was instituting itself as secular? Second, why, given that choice, erase the very event that made a secular identity possible, namely the symbolic "beheading" of the saint? Investigating these questions will allow us not only to disentangle the convoluted relationship between religion, nationalism, and secularism but also to shed light on the dialectic between tradition, mnemonic erasure, and cultural reinvention. One preliminary answer to those questions, I suggest, is that rather than erasing Catholicism or the "French Canadian" identity, the Fête nationale materializes, recodes, and perpetuates vital tensions between Catholicism and secularism, between French Canadian and Québécois national iden-

4. See official website "La Fête nationale du Québec," www.fetenationale.qc.ca/fr/a-propos/histoire, accessed July 15, 2013. See also Chartier and Vaudry (2007). (Since I downloaded materials from that page in 2013, the webpage's address was changed to http://www.fetenationale.quebec/, dropping the ".ca." from its web address. The use of the Internet domain .quebec has become quite popular in recent years. The Gouvernement du Québec websites maintain its "qc.ca" domains.

5. These findings are based on participant observation of St-Jean-Baptiste celebrations in 2007, 2008, and 2009. On selective memory and the invention of tradition in 1970s Québec, see Handler (1988). See also Andréanne Germain's documentary *Pis nous autres, dans tout ça?* (What about us in all this?), which is about Franco-Ontarians celebrating the St-Jean-Baptiste in Québec City. The Québécois interviewed in the film know very little about the history of the holiday besides its pagan origins and do not understand why Franco-Ontarians would care about what they consider to be *Québec*'s national holiday.

tities, and between the social and political institutions of the nation. But before examining the reinvention of the fête and the politics of Québécois identity I provide the reader with the political context necessary for the reader to grasp the meaning, significance, and stakes of that post–Quiet Revolution symbolic politics.

Political Landscape and Agendas in the Wake of the Quiet Revolution

As mentioned in the previous chapter, one of the Quiet Revolution's outcomes was the creation of the Parti Québécois (PQ) in 1968 and the specific articulation of a political program for the independence of Québec. René Lévesque, by the end of the 1960s, had come to the conclusion that political sovereignty was the only path to the rightful development of the nation and thus left the Parti libéral du Québec (PLQ), which remained committed to developing Québec as a province within Canada. The PQ was thus constituted by members of the left wing of the PLQ, who followed Lévesque, and by the moderate wing of the more radical Rassemblement pour l'indépendance nationale (RIN).[6] With the creation of the PQ, the PLQ's position within the broader provincial political field shifted to the center right; not because its policy orientations had changed, but because of the general move to the left in Québec politics. With its left wing gone, the PLQ became a conservative party despite its name. To this day it remains socioeconomically to the right of the PQ, and committed to working within the Canadian federal framework.

The PQ's *raison d'être* was the creation of an independent Québec, and it came to power in 1976 with the promise to hold a referendum on sovereignty. That referendum was held and lost on May 20, 1980. That political project has not ceased to shape the political life of Québec (and Canada), however. In fact, it is safe to say that the political history of post–Quiet Revolution Québec has revolved around the independence question on the one hand, and the place of Québec within Canada on the other. Following the first referendum's strong "no," in 1981 Prime Minister Pierre Elliott Trudeau repatriated the 1867 Canadian Constitution (the British North America Act) from London, and amendments were negotiated by all the provinces of Canada. Although Québec did not agree with some

6. The RIN was dissolved in 1968. Part of its moderate wing joined the PQ, part of its left wing joined the FLP. Its radical elements had joined the FLQ earlier, in 1963. See note 1, chapter 3.

of the proposed amendments and did not endorse the Constitution, the document was ratified in 1982. As the province was legally bound by the provisions of the Constitution Act of 1982 even though it had not endorsed them, many in Québec felt that the ratification had been a betrayal and an unfair imposition. In 1987, negotiations were therefore initiated by the incoming prime minister of Canada, Brian Mulroney, at Meech Lake in Southwest Québec near the Ontarian border, to convince Québec to endorse the 1982 constitutional act. The Meech Lake Accord consisted of a series of amendments to the 1982 Constitution, to be agreed on by the ten provincial premiers. Most concerned a greater decentralization and increase of provincial powers, as well as the recognition of Québec as a distinct society within Canada. For the accord to take effect (and the Constitution to be amended), unanimous approval by the legislatures of the ten provinces was needed by June 23, 1990. On the very last day, Manitoba and Newfoundland rejected the accord, objecting to Québec's status as a "distinct society." This rejection reinvigorated support for independence in the province, and another referendum on sovereignty was held in 1995. That time the results were much closer, with just over one percentage point dividing the "no" from the "yes" camps (see note 15, chapter 1).

After two lost referenda, independence receded in the background of provincial politics, although the "Québec question" did not disappear from the federal agenda. On November 27, 2006, the Canadian House of Commons passed a motion formally recognizing that "the Québécois form a nation within a united Canada" (House of Commons Debates 2006). This symbolic recognition, sixteen years after the rejection of Meech's clause on "distinct society," had little resonance in Québec. It was primarily understood as a gesture in federal electoral games with no potential political-legal traction.

With this wide *tour d'horizon* completed, let us return to symbolic politics and the complex identity reconfiguration taking place in the 1980s and 1990s.

La Fête Nationale as Hybrid

The fate of St. Jean-Baptiste after the Quiet Revolution—first beheaded and then buried by the establishment of a secular national holiday on the saint's name day—marks the rejection of Catholicism as part of the identity of the Québécois nation (in distinction from French Canada). Yet it also evidences the continued presence of a religious temporal order that

FIGURE 4.3 "Nationalization." Lévesque declares, "The first thing we had to nationalize was Saint-Jean-Baptiste Day!" as his vice premier, Jacques-Yvan Morin, enthusiastically agrees, "Obviously!" In the background is a spectacular *fleur de lys* firework (Bibliothèque et Archives nationales du Québec, BAnQ Vieux Montréal, Fonds Jean-Marc Phaneuf, P575).

informs and infiltrates the "secular" one. Although the saint was beheaded and his float destroyed, the St-Jean-Baptiste celebration survived in the guise of a new identity, the Fête nationale.

The choice of June 24 for the national holiday and the rapidity with which it was legally enacted (only a few months after the Parti Québécois was elected) was far from an obvious or predictable sequence of events, as the cynical caricature in figure 4.3 illustrates. It was especially perplexing given the Parti Québécois's agenda and the criticism aimed at the holiday throughout the 1960s. Why bother with the holiday at all, given its complex and contested history? Why not leave it behind altogether, in the kind of "happy forgetting" that Paul Ricoeur called a necessary part of all collective memory (2004)? There are several potential reasons. First, as parliamentary transcripts attest, the continued popularity of the St-Jean-Baptiste holiday—albeit in new forms—and its longstanding tradition militated against simply eliminating it. Lévesque declared: "For over a century now it has been customary to celebrate Saint-Jean-Baptiste Day with an ever-growing feeling of national pride. With its ceremonies and festivities, June 24 . . . is the celebration par excellence of our national character. The Conseil des Ministres has therefore . . . decided . . . that June 24, Saint-Jean-Baptiste Day, will from now on *also* be known as the Fête nationale du Québec. Moreover, [the government] has approved a recommendation . . . to make that day a paid holiday."[7]

Religio-Secular Syncretism

Another possible reason for nationalizing the holiday so quickly was that by doing so, the PQ was *de jure* secularizing it, thereby de facto resacralizing it, an idea I explicate below. As I argued in the previous chapter, St. John the Baptist, as patron saint of the French Canadians of North America, was a sacred religio-national symbol. It was sacred because of both its religious semantics *and* its secular national ones, which were tightly intertwined. In the 1960s, however, the icon's sacredness was doubly forfeited: the religious symbol was secularized by the lamb's removal, and the national symbol was desacralized by discursive and physical attacks. Desecrated and desacralized, the icon became both secular and profane.

In 1977, Lévesque's government officially secularized the holiday by instituting it legally as a national holiday. Once officially stripped of its religious meaning, June 24 could legitimately be envisioned as the holiday of all Québécois, regardless of creed or ethnicity, instead of being the traditional Catholic holiday of the "French Canadians of North America." The nationalization qua secularization of the holiday therefore symbolically made possible a broader, more inclusive, civic vision of Québécois national identity.

That complex process was brilliantly captured by a cartoon in which René Lévesque, dressed in a prophet's robe, is shown sacralizing the saint by nationalizing him (figure 4.4). Paradoxically, it was the legal nationalization of the holiday that, so to speak, consecrated the day as "sacred"

7. *Débats de l'Assemblée Nationale*, Fonds E207, Archives nationales du Québec à Montréal, May 18, 1977, my emphasis.

FIGURE 4.4 “Canonization.” René Lévesque “canonizes” the St-Jean-Baptiste holiday by secularizing and nationalizing it in language evoking Jesus’s foundation of the Church in the Gospel of Matthew (Bibliothèque et Archives nationales du Québec, BAnQ Vieux Montréal, Fonds Jean-Marc Phaneuf, P575).

in a new sense, that of the secular, civic nation. This transition is implied by the *fleur de lys* halo over Jean-Baptiste’s head and by the solemn words Lévesque addresses to the saint: “Jean, on this people and for this people I shall build a country.” The caption puns on the name Jean and the French word *gens*, meaning “people.” This pun in turn is a clever play on the words of Jesus to Peter: “You are Peter, and on this rock I will build my church” (Matthew 16:18), since the name Pierre, the French equivalent of Peter, means “rock” (“Tu es Pierre, et sur cette pierre je bâtirai mon Église”).

Despite the irony, however, the holiday continued to represent a complex religious-secular syncretism. Its intrinsic ambiguities are illustrated by a 1980 photograph of René Lévesque lighting his cigarette from the ceremonial candle used to ignite the traditional St-Jean-Baptiste bonfire,

FIGURE 4.5 René Lévesque lights his cigarette from the candle used to light the St-Jean-Baptiste bonfire. Newspaper clipping found in Bibliothèque et Archives nationales du Québec, BAnQ Vieux Montréal, Fonds Comité organisateur de la Fête Nationale du Québec, E207/6.

which, through its pre-Christian associations, survived the revamping of the national holiday (figure 4.5).

The ritual of lighting the bonfire, until the early seventies the privilege of the Catholic archbishop (figure 4.6), has been usurped by the premier, highlighting the rise of secular power in post–Quiet Revolution Québec.[8]

In another echo of the earlier saint's day ceremony, Lévesque and his wife are accompanied by a young boy unrelated to them and conspicuously reminiscent of earlier depictions of the blond, curly-haired St. Jean-Baptiste. (It had been customary until the mid-1960s for the little boy impersonating the saint to be at the side of the archbishop at the lighting of the bonfire on the eve of the holiday.) The saint's pelt has been replaced

8. In French, the last name Lévesque means "bishop"—hence René Lévesque's common depiction in cartoons as a bishop, and numerous other verbal and visual puns.

FIGURE 4.6 Cover of *L'Oiseau Bleu*, a children's magazine published by the SSJBM. Meant as a pedagogical tool for patriotism, the monthly appeared from 1921 until 1940. On this specific cover, on the occasion of St-Jean-Baptiste Day, "Our national holiday," a scene from New France depicts the colony's governor respectfully handing the ceremonial candle to the archbishop so that he can light another section of the bonfire (Bibliothèque et Archives nationales du Québec, digital collection available at http://collections.banq.qc.ca/ark:/52327/2225698).

by a French striped *matelot* T-shirt. Perhaps most significant, the scene captures the political ambivalence toward the religio-secular symbolism of the holiday in Lévesque's wickedly satirical profanation of the ritual by lighting his cigarette with the ceremonial candle.

The Underdetermined Fête Nationale: Québécois *and* French Canadian?

While the intent might have been to create a sacred-secular holiday, in practice the PQ government created a religio-secular hybrid. They also created an "ethno-civic" one. The phrasing of Lévesque's declaration to the National Assembly that "June 24, Saint-Jean-Baptiste Day, will from now on *also* be known as the Fête nationale du Québec" implied that the secular holiday was not replacing St-Jean-Baptiste Day but rather grafting a new meaning onto it. The implications of his use of the word *also* were not lost on the chief of the conservative (and federalist) PLQ, Gérard-D. Lévesque, who remarked:

> June 24 has always been the holiday of French Canada. We now make [it] the national holiday of Québec. . . . We are fortunate . . . to be able to demonstrate the great solidarity that unites all Québécois, those of French language and culture, and those who belong to other cultural horizons but are no less authentic and real Québécois. . . . A holiday for all Québécois certainly has its *raison d'être*. But . . . the government should certainly not ignore that a very great majority . . . of many non-Québécois throughout Canada remain deeply attached to French language and culture. I would have hoped that the holiday of French Canada could remain an occasion to affirm this great French Canadian solidarity. . . . [But] if I understood the premier's declaration . . . , the word *also* might leave room to associate the national holiday of Québec more closely with the greater community of French language and culture that exists throughout Canada and even North America.[9]

René Lévesque's allusions to St-Jean-Baptiste Day and his use of *also* thus opened the door to an understanding of the Fête nationale as celebration of the new, civic, and inclusive Québécois nation, even as it softened the harsh rupture with the French Canadian social form and those who identified with it.

Other political leaders, while recognizing this territorial civic inclu-

9. *Débats de l'Assemblée Nationale*, May 18, 1977.

siveness, also promoted the idea of Québec as a homeland for Francophone minorities outside the new polity. Rodrigue Biron, from the conservative Union nationale, declared that "in order for June 24 to become a genuine national holiday for Québec, it had to be first of all a holiday for all Québécois, for all those who live in Québec and make a living in Québec, regardless of their ethnic origins, their culture or their language." He added, "The June 24 [celebrations] will show the world that Québec, with respect and in recognition of all its components, has legitimate aspirations and its own identity, *which does not prevent it . . . from radiating beyond Québec, in solidarity with our Francophone brothers throughout Canada*." [10]

The celebration of the holiday was then decentralized, democratized, and subsidized by the government. In 1978, 781 projects from 15 regions were proposed, of which 31 were from "ethnic communities" who had been invited to participate by sharing their own cultural traditions. There were 157 sites of celebrations in Montréal alone and 15,000 bonfires across Québec. An estimated 3.5 million people participated in locally organized events.[11]

While the participation of "ethnic communities" was an encouraging sign for supporters of the Parti Québécois's political project, for others it was troubling. In a letter addressed to François-Albert Angers, the former president of the SSJBM, the representative of the Sherbrooke SSJB decried Québec's nationalization of St-Jean-Baptiste Day. He argued that inviting other ethnic groups had the effect of "diluting *our* holiday" (emphasis mine). Angers responded that in his view, "celebrating Saint-Jean-Baptiste Day as the 'national holiday of French Canadians' better reflected the true meaning of the celebration than the expression 'Holiday of the Québécois'—which does not mean the same thing for everyone. [The former] expresses more clearly what we have always wanted to celebrate: the survival of a people that refuses to disappear, and fights for its national life."[12]

From its very inception, then, the Fête nationale contained a tension between the French Canadian past and the Québécois present, a tension

10. Ibid., my emphasis. The Union nationale was a conservative party in Québec, founded in 1935. Maurice Duplessis led the party from its foundation until his death in 1959, ruling Québec from 1936 to 1939 and 1944 to 1960. The party declined in the 1970s, lost all its provincial seats in the April 1981 election, and was finally abolished in 1989.

11. Letter from Claude Charron, minister responsible for the Fête nationale, to François-Albert Angers, former president of the SSJBM, April 10, 1979. Archives du Centre de recherche Lionel-Groulx, cote P63/a3.8.

12. Letter from Marcel Bureau to François-Albert Angers, June 21, 1979. François-Albert Angers' personal correspondence, Archives du Centre de recherche Lionel-Groulx, cote P63/a3.8.

soon expressed in debates about how to think of Québec's future. Some nationalists now believed sovereignty to be a desirable, even "natural" option. An editorial in a small Montréal newspaper, commenting on the upcoming program of the 1977 Fête nationale, declared that "June 24 no longer needs to be an occasion for confrontation or for reclamation. We now know that we are a people [i.e., a nation]. This week is [instead] the occasion to show that Québec figures in the ranks of the most-industrialized and culturally developed countries" (Jean-Yvon Houle, *La voix métropolitaine*, June 21, 1977). For others, however, French Canada remained a meaningful concept, and continued affiliation with a larger Canada made sense.

The friction between these affinities—French Canadian versus Québécois—was at the heart of the referendum on Québec's sovereignty in 1980. The prime minister of Canada, Pierre Elliott Trudeau (r. 1968–79, 1980–84), much like provincial political leaders for the "no" camp, capitalized on that ambivalence by linking the Québécois independence movement to the wholesale relinquishing of Canada. Addressing a crowd of Québécois who were against the independence of Québec, he appealed to their French Canadian pride:

> It's at the moment when Québec becomes adult, at the moment when the government of Jean Lesage has brought it into the modern era, at the moment when Québec already has technocrats, already has scientists, already has people in all domains, in athletics—the best of the Canada games!—in sports, in culture, in literature!—It's at the moment when Québec is in full possession of its means, that we [French Canadians in Québec] are going to let go of that country [Canada]? . . . Come on! They ["Separatists"] haven't seen anything yet!
>
> It's at this moment, on the contrary, that we are going to say that [we care about] the country our ancestors discovered, that they explored, that they colonized—against all odds, despite a terrible climate; [Our ancestors] who settled very far away and fought as a minority, were deported from Acadia, were stripped of their constitutional rights . . . like in Manitoba.

After describing the heroism of French settlers and the discrimination against their descendants, spread from the eastern coast to the prairies, Trudeau qualifies post–Quiet Revolution's Québécois nationalism as pessimistic, and portrays the desire for independence as motivated by fear of the rest of Canada: "Now that Québec is becoming an adult, now that we are beginning to have muscles, are we going to go back to a pessimistic nationalism?? One that sees the future in black, one that is not afraid—that *is* afraid—of facing the future, one that wants to let go of this Canada and just say, 'Well it's yours, English Gentlemen!'[13] Well, we [the coalition for the 'no'] are not going to say that, and neither are you [voters], I hope!"[14] By recollecting Québécois' recent achievements, past hardships, and exploits, Trudeau appealed to voters' French *Canadianness*. Independence from Canada, in that discourse, is not emancipation but withdrawal; it is the relinquishing of what is "ours" to "English Gentlemen." Voting yes means abandoning the vast expanse of French Canada, a mythical country "discovered, explored and colonized by our ancestors."

The acrimonious referendum campaign had accentuated the differences between French Canadian and Québécois identities, now more or less linked to political parties (PLQ and PQ respectively) and to positions vis-à-vis sovereignty (no vs. yes). Shortly after the defeat of the referendum, the editorialist Yves Leclerc pointed to the general malaise surrounding the Fête as symptomatic of Québec's identity crisis: "Is Saint-Jean-Baptiste the holiday of French Canadians, or that of francophone Québécois? Or that of all Québécois?" (*La Presse*, 10 June 1980). The failure of the referendum highlighted, in the words of another editorialist,

> [the] enduring cleavage between French Canadians, [who] had borrowed the Baptist's name day from the Church, and the new Québécois. . . . The malaise surrounding the Saint-Jean reflects this division. . . . It

13. Trudeau's Freudian slip ("a nationalism that is not afraid" and then, correcting himself, "that *is* afraid . . . of facing the future") is all the more interesting since the "no" campaign focused on people's fear of independence and fomented that fear by depicting apocalyptic economic scenarios in which the elderly would not receive social security or medical treatments, unemployment would rise, and international commerce with an independent Québec would cease.

14. Pierre Elliott Trudeau, from a speech included in *Le confort et l'indifférence* (Arcand 1981; my transcripts and translation). Arcand's editorial documentary analyzes the referendum campaigns of the "yes" and "no" camps. Documentary footage is juxtaposed with an actor impersonating Machiavelli and reciting key passages of *The Prince* to illustrate Arcand's view of the federalist camp's emotional arguments and political tactics to lower the support for independence in Québec and mobilize the population for a no vote. The documentary is available on the website of the National Film Board of Canada, www.onf.ca/film/confort_et_lindifference, accessed August 17, 2013.

> was premature for the Parti Québécois government to declare June 24 the national holiday of Québec. We can have a date, a State budget to organize festivities . . . in all corners of the "province," but the content, or even the meaning itself of June 24, suffers from an emptiness that seems without solution in the short term. . . . Québécois nationalists have emptied the Saint-Jean-Baptiste [holiday] of its religious signification without finding another past worth remembering. (Jean-Claude Leclerc, *Le Devoir*, 19 June 1980)

The survival of St-Jean-Baptiste Day in its phantom form underscores the French Canadian legacy in Québec. "La Fête nationale du Québec" may well be, in official language, "the holiday of all those constituting today's Québec,"[15] but the fact that it is on the feast day of St. Jean-Baptiste clearly expresses a continuity with the Catholic French Canadian past.

Organizational Atomization, Ideological Void

Despite the PQ's intention to turn the holiday into a celebration of Québec, the secularized event was criticized as decentralized, local, and particularist (Yves Leclerc, *La Presse*, 10 June 1980). The SSJBM objected not only to the "scattering" of the Fête but also to the "pathetic absence of rites and symbols that carry national consciousness."[16] What the SSJBM was lamenting was the absence of religious symbols and traditions, for nothing—certainly not the bonfires and concerts—had quite replaced them. This apparent "symbolic emptiness" and lack of a sense of continuity and direction led to renewed efforts to infuse the Fête with meaning. From this perspective, the idea of the new nation needed to be taught and transmitted, with knowledge traveling from the vanguard to "the people"; the nation had to be viscerally rehearsed in order to be made real in minds and bodies (and, not least, voting behavior). As the president of the of Comité organisateur de la Fête nationale du Québec explained a few months later, in what turned out to become a sort of manifesto for instilling the Fête with a national spirit:

15. And as was claimed on the unilingual (French) website of the institution in charge of the holiday's coordination (www.fêtenationale.qc.ca/historique.html, accessed July 23, 2013). The official language in Québec is French, but all government publications are available in English. One wonders why this website is not available in English.

16. Jean-Marie Cossette, president general of the SSJBM, in a memo addressed to the premier of Québec, 11 October 1979, Archives nationales du Québec, P82 1995-01-002\31.

> When one day in a year is dedicated to the celebration of a country, that day becomes the privileged occasion to tighten the bonds that unite all citizens. By seeking inspiration in the past in order to live in the present and project ourselves in the future, citizens of this country, through the national holiday, must be conscious of their values, resources, and, as a result, of their aspirations. All this can be summarized in a single word, PRIDE. If the national holiday has a signification, it is from PRIDE that it must draw its being and its becoming [*son devenir*] . . . The Fête nationale must remain a genuine means of affirmation and stimulation of Québécois PRIDE.[17]

Here the president contends that the Fête's goal is to make people realize the values they supposedly already have: the occasion is not merely the celebration of "who we are" but the *prise de conscience* that "we *are*." In turn, he argues, realizing the existence of the national self and its identity leads to the development of (political) *aspirations*. The Fête, therefore, becomes a pedagogical tool, strategically wielded by planners. To that end, the president concludes, a ceremony with symbols and rituals had to be devised in order to increase the gravitas of the Fête and lend greater homogeneity to the multiple local celebrations of the event.

In response to the common criticism that the holiday celebrations were localized and fragmented, local celebrations were complemented with larger events deemed likely to produce the collective effervescence needed for the creation and maintenance of social solidarity (Durkheim [1912] 1995). A reconceptualized parade and march with papier-mâché sculptures representing "Québécois values" and regions was reintroduced and televised in 1981. No saint appeared in the parade, although a paper statue of the Baptist was built and placed, according to the vice president of Comité organisateur de la Fête nationale du Québec (COFNQ) in a radio interview, "where it belongs," that is, "in front of the St. Joseph Oratory in Montréal."[18] The event, however, left Montrealers lukewarm. In the following years it was replaced with large concerts, which have since become the mainstay of the holiday. These events provide collective experi-

17. "Conference des présidents, samedi, 4 octobre 1980. Allocation du president national," Comité organisateur de la Fête nationale du Québec, Archives nationales du Québec, P82 1995-01-002\319.

18. "Compte rendu d'une entrevue radiophonique concernant le défilé de la Saint-Jean-Baptiste à Montréal," radio interview transcript June 18, 1981. Fonds E207/2, Archives nationales du Québec à Montréal (the transcript contained no mention of which radio station).

ences and a recognizable aesthetic, with hundreds of thousands of people carrying flags and swaying to the sound of popular and patriotic music (figure 4.2).

Even so, the signification of the holiday remained unclear. Throughout the 1980s, the government conducted campaigns to aid people in "reconnecting" with the holiday. A series of vignettes explaining its history were disseminated in print and on the radio. The vignettes addressed diverse aspects of the Fête: the traditional parades, the gradual ethnicization of a pagan and then Catholic holiday in the nineteenth century, the bonfires, and the incorporation of the Québec flag.[19] Additional special sketches were prepared for so-called ethnic communities and Anglophones, and broadcast on the radio by members of those communities.[20]

> The Fête Nationale du Québec and Us, Anglophones
>
> June is fast approaching with the Fête nationale of Québecers on the 24th. We are not very familiar with the celebration of Saint-Jean-Baptiste Day but as residents of Québec not by birth but certainly as whole-hearted Québecers, this celebration involves us too. Many French people, of course, arrived in 1636, when the colony was just beginning; but there were also English, Irish, Scottish, German, Spanish, Greek and so many citizens of other countries of the world besides.
>
> . . .
>
> With the democratization [of the holiday in 1977], came a return to the Fête as it was at the colony's birth with all the people living in the land of Québec joining together and celebrating their relationship to that land. This means the Fête nationale of Québec belongs to us too.[21]

René Lévesque also made special televised addresses on June 24, sending good wishes to the citizens of Québec in French, English, Italian, and Spanish.

19. Untitled document, 1982 E207/98, Archives nationales du Québec; Movement national des Québécois, "Fête nationale 1986: Chroniques sur les traditions de la Fête," P82 1995-01-002\319, Archives nationales du Québec.

20. Movement national des Québécois, "Fête nationale 1986."

21. Untitled document, Archives nationales du Québec, 1982 E207/98. This was the English translation of the generic text for ethnic communities, which was originally written in French. The qualification "not by birth," which in the 1980s could have made sense for recently arrived Latin American, Haitian, or Vietnamese immigrants, was not appropriate for the generic Anglophone population, as a large proportion of Montréal's English speakers could trace their families' presence in Québec for over two centuries.

But the most important population to reach was obviously Francophone Québécois, the former French Canadians, for whom the new Fête nationale still lacked clear meaning or purpose. After the Quiet Revolution, the selective histories of the holiday and the potpourri of traditions described in brochures or on the radio sounded like echoes of a past too distant to be any longer relevant. As noted by the SSJBM in a press release a few days prior to the 1987 St-Jean-Baptiste holiday:

> A national holiday is also very much the expression of tradition. Now, a tradition is what is transmitted from generation to generation; a legacy of the past, in other words, [and] we must say that in Québec an entire generation of Québécois seems to be cut off from that past, which explains the lack of reasons given to celebrate on June 24. . . . It's difficult to celebrate when we don't know what we're celebrating! If the Fête nationale du Québec does not manage to revive [*prendre un nouvel essor*] within a few years, the population of Québec—and mostly that of Montréal, which will be about a third newcomers—will know less and less what it is celebrating. . . . We must also say that this year [many] do not feel like celebrating. A threatened language, a confused constitutional project, an identity continually questioned—there are many uncertainties that are not conducive to a harmonious celebration oriented toward the future.[22]

In the post-referendum years, marred by disputes about the place of Québec in Canada, a new signification for the holiday and the new identity it was supposed to celebrate and elevate was not clearly articulated. No new traditions to successfully link the present with the past were being invented (Hobsbawm 1983). Québec's history lacked a clear narrative people could tell themselves about the history and future of the new nation and their place in it.[23] The Church and the SSJBM had been experts at crafting such a discourse in the nineteenth century and materializing it in everyday objects and grand annual parades. By contrast, the PQ had understood its election in 1976 as a reflection of the fact that the Québécois people already "knew who they were and where they were going" and did not need government assertion or management of their national identity.

22. Communiqué de presse, SSJBM, "La Fête nationale, oui mais," pp. 5–7, June 16, 1987. Archives nationales du Québec, P82 1995-01-002/327.

23. The most extensive and incisive studies of French Canadian and Québécois national narratives, myths, and "collective imaginaries" are by the sociologist and historian Gérard Bouchard (Bouchard 1999, 2004, 2005, 2014).

Re-narrating the Holiday and the Nation

In June 1980, the editorialist Jean-Claude Leclerc decried the fact that "Québécois nationalists [had] emptied Saint-Jean-Baptiste of its religious signification but without finding a past worth remembering." Seven years later, the president of the SSJBM could still agonize over the fact that "an entire generation of Québécois [seemed] to be cut off from the past." The 1990s were marked by attempts at finding or defining a "past worth remembering," and for a specific version of identity that would "stick."

The Sheep Returns

The 1990 St-Jean-Baptiste festivities were especially popular just after the rejection of the Meech Lake Accord. The accord, which proposed reintegrating Québec into the Canadian constitution with a recognition that it was a "distinct society," was voted down by Newfoundland and Manitoba. The announcement was made on June 23, just hours before the traditional St-Jean-Baptiste concert and bonfire on the Plains of Abraham, a large federal park in Québec City with enormous symbolic import as the site of a pivotal battle in the Seven Years' War that resulted in the cession of New France to England.[24] The theme for that year's celebration was "At the Gates of the Nation" (*Aux portes du pays*). Energized by the failure of a treaty intended to formally integrate Québec into the federation, eighty thousand people attended. The highly charged evening included political speeches, poetry readings, and patriotic music.

Diane Dufresne, a popular, extravagant *chanteuse engagée*, sang "Comme un bel oiseau," a song written specifically for the occasion:

> Since all the years that I've wanted to split
> At the hour when all breaks down, I'm really knocked out
> When it was time to act, we believed the worst
> We let it pass, and now we're no better
> One has to stand up straight when one stumbles

24. The Battle of the Plains of Abraham was fought in 1759 between the British navy and the French army just outside the fortifications of Québec City, on land owned by Abraham Martin (hence its name). The battle, which is said to have lasted only about twenty minutes, was the culmination of a three-month siege by the British. Both the French and British generals (Montcalm and Wolfe) died in the battle. It has become a symbol of historical irony and bitterness: although the French Canadians/Québécois managed to lose a country in a mere twenty minutes, in spite of such lost battles, Québécois have not "lost the war."

I'm from a Québec that is taking back its wings
It's time to learn to leave you

. . .
How to understand such a cruel and undignified gesture
Do not ever again wipe your feet on my flag! [25]
You should know I'm not made of ice
And I promise that you won't have my skin
Don't make trouble, I have a good memory
And our hour of glory is soon coming
I'm from a Québec that is taking back its wings
It's no longer time to rest on our laurels

There is so much to do and the death of a king[26]
Who merits remaking the world as our own
There's no expiration date on liberty
But one must deserve it
I'm from a Québec that is taking back its wings
The road is traced, there's nothing to stop me now
From going further than the tip of my nose
And to fly high like a beautiful bird.[27]

The next night, in Montréal, about 100,000 people attended a similar event.[28] The following day, on the 25th, a parade and popular march were held in the streets of Montréal, following a new route. An estimated

25. Dufresne refers to images of a crowd in Sault Sainte-Marie, Ontario, wiping their feet on the Québec flag during the tense negotiations at Meech Lake. The images were widely broadcast in Québec.

26. A reference to the death of René Lévesque, who passed away on November 1, 1987. More than 100,000 people waited in long lines in the cold and rain to view his body lying in state in Montréal and Québec City.

27. "Comme un bel oiseau," live performance on the Plains of Abraham, Québec City, June 23, 1990. Text and interpretation by Diane Dufresne, music by Yves Laferrière. See www.youtube.com/watch?v=deIfASARp1E, accessed June 13, 2014.

28. I was present on the Plains of Abraham on June 23 and on St. Helen's Island in Montréal the following day. Both events were marked by a collective effervescence I have rarely experienced since. The evening of June 23 was especially intense, as the Meech Lake Accord's failure was announced a few hours before the celebrations. The streets were flooded by people of all ages singing, laughing, screaming, and waving flags as if the accord's rejection was a clear sign of what was now to be done. Instead of anger or sadness, the crowds expressed overwhelming joy.

200,000 people participated in the march. Its theme, “Thirty Years of Quiet Power,” commemorated the beginning of the Quiet Revolution. The parade opened with a striking symbol: a three-story-high “Trojan sheep,” pulled by twenty-four little St. Jean-Baptistes of different ethnic origins followed by dancing Aboriginal children (figure 4.7). The stated intent of the artist was to show the changing face of Québec: “A nation, like an individual, must exorcise its images to move on. The sheep is there to tell us that Québec society has evolved” (*La Presse*, June 19, 1990). The director of the committee in charge of the holiday explained to journalists that the sheep “is an extravagant allusion to our adult memory. It’s about the rehabilitation of a symbol that once was negative and to show that Québec regained strength.”[29]

Using the sheep with a twist was also meant to rehabilitate the symbol: “In many countries,” the artistic director explained, “the sheep is a positive image. Here the image of . . . Saint-Jean and his sheep that represents the herd was polluted by negative projections.” Through humor, the sheep was to shatter the mythology of an impotent people. The old parades, the artistic director explained, were “descriptive” (and, his words imply, prescriptive): they spoke more to reason than to the unconscious. His parade was intended to project “positive dreams of victory.” With a black head and a body made of large wooden and steel rings, the sheep was meant to evoke a society still in progress (*La Presse*, June 19, 1990).

The tableau was, however, deeply ambiguous. A Trojan horse (or sheep) is a weapon in disguise, a wolf in sheep’s clothing, the symbol of a stealthy and subversive attack. In this case, however, the bodies implied to have been packed inside the Trojan sheep were not soldiers infiltrated into the enemy’s stronghold, but “ethnic children” pulling the vehicle. The symbolism was unclear at best. Some reporters, on hearing the float’s name and its description at a press conference a few days prior, were concerned by the symbolic confusion and the potential for negative interpretations of the Trojan sheep, such as the implication that minorities were surreptitiously invading Québec (Heinz Weinmann in *La Presse*, June 23, 1990).

In the immediate context of the rejection of the Meech Lake Accord, however, it was not the allusion to the Trojan horse that caught the attention of the viewers but the color of the sheep’s face. The visual allegory of

29. Jean Dorion, president of the Comité des Fêtes nationales de la St-Jean, quoted in *La Presse*, June 19, 1990. Dorion uses the French expression “reprendre du poil de la bête,” a colloquial expression meaning “to regain strength.” By using this expression, with its reference to a “beast,” Dorion was playing on the problematic associations the woolly sheep had acquired in the 1960s.

FIGURE 4.7 Trojan sheep/black sheep, opening the 1990 parade in Montréal (Bernard Brault, *La Presse*, June 25, 1990).

the stigmatized black sheep captured the feelings of the population at that specific historic juncture: Québec rejected by the rest of Canada. The *mouton noir*—sometimes also called la *bête noire* (literally "black beast," meaning bugbear or pet peeve)—became the symbol and expression of Québec in limbo: too timid to vote for its own independence and marginalized within the Canadian confederation.[30]

The Trojan sheep was, however, a prescient material metaphor. Later that fall, the Bloc Québécois was born—a party whose main goals were to represent the interests of the Québécois in federal government.[31] In the 1993 federal elections, the Bloc obtained 49.3% of the Québec vote, which gave it fifty-four seats in the House of Commons, enough to constitute the official opposition to the governing Liberal Party of Canada. The Bloc Québécois was the Trojan sheep that infiltrated Ottawa.

New Icons, Novel Iconography

Various attempts were made to revive the St-Jean-Baptiste parades and marches in new forms in the 1980s and 1990s, but none were popular enough to become established as a new tradition. The most innovative is a carnivalesque march of gigantic artistic puppets of iconic figures and concepts associated with Québec: fathers and mothers of the nation (the founders of Montréal, like Maisonneuve and Jeanne Mance; the Patriots; René Lévesque; and the poet and singer Félix Leclerc); folk characters (the lumberjack, the priest, the peasant, the water diviner); "strong men" such as Louis Cyr and the hockey icon Maurice "The Rocket" Richard; and archetypical ideas, such as winter, log cabins (1994), the St. Lawrence River (1995), language (1996), and the *patenteux* (figure 4.8).[32]

30. See the documentary film by Jacques Godbout, *Le Mouton noir* (1992), available on the website of the National Film Board of Canada, www.onf.ca/film/heritiers_du_mouton_noir. It discusses the Meech Lake Accord and its immediate consequences: the rise of support for Québec's sovereignty, the investigation of constitutional models for Québec, and the creation of the Bloc Québécois. See also Kröller (1997).

31. The Bloc Québécois was founded in June 1991 but originated among a group of Québec MPs who left the Conservative and Liberal federal parties after the failure of the Meech Lake Accord. Its main inspiration and leader was Lucien Bouchard, a former federal cabinet minister in the Mulroney government. Bouchard was the Bloc's leader until January 1996, when he left to become premier of Québec.

32. A *patenteux* is a home inventor. The term comes from the noun *patente* (from the English "patent"). Joseph-Armand Bombardier is probably Québec's most famous *patenteux*. He invented the Ski-doo in his small shop, expanding his company to become a world leader in aeronautics and railway technology. Note the conspicuous ab-

FIGURE 4.8 Giant puppets of hockey great Maurice Richard and strong man Louis Cyr, June 24, 2012 (THE CANADIAN PRESS/Graham Hughes).

Even as the meanings of the Saint-Jean/Fête nationale continued to be debated, a new holiday was instituted in 2002 to reinforce both the civic meaning of the nation and Québec's fight for independence. Under the leadership of the PQ Premier Bernard Landry, the obscure Fête de Dollard was replaced by the National Day of Patriots. The Fête de Dollard commemorated the death of Dollard des Ormeaux, a settler who led a small group of men to fight against Native Americans in 1660. In the nineteenth century, the Church had transformed him into a national and religious hero who fought the "savages," but the holiday in his honor was instituted in Québec only as an alternative to the celebration of Victoria Day, a public holiday observed in all English-speaking parts of Canada to mark the birthday of Queen Victoria. Known as La Fête de la Reine in French, it is observed on the last Monday before May 25 and also serves to officially celebrate the birthday of Queen Elizabeth II. Although the Fête de Dollard was observed on the same date and kept on the calendar after the Quiet Revolution to counter the celebration of English monarchy and colonialism, the teachings about Dollard disappeared from school curricula and

sence of non-French Canadians who played important roles in the history of Québec; there are (as yet) no Anglophones, Jews, or Blacks among the giants.

lost whatever small resonance they once enjoyed.[33] Replacing an obsolete hero's holiday with another day commemorating resistance to the British—and on the very day that the rest of Canada[34] celebrates symbols of British monarchy—was an ingenious move, although it has so far not garnered a major following.[35]

The meaning of the Fête nationale thus remains unclear. That is not surprising. The multivocal nature of symbols and rituals, and their ability to spin out of one orbit of signification into a different one, is what imparts to them their social force to be mobilized by groups with distinct agendas and ideologies. If the Fête nationale were perceived only as an independentist holiday, it might not be celebrated as widely. It is precisely because it is a "traditional" holiday, one that marks the beginning of the summer, that it remains so popular.[36] Most remarkable, though, is the fact that the holiday carries no official signification or ideology. Unlike July 4 in the United States, July 14 in France, or countless other examples, the date of the national holiday in Québec tells no story—or, rather, the story it once told no longer fits, and, no other story has yet replaced it. The new meanings grafted onto the holiday have failed to take hold, lacking the force that established traditions often wield. It remains a holiday of ambiguities: ambiguity about who the Québécois are, where they are going, and how to translate their national identity into a sense of affinity, a reserve of collective memory, or a shared repertory of commemoration that leads to emotional belonging.

The split nature of the holiday also encapsulates the ambiguous place

33. So obscure was the origin of this holiday that children commonly thought that it was "Dollar Day." Though adults raised and educated after Quiet Revolution know that it commemorates "some martyr," they don't know the history behind it.

34. "Le reste du Canada" is an expression used in Québec to emphasize Québec's distinctiveness from the other provinces and territories of Canada. It is such a prevalent expression that Anglo-Canadians have adopted the acronym ROC (for "the rest of Canada") to refer not only to Québécois' outlook, but also to all provinces and territories of Canada except Québec.

35. An official day commemorating the Patriots already existed: it was proposed by the PQ in 1982. The Sunday closest to November 23 was decreed a day "to honor the memory of the Patriots who fought for the national recognition of our people, its political liberty and for a democratic system of governance." But as it was not free of work (unlike Victoria Day/Fête de Dollard), and it was little known.

36. By contrast, Canada Day, July 1, is mostly ignored and used instead as moving day. In Québec most leases end on July 1, so that day and those preceding it are busy with packing and moving. Moreover, because of the widespread partying on June 24, there is little incentive to celebrate again a week later.

of Catholicism in defining Québécois identity. I discussed this in the first part of this chapter but return in the next to examine in greater detail the ways that this ambivalence has been expressed in the patrimonialization of religious heritage and the debate over the "reasonable accommodation" of the religious practices of immigrants.

KEY TROPE *The Sheep*

FÉLIX LECLERC, QUÉBEC'S NATIONAL BARD, WROTE IN 1986:

> We are Québécois,
> Descended from the Old France
> Masters in our own house and far from kings
> After three centuries of patience
> After three centuries of slumber
> Like a flock led to the slaughterhouse
> It was time to wake up
> Before being brought to the salting tub . . .
> Before being salted and cured.

The sheep, during the Quiet Revolution, became the metaphor for what was increasingly perceived by French Canadians as their problematic docility and passivity vis-à-vis "Les Anglais" and the Church. The sheep,

TROPE 4.1 "Because it's that time again . . . happy Saint-Jean-Baptiste!" Normand Hudon, 1960. M997.63.437, © McCord Museum.

as illustrated in trope 4.1, does not realize its alienation, resting placidly in a birdcage. Titled "Because It's that Time Again . . . Happy St. Jean-Baptiste!" the cartoon questions whether servitude should be celebrated, other than through blind habit. The Québécois, in the 1960s, came into being through the active rejection of authority, ambitious economic initiatives, pointed sociopolitical reforms, and creative cultural entrepreneurship. They imagined themselves as the antithesis of the sheep, and as such the sheep remains as a pervasive trope against which Québécoisness is defined and expressed. The sheep is where old fears and national complexes survive. It is a reminder of "who we were" and "who we no longer want to be." The sheep made an ironic comeback as a Trojan/black sheep in 1995, as we have seen in chapter 4, and continues to be used as a warning. To wit, in 2008, political analyst Christian Dufour published a book-length essay on linguistic practices in Québec titled (in French) *Québécois and the English Language: The Return of the Sheep* (trope 4.2). The author argued in the book that openness to English is an atavistic reflex of the conquered.

Three years later, in 2011, Denis Trudel gave the SSJBM's Patriotic Speech, "Let Us Kill the Little Sheep Within Us."[1] In the speech, Trudel wonders when the Québécois's own feeling of linguistic inferiority will disappear: "When an Anglo[phone] meets a Franco[phone], . . . there is reciprocal and tacit acceptation of the submission of one to the other. Linguistically, everything happens as if they were still the bosses and we the employees. They, the possessers; us, the possessed. How to get rid of this submissive stance? How to get rid of this little sheep bleating as soon as its master appears?"

What is key, in the argument put forth by Trudel, is that the responsibility of this uneven linguistic relationship lies with the Québécois' own demons, with the sheep surviving in dark corners of the collective unconscious in spite of significant structural changes since the Quiet Revolution. Hence the need to "kill the sheep." This kind of self-hatred is common in colonized peoples, as we know from the works of Franz Fanon and a long lineage of postcolonial scholarship. In Québec that self-hatred is unconsciously reflected in a constellation of terms that once described the

1. Société Saint-Jean-Baptiste de Montréal, http://ssjb.com/discours-patriotique-2011-il-faut-tuer-le-petit-mouton-interieur-denis-trudel-patriote-de/, accessed January 13, 2012.

TROPE 4.2 This excerpt is reproduced under a license given by Copibec.

French Canadian experience. The nouns *mouton* (sheep), *habitant* (peasant), *colon* (settler), and *zouave* (papal soldier) are no longer merely descriptive or neutral terms, but have become insulting adjectives. "Mouton" refers to one's passivity, "habitant" to low cultural capital, "colon" to gross stupidity, and "zouave" to silliness.

5 Nationalism, Secularism, and Cultural Heritage

ALTHOUGH CONTEMPORARY QUÉBÉCOIS IDENTITY IS A SECULAR one, Catholicism has not vanished from the national landscape, in part because its historical Catholicism—its churches, monuments, and "heritage"—distinguishes Québec from the rest of the Canadian landscape in ways often valued by even militantly secular Québécois. That is, Québec's distinctiveness, within the Canadian federation, depends on its paradoxical combination of a French-speaking and "Catholic" landscape with its secular, generally progressive social policies. To oversimplify for a moment, walking the thin line between "Catholic" and secular distinction has been achieved, I argue, by refiguring religion as culture, heritage, and patrimony.

In this final chapter, I tease apart the ways religion haunts Québec's secularism through an analysis of two important public debates that reveal the challenges posed by this metamorphosis. The first was on the "reasonable accommodation" of diverse cultural communities' religious practices in 2006–8; the second surrounded the Charter of Values/Charter of Secularism proposed by the Parti Québécois in the fall of 2013. I complement these case studies with a study of the "patrimonialization" of religious material culture and practices, a process initiated in the 1990s and which took new forms in the shadow of these public debates.

The Paradoxical Return of Religion

With the drop in religiosity, the expansion of education, and the sexual revolution, fertility rates in Québec began to drop precipitously in the 1960s. In 1996, for the first time in the history of Canada, the population of Québec represented less than 25% of the country's total population, and this figure fell to 23.3% in 2013 (Statistics Canada). Demographic decline, coupled with the two failed referenda on independence, created a significant feeling of insecurity about the linguistic future of the province and, consequently, Québec's place within Canada.

To maintain the delicate linguistic balance in the province and the province's relative weight within Canadian federal structures, Québec government agencies have encouraged the immigration of other Francophone populations. As mentioned earlier, Québec has shared control with the federal government over immigration to its territory, and prior knowledge of French is given weight in the consideration of immigration applications.[1] The recent influx of immigrants has, however, foregrounded the question of the place of religion in Québécois identity, as many newcomers are (or are perceived to be) non-Christian and more religious than Francophone Québécois. A few statistics on the religious and ethnic landscape provide useful context to understand the debates I analyze in later sections of this chapter.

Québec is marked by a large majority of people (83.5% in 2001) who are nominally Catholic but are significantly less religiously observant than Catholics in the rest of Canada. Such "cultural Catholics" are baptized and identify as Catholic in survey data, but rarely (if ever) attend mass or confession. Many couples never marry, even when they have children, without social stigma to themselves or their children. The Catholic Church since the Quiet Revolution is at the margins of social and political affairs. In 2007, among Québécois in the 50–70 age group who spoke French at home and declared themselves Catholic, a mere 8.8% attended mass or other religious gathering once a week. The figures are even lower among younger generations: only 5.8% in Generation X (age 30–50) and 4.1% in Generation Y (age 15–30) attended church weekly. Over 44% of Catholic

1. About 40% of immigrants settling in Québec already know French on arrival: 25% know only French, and about 15% know both French and English (20% know English only, and 40% know neither French nor English). See Québec Government's website "Immigration, Diversité et Inclusion," http://www.micc.gouv.qc.ca/fr/recherches-statistiques/index.html, accessed December 14, 2009. Between 2001 and 2006, slightly fewer than one-fifth of immigrants to Canada settled in Québec.

Francophone Québécois have never practiced any religion at all (Meunier and Witkins-Laflamme 2011). Overall, between 1986 and 2006, 20% of Catholics in Québec went to mass once a month, and 37.3% never attended at all. These rates of observance differ sharply from the rest of Canada, where 42.4% of Catholics attend mass at least once a month. Montréal, moreover, differs significantly from the rest of Québec. Only a slim majority of that city's inhabitants (51%) remains even nominally Catholic. Most of these are not observant Catholics, and 18% of Montréal's residents do not adhere to any religion whatsoever—a rapidly expanding group now well-known in the sociology of religion as the "nones."

The demographics of Montréal are especially relevant here, since the overwhelming majority of immigrants to Québec (87%) have settled in the greater Montréal area, altering the city's ethnic and religious makeup: one-third of Montréal's population today are immigrants (compared with 3.7% in Québec City), and many of them are non-Christian, with about 20% of the immigrant population originating from the Maghreb, Lebanon, Egypt, Iran, and Southeast Asia (Ville de Montréal 2014, 26). Whereas in 2001 Muslims represented 3% of Montréal's population, they now constitute 9%. Jews constitute 4%.

These shifting ethno-religious demographics in a city whose population represents half the population of Québec are perplexing to many and have forced the Québécois to reflect on secularism and their own rapport with Catholicism, just when many thought they had left it behind for good. It is in that sense that religion is making a comeback. In fact, it is a double comeback: as a meaningful category for many new immigrants settling in an overwhelmingly "Catholic" society whose members do not practice, and as a social and political issue debated in the public sphere.

The "Reasonable Accommodation" Debate

As in other places where immigration has sparked debates about the place of religion in the public sphere—such as France, Great Britain, Spain, Germany, the Netherlands, Denmark, and the United States, to name only the most obvious—in Québec secularism is intrinsically related to national identity. Given the complexities of the cultural politics of Québécois identity and the political status of Québec itself, those debates are especially salient there. To what degree can a host society, itself a minority within Canada, accommodate other minorities in its midst without "losing itself"? How good a match is multiculturalism for Québec society? After how long do new immigrants become Québécois in the eyes of the host population, and according to what criteria? The debate about the visibility

FIGURE 5.1 "We are all Québécois, even in Montréal. Happy 24." This 2008 Labatt Bleue beer ad cleverly played on tensions surrounding debates over the religious practices of cultural minorities at that time. It is through festivities (and beer drinking) that ethnic divisions are overcome, "even in Montréal." "Happy 24" is a play on the date of the St-Jean-Baptiste holiday/Fête nationale and the fact that a case of beer containing two dozen bottles is also called a "24" (Christopher DeWolf, urbanphoto.net).

of religion in the public sphere has rapidly metamorphosed into a debate about the very identity of Québec and the challenges it faces as a nation within a federal state.

That debate is no longer solely among Québécois of French Canadian descent, as it was during the Quiet Revolution. It now involves a dialogue with the so-called Other. This dialogue verged on a clash in 2006–7, when several incidents involving religious minorities and Québec's secular majority made provincial headlines. In one, frosted-glass windows were installed at a Montréal YMCA at the request (and expense) of ultra-Orthodox Jews who wished to protect young boys walking to their neighborhood yeshiva from temptations posed by the sight of women exercising at the gym. In another high-profile episode, fathers attending their children's swimming class at the downtown Montréal YWCA were asked to leave the pool area because their presence caused discomfort to Muslim women enrolled in a swimming class at the same time. In a third case, two ambulance attendants were asked to leave the cafeteria at Montréal's Jewish General Hospital, where they were about to eat their lunch, because they had not purchased their food there, and the area where they were seated was considered kosher. In a fourth case, the menu of a popular commercial "sugar shack" (where maple syrup is typically offered in the spring, along with other traditional dishes, many including pork and served family style) was changed to accommodate dietary needs of Muslim patrons.

These four cases concerned individuals and their dealings with specific establishments, both public and private. Many other cases involved the uses and definitions of public space, especially in relation to ultra-Orthodox Jewish groups. For example, disputes arose between some neighborhood residents and the city of Montréal regarding the loosening of parking regulations on Shabbat; the breaching of city codes to erect sukkahs during the Jewish festival of Sukkot; and the deployment of elaborate *eruvim* in Outremont, a neighborhood where the coexistence of ultra-Orthodox and Francophone gentile communities has not always been smooth (Stoker 2003).[2] Two other famous cases concerned Sikh men's wearing of turbans and ceremonial swords (see Stoker 2007), which caused conflicts with rules requiring the wearing of protective helmets on construction sites and a ban on carrying weapons in schools.

These incidents were widely reported in the Québec media, and the accounts were often based as much on incendiary rumors and half-truths

2. An *eruv* (plural *eruvim*) is a symbolic extension of the home that allows ultra-Orthodox Jews to carry objects on Shabbat and Yom Kippur, when they are not allowed to work, or, by extension, to carry or push things outside their homes. *Eruvim* are wires or cords strung around groups of private and public properties, creating an extended private domain. Without *eruvim*, mobility can be significantly reduced for ultra-Orthodox Jews. In Montréal, ultra-Orthodox Jews are concentrated in Outremont, where the *eruvim* link private homes using city electrical poles, a practice many consider to be a safety hazard and others an eyesore. *Eruvim* have also been controversial in London, New York, and New Jersey.

as on documented facts.[3] Thus the media coverage was constitutive of the incidents. What prompted vocal opposition was not so much the requests by religious minorities for special consideration, but the perception that public institutions were overly accommodating to these requests at the expense of the majority. Why should fathers be asked to leave the swimming pool? Why should ambulance personnel be prohibited from eating their ham and cheese sandwiches at the hospital cafeteria? Why should certain religious communities be allowed to violate city building codes or be exempted from school and workplace safety rules? Where do the private and public spheres begin and end? What is a "reasonable" amount of accommodation for a host society to extend toward immigrant minorities? What can or should not be accommodated, and on the basis of what kinds of social claims?

Strictly speaking, a reasonable accommodation is "an arrangement that falls under the legal sphere, more specifically case law, aimed at relaxing the application of a norm or statute in favor of an individual or a group of people threatened with discrimination for one of the reasons specified [in Québec's Charter of Human Rights and Freedoms]" (Bouchard and Taylor 2008c, 289). The duty of accommodation demands that discrimination be present on at least one of the thirteen grounds recognized by the Québec Charter of Rights. Some of these grounds are circumstantial (such as pregnancy or marital status), others are permanent traits of an individual (such as sex, skin color, or disability), still others are sociocultural (such as language or religion). Discrimination alone, however, is not sufficient to warrant an accommodation, because "the duty of accommodation is limited by the realism of the request, that is, by the ability of the organization to accommodate." The reasonable accommodation of a given request is therefore further mitigated by the question of whether "undue hardship" would be placed on the potential accommodating organization. In other words, the duty of accommodation is assessed in relation to the weight of inconvenience posed to the organization to which the request is addressed (Bouchard and Taylor 2008c, 63).

3. Detailed accounts of those cases and dozens more—both the facts and the media coverage—can be found in two chapters of the Bouchard-Taylor Commission's final report: "Chronology of a Crisis" and "Perceptions and the Reality of Accommodation (Bouchard and Taylor 2008a, 45–76). Social-scientific analyses can be found in Stoker (2003, 2007), Bock-Coté (2007), Gaudreault-Desbiens (2009), and Koussens (2009). For journalistic accounts and essays see Geadah (2007), Bégin (2007), Baril (2007), Thompson (2007), Dufour and Heinrich (2008), and Potvin (2008). For a psychoanalytic analyses of the debate, see Clément and Wolfe (2008).

Most requests and their accommodations never become a matter of public record or media scrutiny: they are made on an ad hoc basis—for example, between a student, parents, and teacher; employee and employer; and so forth. Such ad hoc interpersonal resolutions are not considered legal "accommodations" but rather "concerted adjustments." In matters of religion, however, demands for the relaxing of a rule or requests to adapt a law to the specific needs of an individual or community often come under media scrutiny. That the cases reported in the media and which captured public attention involved non-Christian groups, primarily Muslims, Sikhs, and ultra-Orthodox Jews, is telling. Nevertheless, according to the Bouchard-Taylor Commission's report, a significant number of requests for accommodation are also made by practicing Catholics, Jehovah's Witnesses, and Seventh Day Adventists.

These highly publicized incidents involving religious accommodations provoked a backlash. For example, the municipal council of Hérouxville, a small village in Mauricie (population 1,338), adopted a "lifestyle code" governing the behavior of potential immigrants. The document outlined "normal" and acceptable practices in Québec—most of them espousing liberal values and emphasizing gender equality—and controversially stated that "stoning women or burning them alive [was] prohibited, as [was] female genital cutting"[4] This statement was widely reported in international media and vehemently ridiculed at home. It was seen as a source of embarrassment, an example of small-town bigotry not at all representative of Québec as a whole.

Despite the mockery, such gestures were supported by others who feared what the media called a "crise des accommodements." Mario Dumont, the leader of Action démocratique du Québec (ADQ), a neoliberal populist political party, complained in a clever neologism that the Québécois were afflicted by *aplaventrisme*—from *à plat ventre*, "flat on your belly." In a widely disseminated open letter, he wrote that they suffered from "spinelessness," since they passively acquiesced to the requests of those who should be the ones to adapt—those who "when in Rome, should do as the Romans do."[5]

Around the same time, however, André Boisclair, then leader of the

4. Municipalité d'Hérouxville, http://municipalite.herouxville.qc.ca/normes.pdf, accessed August 21, 2007.

5. This was not the first time that Dumont linked the issue of immigrant integration to that of history and national identity. In 2006, for example, he declared in an interview to the *Journal de Montréal* that the Québécois "cannot defend [their] identity with one knee on the ground; [they] fought with too much zeal to carry their identity

left-leaning Parti Québécois, noted that no one had ever requested the removal of the crucifix at the National Assembly even though, in his personal opinion, that religious symbol had no place at such an institution (*Le Devoir*, January 19, 2007). Boisclair opened a Pandora's box. The crucifix became an object of debate among Québécois of all ethnic backgrounds and political stripes and an especially sharp thorn in the Parti Québécois's side when it proposed its Charter of Values, as we shall see in a later section of this chapter. Seen with the benefit of distance, Dumont's and Boisclair's declarations were two sides of the same coin, alternate faces of the ongoing debate about the identity of Québec, during a period of dramatic transformation.

The Bouchard-Taylor Commission

In response to public confusion and discontent over the hazy and ill-defined boundaries of "reasonable accommodation," in February 2007, the Québec premier, Jean Charest (PLQ), announced the establishment of the Commission on Practices of Accommodation Related to Cultural Differences.[6] Known as the Bouchard-Taylor Commission for its eminent commissioners, the sociologist Gérard Bouchard and the philosopher Charles Taylor, the commission was charged with exploring and explicating the meaning and practice of Québec's official secularism in the face of increasing religious pluralism created by diverse immigrant populations.

The commission visited 16 regions of the province in fall 2007, logging 31 days of public hearings. Using a town-hall meeting format, twenty-two citizens' forums across the province (three of which I attended) attracted 3,423 participants.[7] All the hearings were taped and discussed on evening news programs, and the forums were televised live. During a final week-long hearing in Montréal, more than 60 province-wide organizations, such as political parties, trade unions, professional associations, women's groups, ethnic minorities' coalitions, and religious institutions, made statements before the commissioners. Between August 2007 and January

---

and language through the centuries on this continent for all that to stupidly disappear because of a demographic decline" (November 19, 2006).

6. Despite its name, the Parti libéral du Québec is to the right of the Parti Québécois, the sovereignist party in Québec. Contrary to what is often assumed, sovereignists in Québec are on the left, and federalist parties tend to be more conservative socially, economically, and culturally. See p. 119 in chapter 4.

7. For a detailed description of methods and data used for the analysis in this chapter, see appendix C.

2008, the commission hosted a website where briefs could be downloaded and where members of the public could engage the issues and exchange written perspectives. The website was visited more than 400,000 times (Bouchard and Taylor 2008a, 17). Ultimately the commissioners produced a 310-page report assessing the situation and made 37 recommendations to the government. When the much-awaited report was officially released on May 22, 2008, some of its contents had already been prematurely leaked to the press, creating a media frenzy and provoking a whirlwind of political commentary, accusations, and counteraccusations.

The commission's public hearings revealed that the "crisis of accommodations" was not only about immigration and integration but also about Québécois' own relationship to their Catholic heritage and about the very identity and secularity of Québec. The year-long investigation of "reasonable accommodation" turned out to be the most significant critical interrogation of Québécois national identity since the Quiet Revolution, as political figures, public intellectuals, artists, businesspeople, and ordinary citizens all made themselves heard. Québec, so to speak, was put on the couch. The "crisis" gave rise to an entire literature, including journalistic accounts, personal memoirs, academic analysis, and even psychoanalytic diagnoses.

Nearly a quarter of the commission's report was devoted to the factual description of dozens of cases that had been reported in the press or brought up during the commission's hearings, in order to set the record straight. It also contained a detailed portrayal of practices in the fields of education and health, where most of the need for accommodation and most of the conflict tends to arise. The goal was to demystify the extent and nature of requests for accommodation and the alleged over-accommodation of those requests by public institutions. Tellingly, only six of the commission's thirty-seven recommendations pertained to religion specifically. The other recommendations concerned the education of the population about immigrants, integration practices (including greater assistance in finding employment), linguistic policies, and the promotion of "interculturalism," Québec's response to Canada's promotion of multiculturalism.[8]

Multiculturalism, a system founded on the respect and promotion of ethnic diversity, has been widely criticized in Québec for several reasons. First, it is perceived as poorly adapted to the province's particular situa-

8. For an extensive exposé of interculturalism, see Bouchard (2012).

tion and challenges. Unlike the rest of Canada, where only about one-third of the population is of British descent, Québec is ethnically quite homogeneous: about 80% of the population self-identifies as Québécois of French Canadian descent. There is thus a strong attachment to that ethnocultural group's history, traditions, and language, and considerable concern about preserving the language in the face of Anglophone pressures. Second, multiculturalism is commonly understood as an ideological program meant to drown or dilute Québec's distinctiveness, to make it one more tile in the grand "Canadian mosaic." Emphasizing diversity over continuity would also erode Québec's historical status of "founder" (a sentiment, discourse, and political posture shared by First Nations). Finally, since the Quiet Revolution, the Québécois have come to understand themselves as a majority in their own province while remaining a minority within Canada. That double status makes their relationship to multiculturalism and to immigrants especially complex.

For all these reasons, Québec political and cultural élites advocate a different model of interethnic relations in the province. "Interculturalism" attempts to marry ethnocultural diversity with the continuity of the Francophone ethnocultural "kernel." As the Bouchard-Taylor report explained, in the interculturalist model, "The respect of diversity is subordinated to the necessity to preserve the francophone culture of Québec" (2008a, 117). Essential to the future of the nation, according to the report, was the successful integration of immigrants. That outcome was most likely to be achieved through a continued "open secularism" (*laïcité ouverte*) rather than through the adoption of the French republican model strictly enforcing secularism in public life, which they considered overly "rigid" and even "radical." Open secularism is a system whereby institutions and their representatives maintain religious neutrality, but ordinary citizens have the right to practice their religion and request special accommodations insofar as these do not create undue hardship for institutions.

The report therefore recommended the continued goodwill of public agents and authorities to accommodate religiously motivated requests, as long as those did not threaten the neutrality of the state or gender equality, two core values of Québécois society. Concretely, the report proposed that the beneficiaries of state services could continue to wear visible signs of their religious faith and request accommodation of specific needs on a case-by-case basis. State agents such as teachers and doctors could also wear religious symbols in the exercise of their functions so long as those symbols did not prevent them from accomplishing their duties. So, for example, the commissioners opined in their report that it was appropriate for a Muslim teacher to wear the hijab (headscarf) in the classroom, but not the niqab or the burka (full-body coverings) since these latter garments cover the face and therefore interfere with the teacher's communication with children, potentially causing prejudice to the population served by the state.

However, the report recommended that state agents who occupy positions representing state authority or who otherwise exercise coercive power over citizens—such as judges, police, prison guards, and the president of the National Assembly—be prohibited from wearing religious symbols because their very positions "embody the necessary neutrality of the state." That prohibition was proposed in order not to call into question the legitimacy of the civil servant in a position of authority in the eyes of those subject to that authority. These measures would create a secular society where religious Others could find their own place.

In the same vein, the report recommended the removal of remnants of Catholicism in the public sphere, in particular the large crucifix hung over the seat of the speaker at the National Assembly in Québec City, "in keeping with the notion of the separation of Church and State" (Bouchard and Taylor 2008b, 60). According to the report, the crucifix, installed by Maurice Duplessis in 1936, suggests "a special proximity between the legislative power and the majority's religion. . . . It seems preferable that the very site where elected representatives deliberate and legislate not be identified with a specific religion. The National Assembly is the assembly of the entire population of Québec" (Bouchard and Taylor 2008a, 152–53; my translation).

Just hours after the report was officially released, however, Premier Jean Charest proposed a motion to retain the crucifix as symbolic of Québec's religious heritage and culture, its collective memory. That motion was presented by Charest together with the chief of the opposition at the time, Mario Dumont, the politician who coined the term *aplaventrisme*. The motion read, in part: "The National Assembly reiterates its will to promote the language, history, culture and values of the *nation québécoise* and to promote the integration of each and everyone into our nation in the spirit of openness and reciprocity, and it attests to its attachment to our religious and historic patrimony represented by, among other things, the crucifix in the Blue Room and the coats of arms that adorn our institutions."[9]

9. Québec, Assemblée nationale, Procès-verbaux, 38e lég., 1ère sess., n° 87, p. 840 (May 22, 2008).

FIGURE 5.2 Premier Jean Charest responds to the Opposition during the question period on Friday, September 18, 2009. The crucifix over the seat of the National Assembly president is visible in the background (THE CANADIAN PRESS/Jacques Boissinot).

Though the nation is not primordially constituted and certainly changes, Charest argued, it remains historically and culturally constructed, and its history has enduring power.[10] He insisted in television

10. Charest's position was thus closer to Nicolas Sarkozy's notion of "positive secularism" (*laïcité positive*) than to Bouchard and Taylor's "open secularism." Positive secularism supports the separation of church and state but with an emphatic recognition of the civilizing role of the majority's religion. Sarkozy routinely insisted on the Christian heritage of France and Europe, declaring in 2007 that secularism "should not be the negation of the past" and "did not have the power to cut off France from its Christian roots." He added that the secular state teacher (*instituteur*) "will

interviews that the crucifix symbolized that heritage and not the religious beliefs of individual deputies.[11]

For the government of the Parti libéral, the proposal to remove the crucifix from that specific room went too far. The government instead argued that Québec's religious heritage constituted a cultural patrimony, an issue to which I return below.

Secularism Strikes Back

Besides the motion to retain the crucifix at the National Assembly, the PLQ, which had put in place the Bouchard-Taylor Commission, did little, if anything, to address the report's recommendations. The issues of secularism and religious accommodation, however, did not disappear. Numerous political parties proposed bills intended to provide a legal framework for the accommodation of religiously motivated requests. In November 2009, the new official opposition, led by the PQ chief Pauline Marois, proposed Bill 391, "aiming to affirm the fundamental values of the Québécois nation." The proposed bill enshrined gender equality, the primacy of the French language, and the separation of church and state as fundamental values. It also proposed to modify Québec's Charter of Human Rights and Freedoms (Charte des droits et libertés de la personne), the quasi-constitution adopted in 1976. The bill would have added a clause specifying that the charter "must be interpreted within the context of the historical heritage of Québec and the fundamental values of the Québécois nation." The intent behind these rather vague statements would become clear only in the fall of 2013.

Bill 391 was just the start of a longer sequence of proposals. In March 2010, the sociologist Guy Rocher, a key actor in the Quiet Revolution, initiated and cosigned the "Declaration of Intellectuals for Secularism." In that document, the authors argued for "the necessity of an explicit legislative recognition of the State of Québec's secularism, and the inherent prohibition of state representatives to wear conspicuous religious symbols." The authors also demanded that Québec's de facto secularism be in-

never replace the priest or pastor in the transmission of values" in the web-based version of *Le Point* magazine, September 12, 2008 (www.lepoint.fr/actualites-societe/2008-09-12/nicolas-sarkozy-en-appelle-a-la-laicite-positive/920/0/273544, accessed April 14, 2014).

11. See, for example, Jean Charest, interview with Bernard Derôme, Radio-Canada, May 22, 2008, www.radio-canada.ca/nouvelles/National/2008/05/22/003-reax-BT-politique.shtml, accessed May 23, 2008.

stituted de jure, justifying that demand with both historical precedents and historical imperatives: "If the idea of a secular State predates the Patriots, one cannot claim that it is a defensive reaction against recently arrived minorities. . . . Secularism is part of Québec's historic landscape, and its recent achievements define modern Québec." They moreover insisted that "secularism is not a rejection of pluralism [but is rather] an essential condition for it. It is the only way for the equal and fair treatment of all convictions because it neither favors nor accommodates atheism any more than religious faith. Thus understood, pluralism is neither that of minorities nor that of the majority. It is also the necessary condition for gender equality." The declaration concluded with a forceful avowal: "If withdrawal into oneself is not the solution, self-denial is no better. It is important to define the framework of case-based practices of accommodations through our collective values; otherwise the piecemeal requests for accommodation risk shattering the collective accomplishment of our entire society into pieces."[12] By October 18, 2010, when it was submitted to the National Assembly, more than 3,114 university professors, teachers, doctors, and artists had signed the declaration.

During the same period, the PLQ was working on its own legal project, Bill 94, "An Act to establish guidelines governing accommodation requests within the Administration and certain institutions."[13] It was meant to answer some of the recommendations of the 2008 Bouchard-Taylor report and was submitted to the Parliamentary Commission in fall 2010 for review and debate in winter 2011. Its main goal was to establish the conditions under which accommodations could be made for government employees or employees of certain other organizations. Like the PQ's Bill 391, it also recognized the supremacy of the Charter of Human Rights and Freedoms, gender equality, and the state's religious neutrality. It proposed that people providing or receiving services through the state be required to do so with their faces in full view. And like Bill 391, it died a quick death when the Parliamentary Commission's work stalled for no obvious reason other than lack of political and public interest in the issue.

For the sovereignist opposition, the open secularism advocated by the Bouchard-Taylor report, reflected in some articles of Bill 94, was plainly unacceptable. The PQ and many of their adherents advocated instead for

12. My translation of "Déclaration des intellectuels pour la laïcité: Pour un Québec laïque," *Le Devoir*, March 16, 2010.

13. Assemblée nationale du Québec, section sur les travaux parlementaires, www.assnat.qc.ca/fr/travaux-parlementaires/projets-loi/projet-loi-94-39-1.html, accessed July 21, 2014.

a form of secularism in which the state and all its representatives must eschew overtly religious symbols and practices.

Secularism as a National Value

While the debate about religion was ostensibly revived by issues arising from immigration, it quickly became evident that Québécois of French Canadian descent themselves were divided over both the place of religion in the public sphere and the legal form that secularism should take. After a year in power, in summer 2013, the Parti Québécois put the issue back on the political agenda. On September 10, with all possible pomp, they unveiled their proposal for a so-called Charter of Values.

The charter's stated purpose was to affirm the secularity of the state, which was to be accomplished, among others, by a blanket interdiction against state employees' wearing "conspicuous religious symbols" during working hours. In an extensive welfare state like Québec's, that group includes workers as varied as healthcare professionals, teachers, childcare providers, construction workers, and anyone in the private sphere whose work is paid for through government contracts. Another controversial aspect of the project concerned the crucifix at the National Assembly. The charter proposed to "take into account the existence of emblematic and toponymic elements of Québec's cultural heritage that attest to its historical trajectory."[14] It quickly became clear in the ensuing press conferences and interviews with the Minister for Democratic Institutions and Active Citizenship, Bernard Drainville, that the crucifix at the National Assembly would be protected by such a provision. The charter was thus understood by many observers from left and right as having a problematic double standard: prohibiting conspicuous religious symbols associated with religious minorities while protecting those of the majority: the latter were designated as "merely cultural," yet important enough to merit continued display.

During the official announcement and press conference, Premier Pauline Marois stood proudly with Minister Drainville, next to a poster with the slogan, "We Believe in Our Values!" (*Nos valeurs, on y croît!*). The PQ instituted a vigorous public relations campaign to promote their project even before it was officially submitted to the Parliamentary Commission for review. A website with videos of speeches by Drainville, downloadable brochures, and answers to frequently asked questions was

14. "Parce que nos valeurs, on y croit. Document d'orientation." Québec: Government du Québec, September 2013.

FIGURE 5.3 Promotional poster for the Charter of Values. It was plastered all over Montréal, and available for download, with a slew of supporting materials, on a website specifically dedicated to the project, Nos Valeurs (http://www.nosvaleurs.gouv.qc.ca/fr, accessed October 10, 2013). It reads:

Church, Synagogue, Mosque. All this is sacred.
Religious neutrality of the state, gender equality. Just as sacred.
Because we believe in our values.
Québec for all.

"The time has come to rally around our common values. They define who we are. Let us be proud of them." Bernard Drainville, minister responsible for Democratic Institutions and Active Citizenship.

launched the day that the proposed charter was unveiled. Billboards were erected in high-traffic areas of metropolitan centers. The message was straightforward, as illustrated in figure 5.3.

The iconography used, however, was puzzling. The slogan was set on a background of a gray stone wall that evoked various associations: church architecture, commandments written on stone tablets, and the idea that this proposal was already set in stone. Some commentators cynically observed that the PQ was likely to "hit a wall" with the project in which it expressed such ardent faith.

The phrase "We believe in our values" raised more questions. *Whose* values? Those of all Québécois? Of Québécois of French Canadian descent? Of secularists? Moreover, are values so sacred that they cannot be changed or adapted? The name of the project, too, generated so much confusion, opposition, and satire that by the time it was officially submitted to the National Assembly as Bill 60, the charter had been renamed "Charter Affirming the Values of State Secularism and Religious Neutrality and the Equality between Women and Men, and Providing a Framework for Ac-

FIGURE 5.4 Examples of conspicuous religious symbols that state employees would be forbidden to wear during work hours (http://www.nosvaleurs.gouv.qc.ca/fr, accessed October 10, 2013).

commodation Requests." The name was so cumbersome that opponents continued to refer to it as *la Charte des valeurs*, or Charter of Values, while supporters preferred calling it *la Charte de la laïcité*, or simply Bill 60.

Despite serious criticism in the public sphere by intellectuals, civic organizations, and private individuals, the bill officially submitted to the National Assembly on November 7, 2013, basically had the same form as the original draft. It retained the much-criticized prohibition against any state employee wearing conspicuous religious symbols (see figure 5.4) and stated that the crucifix issue could be resolved only by another vote by the National Assembly, since the 2008 motion to retain it had passed unanimously. This provision would effectively allow the crucifix to remain.

Given the opposition to that provision in the preliminary version of the project, most expected that the PQ would soften it in the official version submitted for parliamentary review. Patriarchs of the PQ, including former Québec premiers Jacques Parizeau, Lucien Bouchard, and Bernard Landry, who had previously refrained from commenting on the working document, all denounced the project as regressive and unreasonably rigid. They agreed that the proposed charter, inspired by the French model, was poorly suited for Québec, and they instead supported the model of open secularism advocated in the Bouchard-Taylor report.

Other public intellectuals and scholars pointed out that the charter's model of secularism inherently favored Christians, who are not required to wear religious symbols or specific forms of clothing, or to mark the body with specific signs, and that it was therefore unfair to those who must wear religious symbols (such as the *kippa* for observant Jews or the turban for Sikhs) and to those for whom religious markers have become a sign of cultural belonging to a specific community. Moreover, they asked, why should some have to shed their overt religious symbols in the name of religious neutrality when the crucifix would remain in place at the National Assembly?

For the PQ to affirm and even promote the retention of the crucifix was surprising, contradicting the previous statements of several party leaders. Public figures, editorialists, bloggers, and ordinary citizens criticized the evident double standard of Bill 60. Marches, petitions, and protests colored Québec's autumn. Many argued that the PQ, which ruled in a minority government, was attempting to widen its base by recruiting votes from the right (which typically does not support the left-leaning PQ). Billed by the PQ as a "great step forward," the proposed charter proved to be a highly divisive venture, not only pitting political parties against each other and destabilizing the usual left-right divide but also creating rifts between neighbors and family members.

The proposal gained the support of feminists, LGBT communities, and the secular left—though many tempered their support with a caveat about the crucifix—as well as of xenophobic, anti-immigrant groups and individuals. By flirting with that constituency, however, the PQ ended up losing moderate party members and supporters, who left in droves. Others defected from the PQ when, in the months following the introduction of Bill 60, the party-nominated billionaire businessman Pierre-Karl Péladeau (nicknamed "PKP") to run on its ticket. For those on the left and for unions, PKP's big-boss policies and heavy-handed rebuttal of unions' demands in his large corporations were unpalatable. When PKP and Marois then pronounced the S-word (sovereignty), the PQ lost votes from the right they thought they had secured with the Charter of Values (since the right tends to oppose sovereignty). In April 2014, the party suffered its worst electoral defeat since its creation in 1968. Marois lost not only her premiership but also the seat in her own district. She resigned from the party's leadership shortly thereafter.[15]

15. Despite the initial uproar created by PKP's first public mention of his desire for a sovereign Quebec, which the PQ had been trying to downplay in its campaign,

The debate over the crucifix showed that the significance of the symbol went beyond political campaign gambits. What was at stake was the place of Catholicism and, more broadly, religion in the history and imagined future of Québec. Less explicit but equally present was the semiotic issue of whether a symbol like the crucifix could be softened sufficiently to pass muster with secularists, simply by passing it through the prism of "heritage, "culture," or "patrimony."

The Politics of Religious Tradition and Cultural Patrimony

In a powerful scene in Denys Arcand's acclaimed film *Barbarian Invasions* (2003), a priest and an art dealer meet in the basement of a Montréal church packed to the ceiling with devotional objects. The priest has invited a French-born auction specialist from London to view the desolate, *pêle-mêle* collection. He explains:

PRIEST: You know, at one time everyone here was Catholic, like in Spain or Ireland, and at a one precise moment—in 1966 in fact—the churches suddenly emptied out. . . . So now we don't quite know what to do with this [pointing to religious art and artifacts surrounding him]. The authorities would like to know if any of this has any value. . . .

AUCTION SPECIALIST: Listen, this all certainly has great value for people here, for their collective memory . . .

PRIEST: But is there anything we could sell?

AUCTION SPECIALIST: On the global market? . . . To be honest, I don't think so.

PRIEST: In other words, all this is worthless. I'll show you out.

The scene acutely captures the fate of Catholicism in Québec: to sustain itself, the once-vital Church must sell its devotionalia not even as folklore but as bric-à-brac, the flotsam of a dead religion. It sets the stage for an examination of Charest's 2008 motion to retain the crucifix suspended in the National Assembly, and of why that issue resurfaced five years later in the Charter of Values. In this section, I explore the tensions between the constituting of materials as "art" or cultural patrimony, as opposed to

---

PKP appeared as a potential candidate to replace Pauline Marois at the helm of the party. He was elected Chief of the PQ on May 15, 2015, but resigned from his post on May 2, 2016, for family reasons.

devotional or religious objects, and the challenge of measuring and calibrating value.

Following Martin Riesebrodt, I distinguish here between *religion* and *religious tradition*. Religion is a complex of practices premised on the existence of supernatural powers that offer the promise of salvation. Religion and religiousness—an individual's subjective appropriation of a religion—are notably different from the broader category of religious tradition, "the historical continuity of systems of symbols" (Riesebrodt 2010, xii). Religious tradition may refer to classifications of discourses and practices in terms of theological or symbolic continuity, or to the empirical category of practices understood as having "always already" been performed in that way (Riesebrodt 2010, 77).

Scholars of nationalism like myself are less concerned with the supernatural aspects of religion than with how religious beliefs and practices are yoked to issues of authority, political legitimacy, and social contest. Insofar as religion can be converted into political capital, religious tradition—as a set of discourses, symbols, practices, and material resources—is already thoroughly political. In many cases, it is difficult, if not impossible, to separate traditional religious acts from political ones. When religion is invoked to define "who we are"—a phrase blending religious and political claims and sentiments—it is usually in the form of tradition. The mutual reinforcement or layering of religious and national identities renders them especially resistant to sudden transformation.

The distinction between religion and religious tradition is important, yet it is insufficient for us to disentangle the different registers at which Catholicism is invoked in public (and political) debates in contemporary Québec. I propose to examine the process of *patrimonialization* of religion, that is, the discursive, material, and legal ways in which religious symbols, artifacts, and practices are sacralized as secular elements of the nation and its history. Some of those may already have been secularized by leaving the religious domain proper to enter the realm of religious tradition or cultural religion. Good examples of religious symbols, objects, and practices that were stripped of their religious significations but remained part of social life as cultural religion include the celebration of Christmas and Easter in historically Christian societies, as well as rituals related to life events.

The process of patrimonialization, on the other hand, entails the resacralization of these formerly religious (or culturally religious) symbols, objects, and practices but as *national* symbols, objects, and practices. Debates over reasonable accommodation and the Charter of Values might at first appear to be primarily about the desire to tame particular religious aspirations of immigrants. My sociological focus on the patrimonialization of religion and religious tradition suggests, however, that it might rather be an attempt to preserve "a social state in which Catholicism and secularism [are] united within a single national project" (2011, 675–76), to use the words of sociologist of religion É. Martin Meunier.

Secularizing and Resacralizing Religious Tradition

When Premier Charest proposed a motion in the National Assembly to retain the crucifix just a few hours after the release of the Bouchard-Taylor report recommending its removal, the motion was unanimously adopted by the elected representatives present. How to interpret Charest's action? This was not a display of piety but a tactic reinforcing a policy that sought to patrimonialize religious objects and sites to prevent situations such as the one depicted in Arcand's film (figure 5.5). After countless churches were bulldozed, sold, transformed into condominiums, or simply left to decay for lack of support from dwindling numbers of parishioners (figure 5.6), the state decided in the 1990s to invest in *religious patrimony*.

The government of Québec allocates financial aid and provides expertise to preserve and maintain elements of religious buildings and sites recognized as having "patrimonial value," including structures, materials, furniture, artifacts, artwork, landscape, and monuments. Since 1995, the government has spent $291 million in restoring such religious patrimony.[16] As stated on the website of the Conseil du patrimoine religieux du Québec: "In the eyes of the Québec Religious Heritage Council, Québec's religious heritage is seen as a founding heritage because religious concerns and religious establishments have been present since the origin of Québec society. It is the most universal, the most diversified, and the richest component of our entire cultural heritage. It's also the most visible and most spread out over our territory. It represents a major expression of Québec's culture and an important element of our identity, expressing the social, ethical, and philosophical values of our society."[17]

16. Press Release, Conseil du patrimoine religieux du Québec, Montréal, February 14, 2014, http://www.patrimoine-religieux.qc.ca/fr/actualites/communiques/Budget2013-15, accessed July 22, 2015.

17. Quoted from the Conseil du patrimoine religieux du Québec's English-language site: http://www.patrimoine-religieux.qc.ca/en/financial-assistance/preservation-principles, accessed July 22, 2015. The Cultural Heritage Act was passed on October 19, 2011, as Bill 82. Eligible buildings are those that "are open to the public, were built before 1945 and have recognized heritage value, either by virtue of a list-

FIGURE 5.5 "Agnosticism (What Is Left of Us)," by Simon Beaudry, 2014. An abandoned statue of Jesus, transformed into artwork. Jesus, in that instance, is no longer a sacred, revered icon, but a mere wooden object. It is not blood flowing through Jesus and his sacred heart, but sap. That sap is nevertheless precious enough to be collected through a spigot and a bucket. While the maple leaf has been abandoned by French Canadians and Québécois as an ethnic symbol, the making of maple syrup and family outings to the sugar shack in early spring remains a common traditional practice. Jesus, once faith is gone, is satirically recycled for other sacred purposes.

FIGURE 5.6 The back of what remained of St. Vincent-de-Paul church, Québec City, in 2008. The abandoned church and the site were sold to developers who planned to build a large hotel complex. Graffiti artists painted the interior walls of the façade, visible from the lower town. Pressure groups and committees on patrimony managed to have the city mandate that the façade of the church be incorporated into the hotel structure, but the decision was finally overturned, and the façade was demolished on February 20, 2010 (photograph by the author).

After losing all prestige in the wake of the Quiet Revolution, then, religious heritage was suddenly enshrined as a collective good, and resacralized through the notion of cultural patrimony. In an attempt to inform and educate a public that no longer practiced religion, the state also launched awareness campaigns, posting large banners on religious sites whose preservation was funded by the state with the slogan "Our cultural patrimony, it's sacred!" (figures 5.7–5.8). Another document, a report published in June 2006 by the Commission de la Culture, was titled "*Croire* au patrimoine religieux" (*Believing in* religious patrimony—emphasis in original).[18] It called not for religious belief but for belief in religious tradition as culture. In this reframing, the state was funding and supporting not religion per se but rather the memory of a religious past transformed into the broader and putatively neutral notion of cultural patrimony.[19] By this measure, many secular and even atheist Québécois remain "Catholic." By stressing connections with the past, such strategies reaffirm the predominance of the majority group while confirming that religion is something Québec has left behind, something whose value in the present lies only in its capacity to transmit Québec's past.

Patrimonial Practices?

It should be no surprise that while some promote religious patrimony qua cultural heritage to solidify Québécois's secularity in a diversifying society, others use it to promote a different vision of Québécois identity, one that remains closely tied to its French Canadian antecedents. This became evident in a controversy over prayers recited before the opening of municipal meetings in the town of Saguenay, in northeastern Québec (pop. 145,000). In article G3, the Bouchard-Taylor report recommended the abolition of prayers in public offices, a practice that had persisted in some places despite the otherwise far-reaching secularization of political institutions during and after the Quiet Revolution. Prayer was abolished in

---

ing in the Inventaire des lieux de culte du Québec (ILCQ) or under Québec's Cultural Heritage Act." See website of Conseil du patrimoine religieux du Québec, http://www.patrimoine-religieux.qc.ca/en/financial-assistance/religious-heritage-restoration, accessed July 22, 2015.

18. These slogans are almost identical to those used seven years later by the PQ to promote its Bill 60: "Because we believe in our values" and "Our values are sacred."

19. The state does not fund the restoration and preservation of Catholic sites exclusively: it funds projects of other religious communities insofar as they are recognized as religious patrimony, and the website of the Conseil is careful to showcase diversity. Because of the sheer number of Catholic sites in Québec, however, these constitute the overwhelming majority of projects funded.

FIGURE 5.7 Notre-Dame-des-Victoires church, Place Royale, Québec City, 2008. One of the oldest stone churches in North America, its construction began in 1687 and was completed in 1723. Initially dedicated to L'enfant Jésus, the church was renamed Notre-Dame-de-la-Victoire after the Siege of Québec, and Notre-Dame-*des*-Victoires (plural) in 1711, when the sinking of a British fleet was attributed to miraculous intervention. It is an important symbol of French resistance and victories over the British (photograph by the author).

FIGURE 5.8 Notre-Dame-des-Victoires church, Place Royale, Québec City, 2008. The government-sponsored poster informs passers-by that the church has received a $78,000 subvention as part of the patrimony program. Below it, a plaque permanently affixed to the wall informs (French-speaking) visitors that "Place Royale [is] the cradle of New France. Here, on these grounds, Samuel de Champlain founded Québec City in 1608" (photograph by the author).

1973 at Parliament, but it was at least intermittently retained in Saguenay and now was defended by a vocal mayor who turned the ritual into his personal religious and political crusade. The prayer he recited until 2008 at the beginning of municipal council meetings at City Hall went as follows:

> [Opening with Mayor crossing himself, then reciting]
>
> In the name of the Father, Son and Holy Ghost:
>
> O God, eternal and almighty, from Whom all power and wisdom flow, we are assembled here in Your presence to ensure the good of our city and its prosperity. We beseech You to grant us with the enlightenment and energy necessary for our deliberations to promote the honor and glory of Your holy name and the spiritual and material well-being of our town.
>
> *Ainsi soit-il*. Sign.[20]

On July 22, 2008, Alain Simoneau, a Catholic-born atheist who declared his apostasy in 2007, requested that the prayer be abolished. Although the city rejected his request, it amended its bylaws with a revised prayer three months later:

> *As soon as the person who presides over the assembly enters the deliberation room, council members who wish to do so shall rise to recite the traditional prayer, whose text is reproduced here*:
>
> God almighty, we thank You for the numerous graces that you have given to Saguenay and its citizens—liberty, the possibility to prosper, and peace. Guide us in our deliberations as members of the municipal council and help us to be mindful of our duties and responsibilities. Grant us the wisdom, knowledge and understanding that will allow us to preserve the advantages that our town enjoys so that all may benefit and that we may take wise decisions. Amen.

20. As cited in the Saguenay (ville de) c. Mouvement laïque québécois, 2013 QCCA 936, Greffe de Québec 200-09-007328-112 (150-53-000016-081), §17. The mayor, born in 1948, used the traditional, pre-Vatican II *Ainsi soit-il* instead of Amen to conclude the prayer. My translation.

In order to allow council members and private individuals who do not wish to be present during the recitation of the prayer to come back into the room, the President of the Assembly will declare the session open two minutes after the prayer's recitation has ended.[21]

Not satisfied, Simoneau joined with the Mouvement laïque québécois to sue the city. On February 9, 2011, the Tribunal des droits de la personne ruled that the plaintiff had suffered prejudice through the recitation of the prayer and ordered the cessation of the practice as well as the removal of all religious symbols from the Saguenay City Hall meeting rooms. It also fined the city $15,000 and ordered it to pay another $15,000 in personal damages to the plaintiff. The judgment was positively received in the public sphere, but Mayor Tremblay appealed, and on May 27, 2013, the Court of Appeal reversed the initial ruling in a brief of 44 pages.[22] In his detailed opinion, Judge Guy Gagnon argued that Simoneau had not suffered discrimination from the practice and that in any case the prayer was patrimonial rather than religious. The following passages of Gagnon's main opinion illustrate the criteria and reasoning applied to distinguish between religion, religious tradition and cultural patrimony:

> §63 [The state's] obligation to be neutral can only be realized by a delicate yet inevitable arbitration between the common good that the state is supposed to defend—including the safekeeping of its cultural heritage—and the right of each [citizen] to have his or her moral convictions respected.
>
> §64 However, in Québec nothing like a Charter of Secularism exists. In the absence of such an official statement of the values that the state intends to protect, within the framework of its obligation to be [religiously] neutral, we must follow the liberal rule according to which a religiously neutral state essentially means that no religious viewpoint is imposed on citizens, that government actions in all forms are devoid of such influence, and that it is truly so.
>
> §65 This objective does not require that society be sanitized from all confessional reality, including that related to its cultural history. On

21. As cited in the Saguenay (ville de) c. Mouvement laïque québécois. 2013 QCCA 936. Greffe de Québec 200-09-007328-112 (150-53-000016-081), §22.

22. Ibid.

> that point, we must recognize that certain historic values of Québec society remain compatible with some of today's values that are said to be neutral and universal.
>
> . . .
>
> §68 . . . Though the history of Québec society, symbolic references included, should not silence currents of thought that are different from those that animated it at the beginning, *we still cannot ignore the patrimonial reality without risking that [Québec society] cut itself off from the bases that shaped its evolution.* In that sense, the absolute neutrality of the state does not seem possible from a constitutional point of view (my emphasis).
>
> §70 [P]ractices that were once intimately linked to identifiable religious dogmas have since been secularized. Seen in this new context, they cannot . . . be eliminated in the name of a draconian conception of the state's neutrality. What purpose would it serve if those practices, in spite of their initial signification, are now merely passive historical witnesses?
> . . .
>
> §72 . . . [A] contextual analysis requires that we take religious diversity and each [citizen]'s moral beliefs into account, while reconciling this imperative with the cultural reality of [Québec] society, including references to its religious heritage.

The judge then explicitly referred to the Government of Québec's 2008 motion to retain the crucifix at the National Assembly, noting that "surely it was aware of its duty to remain religiously neutral" (§72). Taking this precedent as his point of departure, and highlighting the fact that the National Assembly motion had been adopted through a unanimous vote, the judge then cited other examples of religious symbols and imagery that had been secularized: the theist references in the national anthem of Canada and "the white cross on Québec's flag, supposed to symbolize the faithfulness of the first Francophone Québécois to the religion of their ancestors (Catholicism)" (§103). "These forms of religious particularism which we find here and there in public space are *nothing more than historical manifestations* of Québec society's religious dimension. Once viewed from the proper perspective, they cannot compromise the neutrality of different state apparatuses" (§104, my emphasis). By defining practices as symbols, symbols that were, in his view, both nondenominational and patrimonial,

Justice Gagnon concluded that the prayer could not pose a threat to the neutrality of the city and reversed the decision of the Tribunal des droits de la personne (§108). He then extended his judgment to the issue of material religious symbols, notably a crucifix and a statue of the Sacred Heart in other rooms of City Hall, explicitly citing (out of context) a passage of the Bouchard-Taylor report in which the commissioners distinguished between symbols that were "properly" religious and therefore problematic and religious symbols that had become merely "patrimonial" (§118): "For example, the cross on Mount Royal does not signify that Montréal identifies with Catholicism, and does not demand that non-Catholics act against their conscience. It is a symbol that reflects a chapter of our past. *A religious symbol is therefore compatible with secularism when it is a historic reminder rather than a sign of religious identification by a public institution*" (Bouchard and Taylor 2008a, 152; emphasis in original).

Citing the artistic and patrimonial value of the crucifix in question, Judge Gagnon rejected the proposal to remove it. He explained, for example, that the crucifix in Saguenay, dating from the 1980s, came from a known artist from the region who had testified that his sculpture "had no religious objective": in his testimony, the artist explained that the work did not represent a dead Christ and that, moreover, Jesus was "not *nailed* to the cross" (§121; emphasis in the original). Throughout, the judge used the terms *artwork* (*œuvre*) and *sculpture* in regard to the crucifix in an attempt to secularize it.

Gagnon then cited an expert witness, a professor of theology, who testified that this "artwork did not follow canonical norms of a crucifix" but was instead closer to an "art form that has a certain aesthetic value related to a religious past" (§124).

Such arguments provided sufficient evidence, in Judge Gagnon's view, that "the religious symbol is for a large segment of the population stripped of its religious connotation and that [its] presence merely underlines a historic cultural heritage that in no way interferes with the City's religious neutrality" (§125). To affirm that interpretation, he returned once more to the vote to retain the crucifix in the National Assembly (§137). Finally, he explained that there was no evidence that those visual symbols were used for veneration or contemplation by observers in any sense that could threaten the neutrality of the city (§140). Taken as a whole, the judge's arguments emphasized the artistic, noncanonical nature of the crucifix and its lack of religious signification. It was thus a secular, "neutral" object but nevertheless sacred in the sense that it represented an essential part of "our past."

It is important to underscore the two lines of arguments made by Judge Gagnon to reject the plaintiff's claim of infringement on his freedom of conscience: first, reciting a prayer before a council meeting, or of hanging a crucifix in a room, is a *patrimonial* practice. As such, it is not necessarily religious. Second, the prayer and the crucifix themselves are unproblematic, since the prayer is supposedly nondenominational and the crucifix is a work of art.

A second judge, Judge Hilton, supported the main opinion regarding the prayer but noted that the issue of religious symbols was thornier, since it dealt not with a "non-denominational prayer that lasts 20 seconds and is recited before the formal opening of the municipal council meeting, but the permanent presence of religious symbols in two of the three meetings rooms of City Hall" (§164). Here Judge Hilton cited a key passage from the Bouchard-Taylor report on the crucifix at the National Assembly to justify his position and oppose that of Judge Gagnon: "In spite of the motion about religious symbols that was unanimously accepted by legislators, the Bouchard-Taylor report pointed out in the very chapter cited earlier by Judge Gagnon in §118, that the presence of a crucifix above the seat of the National Assembly's president 'implies a special proximity between the legislative power and the majority's religion.'" Judge Hilton was being diplomatic in order to not contradict his colleague too forcefully, merely underlining that he had been selective in his reading of the Bouchard-Taylor report. In fact, Bouchard and Taylor had explicitly cited the prayer as an example of practices that should be abolished on the very page where they discussed the example of the Mount Royal cross: "We must avoid maintaining practices that in point of fact identify the state with a religion, usually that of the majority, simply because they now seem to have only heritage value. The prayers recited at the beginning of municipal council meetings or the crucifix hanging above the president's chair in the National Assembly of Québec come to mind" (Bouchard and Taylor 2008c, 152). Whether because of their religious or their patrimonial status, the court deemed the symbols sacred.[23] Through the examination of their status as material objects and embodied practices, indeed, the crucifix and the prayers acquired an additional layer of meaning, becoming political symbols. The same was true of the crucifix at the National Assembly.

23. That judgment, however, was reversed by the Supreme Court of Canada on April 15, 2015. I discuss the judgment in the book's conclusion.

Duplessis's Crucifix

The 2008 motion to retain the crucifix at the National Assembly became a legislative point of reference on both the secular nature of that object and its sacred patrimonial value. The crucifix was largely invisible for most of the twentieth century, but in recent years it has taken on a new signification. Its trajectory as a material object and a contested symbol highlights the blind spots of Québec's engagement with religion.

In 1936, when the fall legislative session opened at the beginning of Premier Maurice Duplessis's tenure, a crucifix was hung on the wall over the assembly president's seat. It is impossible to ascertain whether Duplessis himself requested its installation and, if so, what he might have intended by it. In any case, those opposing the presence of the crucifix in Parliament today call it "Duplessis's crucifix."

As Gaston Deschênes (2007) has shown, the installation of the crucifix in 1936 was uncontroversial and indeed went almost unnoticed at the time. It was nevertheless the prelude to further and more telling demonstrations of Duplessis's conservative Catholic conception of French Canadian Society, argues Martin Rochefort (2008, 22). According to him, the crucifix acquired a symbolic significance related specifically to the alliance between the Church and the Duplessis government. As detailed in chapter 1, this period is commonly referred to as the Great Darkness (*Grande noirceur*).

The crucifix was first brought to public attention in 2007 by André Boisclair, then leader of the PQ, in the context of rising public discontent over reasonable accommodation. It remained in the spotlight throughout the work of the Bouchard-Taylor Commission and was specifically mentioned in the commission's report as an example of religious symbols that should be removed. Charest's immediate proposal to retain it as a patrimonial object, and, later, the PQ's invocation of the Charter of Values to affirm that status have kept the crucifix at the center of questions about and debates over the place of Catholicism in contemporary Québec. It is worthy of note that the crucifix was not associated with Duplessis until its mention in the Bouchard-Taylor report.

What is perhaps most surprising is that the crucifix survived both the Quiet Revolution and the political and institutional changes of 1968. In that year, Québec's bicameral legislature was abolished. The upper house, the Legislative Council, was dissolved, and the lower house, the elected Legislative Assembly, was renamed the National Assembly. According to

Deschênes, the crucifix in the Legislative Council's meeting chamber, the Salon Rouge, was placed in storage. When the National Assembly's Salon Bleu underwent a renovation and restoration in 1984, the crucifix installed during Duplessis's tenure was replaced.[24] The new crucifix, fashioned by the artisan Romuald Dion, was made of mahogany to match other woodcarvings in the Salon Bleu. Despite the artist's claims to originality in his positioning of Jesus on the cross, no one paid it much heed (Pelletier 1988). That is perhaps why André Boisclair indicated the irony in the tendency of Québécois to criticize the religious practices of other cultural communities while they did not even notice their own.

When attention was brought to the crucifix more than two decades later, its religious semantics had to be toned down and its presence justified by other arguments. Premier Charest insisted that it was a patrimonial symbol that signified both Québec's religious history and the role of the Quiet Revolution in leading the people out of that history. Others claimed that the object was patrimonial and not religious by virtue of its new, artistic form, secularized and resacralized as patrimonial. The crucifix was turned into a putatively neutral object empty of religious signification but rich in historical value.

Holy Men and Femen

The assertion that the crucifix is now only a symbol of cultural patrimony has been challenged by both religious and secular groups. In response to mounting arguments about the appropriateness of the crucifix in the Salon Bleu, the Assembly of Catholic Bishops of Québec issued a statement noting that its presence there was by the vote of "elected representatives respecting the population's opinion" and that they would respect any decision to remove it. But they also challenged the notion that the crucifix had only secular significance: "The crucifix represents the ultimate act of love, that of Christ giving his life for the world's salvation. It is venerated by millions of Christians from all nations and by a great majority of Québécois. It is neither a museum artifact nor merely a souvenir from the past, or a patrimonial element. It must be treated with all the respect due

24. The whereabouts of both the Salon Rouge crucifix and the original Salon Bleu crucifix are uncertain. Deschênes cites a 1986 newspaper article claiming that the original 1936 crucifix was in the collection of the Parliament's museum, but he notes that it was not exhibited. According to Deschênes, both are most likely in a dusty storage bin somewhere.

a fundamental symbol of Catholic faith. Deputies must insure that it be that way."[25]

Some secular critics also disputed the idea that the crucifix was a neutral historical symbol, and they were less discreet than the bishops in expressing their opposition to it. On October 1, 2013, Premier Pauline Marois was interrupted during the question period of the National Assembly when three bare-chested, flower-crowned activists from Femen, an international feminist group, started shouting from the gallery, "Patrimoine au Musée!" and "Crucifix, décâlisse!"[26] A rough translation from Québec French to English of that second slogan is, "Crucifix, get the hell out!" But the translation loses much of the original's brilliant and complex juxtaposition of the sacred and the profane. To understand this requires a short detour into cursing practices in Québec.

In France and elsewhere in the world, profanities tend to refer to sex and scatology. In Québec, by contrast, such terms are almost exclusively deformations of names of sacred objects, rituals, or names: *calice* (chalice) becomes *câlisse*; Christ becomes *criss*; *tabernacle* becomes *tabarnak*, and so forth. There exists, in addition, a hierarchy of these profanities as well as a series of euphemistic variants. For example, *câlisse* becomes an acceptable expression when transformed into *câline*, just as *criss* becomes *crime* and *tabarnak* becomes *tabarnouche*. Those words, like *fuck* or *shit* in English, can act as noun, adjective, verb, and adverb, sometimes in a single sentence. The representatives of Femen, therefore, were using a verb derived from one sacred object (*dé-câlisse*, from *chalice*, to signify "get the hell out") to argue for the removal of another sacred object (the crucifix).

While these curses are considered vulgar—their use would be unthinkable in a professional context—they are no longer generally seen as blasphemous. But the Femen protesters' juxtaposition of the crucifix and the swearword *décâlisse*, shouted at the National Assembly during the premier's speech by half-naked women, was shocking. The women were immediately apprehended by guards who escorted them out of the Salon Bleu and tried to cover their chests and immobilize them as the women continued their chant, "Crucifix, décâlisse!"

The women were charged with nudity, indecent exposure, and disrupting public order. A few hours later, the group posted a statement on its Facebook page: "Crucifix from the Great Darkness, a painful memory,

25. Pierre-André Fournier, archbishop of Rimouski, president of the Assembly of Catholic Bishops of Québec, November 8, 2013.

26. See YouTube clip "Québec; Les Femen à l'Assemblée Nationale: 'Crucifix, décâlisse!'" http://www.youtube.com/watch?v=8e0ZrIlxTq4, accessed May 1, 2014.

FIGURE 5.9 A Femen activist standing in front of the bronze statue of Maurice Duplessis outside the Parliament building, a few days prior to their action at the National Assembly (personal interview with Morgane Mary-Pouliot, June 16, 2015). The placard reads, "I am dead, but my crucifix stands for me." To Femen, the so-called Duplessis's crucifix, on the wall above the seat of the National Assembly's president, represents Duplessis's ideological oppression and duplicitous connection with the Catholic Church. On the woman's torso is the call for purging the remnants of Catholicism and the symbols of Duplessis's "Great Darkness": "Let us decrucify ourselves" (photo by Yannick Fornacciari, Femen, with his permission and that of Morgane Mary-Pouliot, former Femen activist).

FIGURE 5.10 "The Crucifix at the National Assembly," by Garnotte, published in *Le Devoir* on August 31, 2015. The PQ leader and Québec Premier Pauline Marois is nailed to a cross against a blue background (to evoke the Salon Bleu). Above her head is the inscription "Charter of Values," for which she has been crucified.

especially for women. This renewal of the pact between Church and State is no heritage to cherish. No to a government that accepts religion in its midst. Yes to the State's secularity!"[27]

In the context of these events, the crucifix, which the PQ had perhaps envisioned as an asset to boost support from the right, became a thorn in the party's side. A caricature published in *Le Devoir* a few months before the April 7 elections, in which the PQ suffered a crushing defeat, turned out to be prophetic: the PQ was crucified and Marois nailed to the Parliament's crucifix, chastised for the Charter of Values.

27. The Facebook page of Femen Québec has since been taken down by Facebook administration because of its photographs of semi-nude women. The content cited above was accessed on October 2, 2013.

6 Conclusion

Toward a Cultural Sociology of Identity Transformation

At the cultural and ideational level, the Quiet Revolution marked the birth of the Québécois nation. The borders of the national community were reimagined around Québec instead of around Canada as a whole. Catholicism was abandoned as an important or even desirable national trait; instead, secularism was enshrined as the key value of the newly defined nation. A rising generation of intellectuals, politicians, artists, and social activists explicitly rejected the notion of ethno-religious survival; the goal was not to survive but to *develop*. The Church was no longer perceived as a bulwark but rather as a barrier to the achievement of that goal. It had controlled social services, supported political authorities, promoted large families, and glorified an agrarian economy of subsistence. None of these projects fit the Quiet Revolution's program. The provincial state was now conceived of as the instrument of modernization and national development, equipped to represent the interests of the new Québécois nation within or alongside the Canadian federal structure.

While the Quiet Revolution is a story of the secularization of national identity, it would be fallacious to assume that a secular identity emerged explicitly to replace a fading religious one. Such causal assumptions are common in the study of nationalism.[1] Eric J. Hobsbawm, for example, explained the existence of Québécois nationalism since the 1960s as a response to the Quiet Revolution's "social cataclysm," which created a "disorientated generation hungry for new certitudes to replace the collapsing old ones," such that "the rise of militant separatism was a surrogate for the lost traditional Catholicism" ([1992] 1995, 172). If nationalism in Québec could be reduced to a simple causal relation—which it cannot—a more plausible argument is precisely the opposite: the secularization of society was not the cause of the nationalist movement but rather its consequence. The collapse of the Church as a crypto-state and the rapid secularization of society were both the results of emerging Québécois nationalism. A new wave of nationalists arguing for a novel national project centered on Québec were instrumental in initiating the break with the Church and building a welfare state. As I have shown, the struggle over, and the ultimate assault on, the figure of St. Jean-Baptiste by left-wing activists were an integral part of that process.

Materiality and Performativity

The reconfiguration of national identity in the 1960s was carried out not only in institutions and through the renegotiation of Church-state relations, but also through an aesthetic revolt led by left-wing nationalists who rejected one vision of the nation and proposed another. That rejection was effected in discursive repudiations, material reworkings of symbols, and narrative reversals. In the course of a decade, parades became the stage for protests that chipped away at the iconic foundation of ethno-Catholic French Canadianness.

We know that material symbols are not merely reflective and derivative of structures but also constitutive of those structures (Sewell 1996). A rich and diverse scholarship (e.g., Turner 1967; Geertz 1973; Swidler 1986; Hunt 1986; Ozouf 1988; Kertzer 1988; Sewell 1996, 2005; Zubrzycki 2006) has convincingly demonstrated the importance of symbols and rituals as vehicles of identity formation. They not only express, but also create and propel political transformations, or, to borrow Weber's metaphor, switch the track of such transformations. The question that had not been fully examined in that literature, however, is why that is so.

1. See, for example, Durkheim ([1912] 1995), Hayes (1960), Kohn (1946), Gellner (1983), and Hobsbawm ([1992] 1995). See Zubrzycki (2006, 18–22) for a critique of that argument.

I showed in this book that new identifications are made possible through social actors' implicit faith in the transformative power of icons. But, in contrast to Alexander's theory of iconic consciousness (2008; Alexander et al. 2012), I demonstrated that this attribution of power to objects is not totemic, in Durkheim's formulation—the sacralization, in a material object, of society *as it is*—but rather polemical—the pressing of claims, through symbols, about how society *should* (or should not) be. Symbols serve to highlight, magnify, and exaggerate particular features of national identity. These effects, in turn, allow social actors to contest given representations and narratives and articulate new ones. Their embodiment in material form enables actors to handle, mold, elevate, turn, fragment, and invert them. In the case of St. Jean-Baptiste, it was the material form of the *tableau vivant* that allowed the lamb to be removed, the saint to "grow up," the float to be overturned, and the saint to be beheaded. Visual, aural, and material forms are as important as narrative for the expression of ideology. Such forms sometimes even alter ideologies and discourses to fit them to their own molds.

These formal transformations are part of a complex chain of signification within performative events. For example, the action of verbally criticizing the lamb brought about another action, the removal of the lamb from the tableau. Once materially altered, the icon was secularized, and that shift rendered St. John the Baptist vulnerable to further attacks—now physical as well as verbal.

The very materials the symbol was made of were also both representative and constitutive of its increasing vulnerability, as is shown in the succession from the human flesh and blood of the "petit Saint Jean-Baptiste" to the majestic bronze statue, the modern wooden sculpture, and its final, fragile papier-mâché rendition. The ever more transitory constitution of the saint foreshadowed and mirrored, but also invited and precipitated, his demise. The saint's transient materiality in the last parade turned his toppling into a beheading. And this transformation, in turn, facilitated the interpretation of the statue's destruction as a murder, adding to the discursive impact and the capacity of the happening to augur a social *event*. Over a decade, thus, the saint was *de*-incarnated until it disappeared, returning only in phantom form after the nationalization of June 24th as the Fête nationale.

The manipulations of the material form of the icon, and the chains of signification they created, were rendered especially powerful through their animation and exhibition in parades. It was the prominence and popularity of the parades that rendered the icon's weakening and final transfiguration so potent. In fact, the beheading of the statue was transformative only because of the parade, which caused the event to be witnessed by the largest mass-media audience possible in Canada in the late 1960s. The very public nature of these ritual performances, with sound and visual images communicated to large groups en masse, reproduced and circulated in mass media the following days, and then remembered and interpreted according to shared scripts—all of this was central to, even constitutive of, the historical event and its transformative consequences. The events were not only reflective of, but also integral to, the process of "social becoming" during the Quiet Revolution (Sztompka 1993).

We can grasp the full significance of the "beheading" only by carefully taking into account material properties of the icon and its symbolic configuration with the lamb, tracing the slow movement of the float in parades through its manifold instantiations over nearly a decade, and analyzing the particular discursive and visual narration made of the event in the press and its interpretation in the public sphere. Without paying attention to these multiple dimensions of aesthetic revolt, it would be difficult to explain how a new national identity could dislodge another one so rapidly and forcefully. One conclusion of this study, then, is that the force of symbols resides not only in their content but also in their form and the stages on which they are displayed and contested.

Sacrality and Eventfulness

Mona Ozouf (1988) has argued that festivals in revolutionary France were designed to effect a transference of sacrality, because a society must sacralize the act of its own creation. But in the case of the Fête nationale, the symbolic foundational moment—the assault on the float, the "beheading" of the saint, and the abolition of the parade—far from being remembered and sacralized, have been forgotten.

While the effacement of the association of today's Fête nationale with the saint's name day is not surprising, what is puzzling is the mnemonic erasure of the very moment that enabled the transition from a Catholic French Canadian to a secular Québécois identity. I suggest that this occurred because the events of 1969 made possible the social but not the political establishment of Québec as a nation. From that perspective, the celebration of the Fête nationale on June 24 actually monumentalizes the failure of the sovereignist national project and the deep ambivalence toward it among even so-called *Québécois de souche* (old-stock Québécois), since the continued use of the saint's name day as the national holiday indexes the conspicuous absence of an independence celebration for Québec. The precursor was beheaded, the Lamb of God sacrificed, yet no new covenant was announced.

With no national foundational moment to ritualize, in 1977 the PQ instead nationalized and secularized the St-Jean-Baptiste observance. This undertaking turned out to be symptomatic and perhaps even prophetic of the ambiguous nature of Québécois identity—officially defined around territory and language but still attached to some of the traditions and customs of French Canada. The nationalization qua secularization and sacralization of the holiday in fact created part of the ambiguity, as the organization responsible for coordinating the celebrations sought new forms of observance and tried to devise a new national aesthetic without successfully forging that fictitious link with the past that Hobsbawm (1983) has shown to be so potent. The Fête nationale drew attention to a political and ritual void in the nation it was supposed to celebrate. In fact it remained a deeply French Canadian holiday, dressed and powdered as Québécois: that is to say, a holiday that today is celebrated primarily by Québécois of French Canadian origin who no longer know why they celebrate themselves on that specific day.

The Fête nationale also symbolizes the very ambiguity of Québec's "national" status, since Québec is not a sovereign state, even though it very much speaks and acts as one. This ambiguous status is reflected in the enfeebled nationalization of the St-Jean-Baptiste holiday, since the holiday cannot celebrate the establishment of a nonexistent sovereign state. On June 24, two conflicting rituals are conflated: the name day of St. Jean-Baptiste, which celebrates the cultural and ethnic survival of the French Canadians in Québec, and the Fête nationale, which celebrates the fact that the Québécois of French Canadian descent have overcome their minority status to become a majority in Québec, "masters in their own house." The tension between those identifications manifested itself in the 1980 and 1995 popular referenda on the sovereignty of Québec as well as in the St-Jean-Baptiste holiday/Fête nationale every year. Discourses and debates *about* the holiday have themselves become a yearly ritual of reflection on Québécois national identity.

Religion, Secularism, and the Politics of Heritage

The split nature of the holiday also encapsulates the ambiguous place of Catholicism in defining Québécois identity. I have explored the ways that this ambivalence has been expressed in the patrimonialization of religious heritage, the debate over the "reasonable accommodation" of the religious practices of immigrants and the Charter of Values/Charter of Secularism.

From that analysis, it becomes clear that Catholicism as a religion may have lost its centrality in Québécois' personal lives, and the Catholic Church may have been marginalized to the extent that it is not even a significant interlocutor in the debates I have analyzed; but when encountering religious "others," most Québécois remain surprisingly Catholic in their secularism. That is, their secularism is defined and articulated through and sometimes against that religion: they are "recovering Catholics," one could say. The reactions of many to religion in general come from deep personal grievances about their Catholic upbringing as well as from broader political, sociocultural resentment toward the role of the Church in Québec until the Quiet Revolution. From a more scholarly vantage point, we might say that Catholicism continues to define the issues with which they disagree. Paradoxically, this is a form of religious belonging, since the rejection of the faith can be articulated only in Catholic terms. The Québécois remain "Catholic in their secularism" precisely because they rejected Catholicism in favor of secularism during the Quiet Revolution. Their story is one of *overcoming* Catholicism. As a result, they often tend to view religion—as a category—with great suspicion. Yet although they have relegated Catholic doctrine largely to the past, Catholicism as religious tradition continues to inform who they are, in a broad cultural way, even if only because Catholicism was a key element of who they *were*.

Québec may have undergone a thorough secularization, then, but religion survives either in defining a collective "us"—former or cultural Catholics—against a certain non-Catholic "them," or in defining an irreligious "us" against a religious "them." The commissioners' recommendation to remove the crucifix at the National Assembly, along with earlier requests by left-leaning sovereignist politicians, however, suggests an awareness of the tension between a secular Québécois identity and its Catholic French Canadian origins. Just as the crucifix remains in place, "as a symbol of Québec's religious heritage and cultural patrimony," Québécois display a profound ambivalence toward their religious past. That has never been more evident than in the heated arguments over the PQ's Charter of Values and the positions expressed by those who insist on enshrining the heritage of the Quiet Revolution and its forceful rupture with religion. Those groups, such as the Mouvement laïque québécois and the Intellectuels pour la laïcité, supported the Charter of Values (albeit minus the crucifix) and argued for the official establishment of a "truly secular" society in which religious individuals and groups have no special rights under the law.

For these citizens, the reasonable accommodation of cultural minorities' religious practices is a problematic practice. The Bouchard-Taylor Commission's proposal for "open secularism" (*laïcité ouverte*) was rejected by both the federalist right and the sovereignist left, and the commission's report was for the most part ignored and soon forgotten. The issue returned with a vengeance, however, in the PQ's proposed Charter of Values, the public reaction to it, and the party's humiliating electoral defeat in April 2014.

In this context, the meaning of religion and religious tradition in Québec, and the challenge of building a secular and religiously plural society from a formerly religious and religiously homogenous one, become clearer. The debates over reasonable accommodation and the Charter of Values were not "just" about religion, or about the religious and the secular. They prompted a reexamination of the way in which the secular was born in that society, a reflection on the religious and political systems out of which—and against which—the secular was born. Just as *Catholicism* carries a range of significations, occupies diverse social spaces, and achieves various levels of political valence in different national and historical contexts, *secularism* is defined in relation to specific religious systems and articulated in relation to specific political structures. These institutions are themselves historically constituted and not readily amenable to, say, the French notion of universal values, the U.S. model of multiculturalism, or other importations from abroad.

What appeared to be a debate about a secularism threatened by the religious otherness of immigrants, then, was also—perhaps even primarily—about the examination of Québec's religious past and its forceful yet incomplete break with that past during the Quiet Revolution. The religions ostensibly at the center of the debates were the usual suspects in similar debates in Western Europe: Islam, Orthodox Judaism, and Sikhism. But it was Catholicism, at once in the center and at the edge of those debates, that truly defined them. Although suspended outside the frame of the discussion, like the crucifix hanging in the Salon Bleu, that religion was the tacit norm against which the others were compared and evaluated. The crisis over reasonable accommodation and the debates over the Charter of Values were shaped by the past dominance of Catholicism and the Church in Québec: one the one hand, the negative valuation of that religious past, and on the other, the realization that this past was rigorously formative. Québec's "religious others" were, unfortunately, injured in a mostly intramural contest.

Beyond Québec, this analysis shows how important it is to study "religion beyond religion," that is, as it is imbricated in various social, political, and cultural processes. Although the debates over reasonable accommodation seemed to center on religion, the core of the controversy was the nation. Looking at these debates only through the lens of religion, we would miss the intricate and subtle ways in which religion still matters in Québec.

In this work I have sought to recover and recenter an event mostly absented from narratives of the nation, namely the aesthetic revolt of the 1960s Quiet Revolution, and to show why and how some of the ambiguities of the period and the few years following it still shape debates over national identity in Québec today. I have demonstrated that the tension between religion and secularism is but one piece of a larger puzzle, and moreover, a piece whose borders are shaped by the overall puzzle of the national question in Québec.

A year after the debate over the Charter of Values and the subsequent defeat of the PQ, in the spring of 2015, the Supreme Court of Canada overturned the decision by Québec's Court of Appeal holding that the prayer recited before municipal council meetings in Saguenay did not infringe on the freedom of conscience of the plaintiff, since the prayer was a patrimonial practice. The Supreme Court of Canada ruled instead: "If the state adheres to a form of religious expression *under the guise of cultural or historical reality or heritage, it breaches its duty of neutrality*. If that religious expression also creates a distinction, exclusion or preference that has the effect of nullifying or impairing the right to full and equal recognition and exercise of freedom of conscience and religion, there is discrimination."[2] The Court referred to the Bouchard-Taylor report's insistence that "we must avoid maintaining practices that in point of fact identify the State with a religion, usually that of the majority, simply because they now seem to have only heritage value" (2008c, 152). After extensive examination of the case, the court reinstated the Tribunal de la Personne's 2011 order "to cease the recitation of the prayer in the chambers where the municipal council meets" (§356, cited in Supreme Court of Canada decision, §164).

2. §78, Supreme Court of Canada, File No. 35496, Mouvement laïque québécois c. Saguenay (Ville) and Alain Simoneau, 2015 CSC, April 15, 2015. Official English translation, my emphasis.

KEY TROPE *The Flag*

THE PATRIOTS' FLAG WAS THE FIRST CANADIAN FLAG, ALTHOUGH it was never adopted officially to represent the polity (see figure 2.1). It is used on some occasions in Québec—on the National Day of Patriots, for example, which is celebrated on the Monday preceding May 25th (see chapter 4) and it can sometimes be seen on June 24th. The Patriots' flag was also used in the 1960s as an emblem of independence movements and a rejection of religious nationalism. In that period, the FLQ added the peasant-patriot to the center of the flag, the so-called Old Patriot (*le vieux de '37*), thereby commemorating the Rebellions and the anticolonialism that motivated them (plate 1).

A recent reinterpretation of active citizenship is visually articulated on a poster promoting Patriots' Day. The silhouette, posture, and movement signify that the Old Patriot has been transformed into several modern-day activists: an environmentalist, a musician, a writer, a filmmaker/sound recordist, and a protester. Québécois national identity is presented as active, engaged citizenship, against the colors—and ideals—of the nineteenth-century Patriots (plate 2). Women are among the active citizens; moccasins have been traded in for Chuck Taylors, but the *tuque* and *ceinture fléchée*, traditional items of clothing, remain. The background of the flag appears to be wood, the grain of the nation, presented not in the form of the romantic tree but as a construction material, with screws visible at the edge. The text, *En avant!* ("Forward!"), explicated by an asterisked note, was the motto of *les fils de la liberté*, adopted on October 4, 1837.

After the defeat of the Patriots and the retreat of the republican agenda, the tricolor "creole" flag was abandoned and the flag of Carillon—a national relic rescued from the battle of Carillon (now Ticonderoga), where the French defeated the British in 1758—resurfaced (plate 3). It later inspired the creation of the Sacré-Coeur flag, a religious-patriotic flag mixing Catholic iconography (the white cross and the sacred heart) with French royal insignia (the *fleur de lys*) (plate 4). In 1948, almost two decades before Canada decided to have its own flag (the Maple Leaf), the Province of Québec adopted the *Fleurdelisé* as its flag, removing the sacred heart but keeping the French royalist colors and symbols (plate 5).[1]

1. Until 1965, when the Maple Leaf was adopted as the official flag of Canada, Canada had no national flag per se. It either used the flag of the United Kingdom (the

In Québec, however, the flag was read not as a royalist symbol but merely as "French" and Catholic. The current flag of Québec quickly became the symbol of the French Canadian and then Québécois nation. Although, as we have seen in chapter 2, the maple leaf was originally embraced as the symbol of the (French) Canadiens, it is now widely understood as (and often rejected as) a symbol of Canadians. The *Fleurdelisé's* blue is easily opposed to the Maple Leaf's red.

The *Fleurdelisé*, it is important to note, resonates with people regardless of their political orientation. It does not signify support for independence but rather marks national belonging more broadly. It is the "unmarked" flag in Québec, ubiquitous, often even unnoticed. It is flown on government buildings and many private residences; it adorns key rings, bumper stickers, mugs, and other commercial items, representing what Michael Billig has aptly termed "banal nationalism" (1995).

Tension has recently been noted, however, between the Québécois civic and secular project—most prominently during the debates over the Charter of Values/Secularism (plates 6 and 7). It is in that broader context that we can make sense of a new generation of activists and graphic designers that have proposed to revise the flag. The visual artist Simon Beaudry, cofounder of the Collectif identité québécoise, designed a flag that he believes better represents the goals and ideals of modern Québec than the *Fleurdelisé*. His "Unilys" (plate 8) unifies the elements that are divided by the cross, making the lily, the symbol of the nation, much bigger and more central. The removal of the religious (specifically, Catholic) element of the current flag foregrounds the strength and significance of the nation.

Union Jack), or the so-called Red Ensign, which is a red flag with the Union Jack on the top left corner and Canada's coat of arms on the middle portion of the right half.

PLATE 1 *Le vieux de '37*, by Henri Julien, 1904. Inspired by a poem of Louis Fréchette, the patriot wears and carries the typical attributes of French Canadians at that time: a pipe in his mouth, a carbine, a *tuque* on his head, a woven belt (*ceinture fléchée*) at his waist, and moccasins on his feet.

PLATE 2 Poster "En avant!" by Simon Beaudry, 2010. Produced by Mouvement National des Québécois (MNQ), photograph by Alain Desjean.

PLATE 3 Bannière de Carillon, reproduced in 1984 for the 400th anniversary of Québec City's Foundation. On June 24, 1848, officials from the Société Saint-Jean-Baptiste paraded in the streets of Québec City with that banner. Half a century later, Papal Zouaves reproduced details of the banner on their own flag and became "protectors" of relics from the original banner, now kept at the Musée de l'Amérique francophone (photo: Marc-André Grenier, Assemblée nationale du Québec).

PLATE 4 Sacré-Coeur flag on unofficial stamps. Such stamps were typically added next to official Canada Post stamps to promote some holiday, tradition, or ideals. Here, the stamp is used in a campaign to stop the use of blasphemous words (see chapter 5). "Blasphemy is offensive to Faith. Combat it." Politeness and Patriotism are equally important values. Note the use of the maple leaf on each corner of the stamp. Musées de la civilisation, gift from Jean and Louis Pelletier, 1997.9116.1.

PLATE 5 Official flag of Québec since 1948, the *Fleurdelisé*. "Le fleurdelisé: reflet de notre histoire en Amérique," http://www.drapeau.gouv.qc.ca/drapeau/images/images.html, accessed July 7, 2014.

PLATE 6 "Minister Drainville wishes to ban ostentatious religious symbols: 'Let's set an example!'" The cartoon, showing a version of the Québec flag with the cross removed, is ironic, since Martin Drainville, minister of Democratic Institutions and Active Citizenship (2012–13) and primary author and promoter of the Charter of Values/Charter of Secularism, actually argued for keeping the crucifix at the National Assembly and never suggested removing the cross from the flag. It is that double standard that the cartoonist Garnotte is emphasizing here (Garnotte, *Le Devoir*, August 21, 2013).

PLATE 7 Femen activist, in a pose evocative of the Virgin Mary with the Québec flag serving as a veil, 2013. The Femen crown of flowers and ribbons (itself borrowed from Slavic folk costumes and emphasizing both virginity and fertility) holds the flag-veil in place. It is the flag as veil that transforms the woman into the Virgin Mary; it is the flag as nation that sacralizes her body; that transforms the woman into a saintly figure. The slogan on her bare chest (what Femen calls the "body-poster") reads, "Let us decrucify ourselves." Femen considers religion in all forms to be a part of patriarchal oppression, and the group declares "sextrism and atheism" as its cornerstone values. For Femen Québec, Québec society can be secular only if it purges itself of remnants of its religious past, including the crucifix at the National Assembly. Femen Québec managed to powerfully mix contested symbols in its ironic protests, juxtaposing the sacred and the profane in their discourse and bodily aesthetics (photo: Morgane Mary-Pouliot, former Femen activist, with her permission).

PLATE 8 Unilys flag by Simon Beaudry, 2008. 180 cm x 120 cm. Ink on fabric.

It is too soon to know what direction or flavor the debate over religion, religious symbols, and religious tradition will take in the years to come, but what is certain is that this issue is unlikely to disappear, and it is reshaping the political landscape, destabilizing previous categories such as the "left" and the "right," and reshuffling political allegiances, as we have seen in the previous chapter. Religion, in its manifold incarnations, continues to inform public debates and policies in post–Quiet Revolution Québec. My hope is that this book has convincingly conveyed that the politics of secularism in Québec can be understood only in conjunction with the forces of national identity and the history of Catholicism in that society, and that attention to oft-overlooked phenomena such as aesthetic revolts can broaden and deepen our understanding of the process of cultural identity transformation.

APPENDIX A: HISTORICAL CUES

1534–42: Jacques Cartier discovers the St-Lawrence Seaway and River.

1534–1763: New France.

1608: Founding of Québec City and New France by Samuel de Champlain.

1642: Founding of Montréal.

1737: Opening of the *Chemin du Roy*, a road linking Québec City and Montréal.

1756–63: Seven Years' war (known in the United States as the French and Indian war).

1758: Victory of Marquis de Montcalm at Carillon.

1759: Battle of the Plains of Abraham.

1760: The English take Montréal.

1763: Act of Paris. New France is officially ceded to England.

1763–91: Province of Québec.

1774 Quebec Act.

1776: American Revolution. It has a significant impact on the Province of Québec as it diffuses revolutionary ideals.

1783: Treaty of Versailles, which recognizes the independence of the United States of America. Many of those who remain loyal to the King of England leave and settle in Canada. The arrival of those "Loyalists" considerably shifts power relations between French- and English-speakers in Canada.

1789–92: French Revolution. Church property is confiscated, members of the ecclesiastic hierarchy are killed. Many conservatives seek refuge in the Province of Québec.

1791–1841: Constitutional Act. Creation of Lower and Upper Canada, known as "The Canadas."

1800–1848: National movements in Europe and in Latin America. *Canadiens* pay attention to insurrections of peoples they feel live in political situations similar to theirs, such as Ireland and Poland.

1806: Founding of the Patriot newspaper *Le Canadien*.

1826: Founding of Bytown (Ottawa).

1834: Publication of the Patriots' 92 Resolutions, demands for political reform in the British colony.

1837–38: Patriots' Rebellions.

1838: Lower Canada declares independence. Rebellions are crushed.

1839: Durham's Report.

1840–41: Act of Union is passed in London in 1840 and proclaimed in 1841.

1842: Beginning of St-Jean-Baptiste processions.

1841–67: Province of Canada, also known as The United Canadas.

1867: Adoption of the British North American Act in London, which creates the Dominion of Canada. Confederation.

1867–: Canada.

1868: Québec *Zouaves* go to Rome to defend the papal estates after Garibaldi's 1867 invasion.

1868: Mgr Bourget excommunicates members of the liberal *Institut Canadien*.

1901: The fertility rate of Québec is approximately 5.31.

1910: Founding of the newspaper *Le Devoir* by Henri Bourassa. The daily argues for the autonomy of Canada vis-à-vis England, equal rights between French and English Canadians, as well as faithfulness to Roman Catholicism and the French language. In the second half of the twentieth century, *Le Devoir* adopts a new nationalism oriented toward the modernization of society.

1924: First thematic St-Jean-Baptiste parade organized by the SSJBM.

1936–39,
1944–59: Maurice Duplessis is Premier of Québec.

1948: The *Fleurdelisé* is voted official flag of Québec.
Publication of Émile Borduas and colleagues' *Total Refusal* (*Refus Global*).

1952: Creation of Radio-Canada, the French-language branch of the Canadian Broadcast Company.

1955: Riots in Montréal after star hockey player Maurice "The Rocket" Richard is suspended.

1959: September 7, Death of Maurice Duplessis.

1960: June 22, Jean Lesage is elected premier.
Beginning of the Quiet Revolution.
Foundation of the RIN.

1961: The population of Québec is 5,259,211.
- 35% are younger than 15.
- 5.8% are older than 65.

Beginning of the Parent Commission on Education.

1963: Founding of Front de libération du Québec.
Founding of the journal *Parti-pris*.

1965: The Maple Leaf is officially adopted as the flag of Canada, replacing the Red Ensign. It quickly becomes popular throughout the country except in Québec, where the *Fleurdelisé*, officially adopted almost two decades earlier, is firmly established.

1966: Opening of the Montréal Metro, the city's underground rapid transit system.

1967: World Exhibition is hosted in Montréal (Expo '67).

July 24–27, de Gaulle visits Québec.

Lévesque leaves the Parti liberal.

1968: June 24, Violent parade, nicknamed "Truncheon Monday."

August, Michel Tremblay's *Les belles-soeurs*, written in joual (Montréal's working-class dialect) is performed on stage.

October, Lévesque founds the Parti Québécois.

Pierre Vallières publishes *White Niggers of America: The Precocious Autobiography of a Quebec Terrorist*.

Québec's legislative assembly is officially renamed the National Assembly.

1970: May 12, Election of Robert Bourassa.

October Crisis: The FLQ kidnaps Pierre Laporte, PLQ minister, and British diplomat James Richard Cross. Laporte is killed on October 17. The War Measure Act is decreed by Ottawa. Cross is freed in December.

1976: PQ wins provincial elections. René Lévesque becomes premier of Québec.

1977: June 24th is legally adopted as Québec's legal national holiday.

Bill 101 is adopted.

1980: May 20, First Referendum on Québec's sovereignty.

June 27, *O Canada* is proclaimed national anthem of Canada on its centennial.

1981: November 5, repatriation of the 1867 constitution.

1982: April 17, Constitutional Act.

1987: Fertility rate is at 1.37.

November 1, René Lévesque dies.

1990: June 23, Failure of the Meech Lake Accord.

1991: 76.5% of couples under the age of 25 are unmarried.

1994: For the first time, the population of Québec is less than 25% of Canada's population.

1995: Second Referendum on sovereignty.

2007–8: Debates and inquiry of Reasonable Accommodation.

2013: Charter of Values/Charter of Secularism/Bill 60 is proposed.

2014: PQ is defeated, Charter abandoned.

APPENDIX B: PARADE THEMES

1924 Ce que l'Amérique doit à la race française
[What (North) America owes the French race]

1925 Visions du passé. Coutumes et traditions ancestrales au Canada francais
[Visions of the past]

1926 Hommage aux Patriotes 1837–1838
[Homage to the Patriots 1837–1838]

1927 Quatre siècles d'histoire
[Four centuries of history]

1928 Nos chansons populaires
[Our folk songs]

1929 Les contes et les légendes du Canada français
[Folktales and legends of French Canada]

1930 Je me souviens
[I remember]

1931 Vive la Canadienne
[Long live the Canadian woman]

1932 Glorification du sol
[Glorification of the land]

1933 *No parade*

1934 Les anniversaires, Histoire, Progrès
[Anniversaries, history, progress]

1935 Le Saint-Laurent et les Grands Lacs
[The St. Lawrence River and the Great Lakes]

1936 Les voix du passé—Évocation de nos poètes disparus
[Voices of the past: Evocation of our long-gone poets]

1937 Ô Canada! Mon pays, mes amours
[O Canada! My country, my love]

Source: Fonds P81, Archives nationales du Québec à Montréal

1938 Les pionniers de la prose au Canada français avant 1900
[Pioneers of prose in French Canada before 1900]

1939 Le Canada français est resté fidèle
[French Canada has remained faithful]

1940 Leçons d'énergie
[Lessons of energy]

1941 Hommage à la famille paysanne canadienne-française
[Homage to the French-Canadian peasant family]

1942 Naissance d'une ville catholique et française au XVIIIème siècle: Ville-Marie
[Birth of a Catholic and French city in the eighteenth century: Ville-Marie (Montréal)]

1943 Hommage à la mère canadienne
[Homage to the Canadian mother]

1944 Hommage à l'éducateur
[Homage to the educator]

1945 Les groupes français d'Amérique
[(North) America's French groups]

1946 Les Canadiens français et la science
[French Canadians and science]

1947 La patrie, c'est ça
[That's what fatherland is about]

1948 La cité
[The city]

1949 L'expansion française en Amérique
[French expansion in America]

1950 Le folklore
[Folklore]

1951 Le Canada français dans le monde
[French Canada in the world]

1952 Notre héritage culturel
[Our cultural heritage]

1953 Nos richesses économiques
[Our economic riches]

1954 Fidélité mariale
[Faithfulness to Mary]

1955 L'Acadie rayonnante
[Radiant Acadia]

1956 Le visage du Canada français
[The face of French Canada]

1957 Sa majesté la langue française
[Her Highness the French language]

1958 Champlain, père de la Nouvelle-France et Québec, capitale du Canada français
[Champlain, father of New France and Québec City, capital of French Canada]

1959 Le Saint-Laurent: la route qui marche
[The St. Lawrence River: the road that works]

1960 La présence canadienne-française
[The French Canadian presence]

1961 Hommage à la femme canadienne-française
[Homage to the French Canadian woman]

1962 L'épanouissement du Canada français
[French Canada's blossoming]

1963 Joie de vivre

1964 Le Canada français, réalité vivante
[French Canada, a living reality]

1965 Montréal, ville dynamique
[Montréal, dynamic city]

1966 La présence canadienne-française dans le monde
[The French Canadian presence in the world]

1967 La vocation internationale du Québec
[Québec's international vocation]

1968 Québec '68

1969 Québec, mon amour
[Québec, my love]

1981 Les forces vives
[Vital forces]

1988 Une démocratie à venir, à bâtir, à préserver
[A democracy to come, to build, to preserve]

1990 Le Québec: 30 ans de puissance tranquille
[Quebec: 30 years of quiet power]

1991 La marche des géants
[The march of giants]

1992 Sept moments de notre histoire
[Seven moments of our history]

1993 Clin d'oeil à la chanson québécoise
[A wink at the songs of Québec]

1994 Gens du Pays
[Countrymen]

1995 Le fleuve
[The (St. Lawrence) river]

1996 Reflets du Québec
[Reflections of Québec]

1997 Une équipe d'étoiles
[A team of stars]

1998 Hommage à la communauté chinoise
[Homage to the Chinese community]

1999 Hommage aux communautés des Caraïbes
[Homage to Caribbean communities]

2000 Hommage à la culture autochtone
[Homage to Aboriginal culture]

2001 *Cancelled*

2002 Fêtes et festivals québécois
[Quebec's holidays and festivals]

2003 Sur mon chemin j'ai raconté.
[On my path, I have told]

APPENDIX C: METHODS AND SOURCES

Beheading the Saint is based on a variety of data. This appendix is meant to provide detailed information on these data, their sources, and how they were collected and analyzed.

Chapters 2, 3, and 4

The first three empirical chapters of the book, chapters 2, 3 and 4, are focused on the iconic making, iconoclastic unmaking, and iconographic remaking of the St-Jean-Baptiste holiday, its symbols and attending practices over time. In chapter 2, I consider five dimensions of St. Jean-Baptiste as a cultural object: 1) the historical, political, and social *contexts* of its creation, interpretation, use, and transformation; 2) its *content*—that is the ideologies and significations that "fills" it; 3) its visual and material *form*; 4) the discourses and *contests* about it, both concerning its content and form; and 5) how public *performances* with the object are represented, depicted, reproduced in the media, and interpreted in the public sphere. Correspondingly, I conducted extensive archival research and analyzed a wide and varied corpus of original data on St. John the Baptist and the annual celebrations of June 24th:

- *Iconographic representations of the patron saint* on religious paintings, commemorative coins and medals, prayer cards, advertisements, and cartoons; religio-national artifacts such as sculptures, statues, processional banners and flags; and audiovisual documents of the St-Jean-Baptiste processions, parades, and protests from prints, photographs, documentaries, televised broadcasts, and amateur footage.
- *Official documents* from the Société Saint-Jean-Baptiste de Montréal (SSJBM), the institution in charge of—among many other things—the organization of the holiday's rituals and festivities, including meet-

ing minutes, correspondence, processional protocols, parade themes, float projects, legal briefs, sponsorships, and accounting.

- *Public debates about the saint and the holiday* found in newspapers' editorials and letters to the editor, political speeches, pamphlets and manifestos, political cartoons and graffiti, as well as in religious sermons and pastoral letters. I used photographic and cinematographic records of protests, collecting photographs of banners and placards carried by protesters.

These data were collected through archival research conducted between 2006 and 2009. I have visited seven archives in Montréal and Québec City, and systematically consulted two more available online. I leafed through several dozen boxes of documents, watched amateur films of parades, documentaries, and film-essays on the parades, as well as purchased television broadcasts of the 1968 and 1969 parades, transcribing the narration myself. In addition to more than 1,000 pages of photocopied archival documents and more than 700 scanned or photographed images of the saint and parade floats, I personally observed a multitude of artifacts, paintings, stamps, medals, and devotional objects at the Réserve of the Musée de la Civilisation and the Musée de l'Amérique francophone in Québec City, where I conducted fieldwork in July 2008.

Official documents, correspondence, leaflets, and manifestos provide unusually rich and varied data for the analysis of debates surrounding the national icon, the parade, and French Canadian identity. In addition to those, I also analyzed coverage of, and debates about, the annual parade and its namesake in newspapers representing diverse ideological positions and political options, as well addressing different subsets of Québec's population. Most of those consulted were dailies (*L'Action catholique, Le Devoir, Le Journal de Montréal, La Patrie, Le Petit Journal, La Presse, The Gazette, The Montreal Star*), and my sample included all issues published during the two weeks preceding and following the annual celebration of St-Jean-Baptiste Day, when the debates about the event were most likely to occur and controversies to be covered, from the beginning of the Quiet Revolution until the first referendum on Québec's independence (1959–81). I systematically reviewed those newspapers on microfilm at the library of Laval University in Québec City during summer 2008, scrolling through every single page of an issue, downloading, printing, or photographing relevant articles, noting the prominence of the story on the page, paying attention to photographs accompanying it and other stories or advertisements next to it, providing "extra-textual" evidence that search engines and software do not. Of the eight newspapers I consulted, two catered to the Anglophone population of Montréal and were therefore in English. While debates were typically not occurring in the pages of those publications (because they concerned French Canadianness and were not involving Anglo-Canadian Montrealers), as parades became the site of contestation and occasion for violent protests, *The Gazette* and *The Montreal Star* started covering them more attentively. Editors sometimes used the St-Jean-Baptiste celebrations as an occasion to explain to English-speaking Montrealers the cultural politics of the Quiet Revolution. As such, I found them to be relevant sources. I also consulted the newsletter of the SSJBM, *Le Bulletin national*, as well as the monthlies *Parti-pris* and *Cité libre*, which were influential political journals. Together, these different kinds of data from multiple sources also allowed me to carefully track, through time, the transformation of the icon and the dialogical relation between discourse, aesthetics, and performance.

Archives Consulted

Archives nationales du Québec (in Montréal)

- Fonds P82, archives of the Société Saint-Jean-Baptiste de Montréal
- Fonds E207, archives of the Comité organisateur de la Fête Nationale du Québec
- Fonds P161, archives of the Mouvement national des Québécois
- Fonds P575, archives of Phaneuf, cartoonist

Archives nationales du Québec (in Québec City)

- P769, S2
- P858 Fonds Gilles Grégoire
- Division des archives photographiques
- Films of parades from the 1930s–1970s
- Films of celebrations 1980s–90s

Centre de recherche Lionel-Groulx (in Montréal)

- Fonds François-Albert Angers P63/A1,31

Musée de la civilisation (in Québec City)

- Prayer cards, paintings, parade floats

Musée de l'Amérique francophone (in Québec City)

- Vestments, flags, icons, devotional objects
- Collection Gaston Fiset-aquarelles of 58 floats for the St-Jean-Baptiste parades, 1950–1968

- Collection Philippe-Lachance: Artifacts of popular devotion—pious images, prayers cards, medals and rosaries
- Collection des Zouaves pontificaux de Québec

Archives de Radio-Canada (in Montréal)

- Television broadcast, 1968
- Television broadcast, 1969
- Images non-broadcasted of the 1968 parades

Archives de folklore de l'Université Laval

- Religio-patriotic iconography
- Photographs of floats

Archives photographiques Notman, Musée McCord

- Available online, http://www.musee-mccord.qc.ca

Maine Historical Society

- Available online, http://www.mainememory.net

Mouvement national des Québécoises et Québécois

- Annual reports, memorabilia, unpublished survey data

Chapter 5

My analysis of the debates over reasonable accommodation is based on briefs submitted to the Commission, observation of the Commission's work, informal interviews with participants and key actors, as well as a review of important interventions in the press and blogosphere during and after the debate. My research assistant and I read and systematically coded a sample of the briefs, representing a third of the entire corpus of all briefs submitted and made available for download on the commission's website http://www.accommodements.qc.ca.

I observed the commission during a week-long series of hearings and meetings in Montréal in November 26–30, 2007, which also included two evening citizens' forums (one in French, the other in English). I also watched Radio-Canada's coverage of the hearings, the press conference upon the publication of the report, parliamentary discussions of the report, and various interviews with the commissioners and politicians, which were available online (http://www.radio-canada.ca/nouvelles/National/2007/09/10/004-Bouchard-Taylor-Antenne.shtml).

During my week-long observation of the Commission's hearings in Montréal, I also conducted informal interviews with participants who presented briefs as well as with "ordinary citizens" present at the hearings.

Data at the basis of my analysis of the Charter of Values consisted of:

- Bills proposed (Bill 391, Bill 94, and Bill 60), transcripts of parliamentary debates and briefs presented to the Parliamentary Commission by individual citizens, representatives of different interest groups and other organizations, as well as videos of their formal presentation by their author(s) at the parliament and the following informal discussion between the author(s) and members of the Commission.
- Op-ed pieces on the Charter published in the Francophone press (*Le Devoir, La Presse, Le Journal de Montreal*, and *Le Soleil*), as well as countless opinion articles and blogs originally posted on the Huffington Post Québec or reposted there from other political blogs and websites.
- Advertisements distributed by the government to promote the Charter, caricatures related to the Charter in the press, placards carried by pro- or anti-Charter activists, and Femen photographs posted on their Facebook page.
- Survey data on the Charter.

REFERENCES

Filmography

Archival Films and Documentaries

Arcand, Denys. 1981. *Le confort et l'indifférence*. Office national du film du Canada.

Clairoux, Jacques. 1977. *77 juin*. FC09494. Archives nationales du Québec à Québec.

Cyr, Luc, and Carl Leblanc. 2005a. *Les feux de la Saint-Jean*. Ad Hoc Films and Télé-Québec.

Cyr, Luc, and Carl Leblanc. 2005b. *Le Chemin du Roy*. Ad Hoc Films and Télé-Québec.

Dansereau, Fernand. 1973. *La Parade*. Office du film du Québec. FC09550. Archives nationales du Québec à Québec.

Falardeau, Pierre. 1985. *Le temps des bouffons*. https://www.youtube.com/watch?v=SiJGQYd6KwO

Falardeau, Pierre. 2001. *15 février 1839*. https://www.youtube.com/watch?v=aPIGxCI8MB4

Germain, Andréanne. 2008. *Pis nous autres, dans tout ça?* Office national du film du Canada.

Godbout, Jacques. 1992. *Le mouton noir*. Office national du film du Canada. www.onf.ca/film/heritiers_du_mouton_noir

Godbout, Jacques. 2002. *Les héritiers du mouton noir*. Office national du film du Canada.

Labrecque, Jean-Claude. 1967. *La visite du Général de Gaulle au Québec*. http://vimeo.com/25725959

Labrecque, Jean-Claude, and Claude Jutra. 1976. *Québec-fête, Juin '75*. Office du film du Québec. FC08259. Archives nationales du Québec à Québec.

Martin, Marcel. 1959. *Jour de juin*. Office national du film du Canada. http://www.onf.ca/film/jour_de_juin

Mercier, Jean-Francois, and Lise Payette. 1989. *Disparaître. Le sort inévitable de la nation française d'Amérique?* Office national du film du Canada.

Nova Films. 1957a. *Parade de la Saint-Jean à Montréal*. FC89-328. Archives nationales du Québec à Québec.

Nova Films. 1957b. *Parade de la Saint-Jean à Québec*. FC89-255. Archives nationales du Québec à Québec.

Proulx, Maurice. 1942. *Parades de la Saint-Jean-Baptiste (à Montmagny)*. FC01785. Archives nationales du Québec à Québec.
Société Radio-Canada. (1954) 1968. *Fêtes de la Saint-Jean à Montréal*. FN90-607. Archives nationales du Québec à Québec.

Fiction

Arcand, Denys. 1989. *Jésus de Montréal*. Centre national de la cinématographie.
Arcand, Denys. 2003. *Les invasions barbares*. Pyramide Productions and Cinémaginaire Inc.

Literature

Lalonde, Michèle. (1970) 1974. *Speak White*. Montréal: Éditions de l'Hexagone. Translated by D. G. Jones, "Speak White." *Ellipse* 3 (3): 24–31.
Lec, Stanisław Jerzy. (1957) 2015. *Myśli nieuczesane*. Kraków: Wydawnictwo literackie.
MacLennan, Hugh. (1945) 2008. *Two Solitudes*. Toronto: New Canadian Library.
Tremblay, Michel. 1968. *Les belles-soeurs*. Vancouver, BC: Talonbooks.

Music

Dufresne, Diane. 1995. "Comme un bel oiseau." Text and interpretation by Diane Dufresne, music by Yves Laferrière. www.youtube.com/watch?v=deIfA-SARp1E
Mes Aïeux. 2006. "Dégénérations." On *Tire-toi une bûche*, Victoire, compact disc.

Primary Accounts, Speeches, Reports, and Essays

Asselin, Olivar. (1913) 2002. *Pensée française*. Bibliothèque électronique du Québec. http://beq.ebooksgratuits.com/pdf/Asselin-pensee.pdf
Assemblée des évêques du Québec. 1979. *Le peuple québécois et son avenir politique: Message pastoral des évêques du Québec sur l'évolution politique de la société québécoise*. Montréal: Assemblée des évêques du Québec.
Bégin, Monsignor. 1908. *Mandements des Évêques de Québec*. Québec: Archevêché de Québec.
Borduas, Paul-Émile. (1948) 1974. *Le refus global*. Montréal: Éditions Parti pris.
Bouchard, Gérard, and Charles Taylor. 2008a. *Fonder l'avenir: Le temps de la conciliation. Rapport*. Québec: Gouvernement du Québec.
Bouchard, Gérard, and Charles Taylor. 2008b. *Building the Future: A Time for Reconciliation. Abridged Report*. Québec: Gouvernement du Québec.
Bouchard, Gérard, and Charles Taylor. 2008c. *Building the Future: A Time for Reconciliation. Report*. Québec: Gouvernement du Québec.
Bourassa, Henri. 1916. *Hier, aujourd'hui, demain: Problèmes nationaux*. Montréal: s.n.
Chartier, Daniel, and Catherine Vaudry. 2007. *La fête nationale du Québec. Un peuple, une fierté*. Montréal: Mouvement national des Québécoises et Québécois and Lanctôt Éditeur.
Chouinard, Honoré-Julien-Jean-Baptiste. 1881. *Fête nationale des Canadiens-Français célébrée à Québec en 1880: Histoire, discours, rapports, statistiques, docu-*

ments, messe, procession, banquet, convention. Québec: L'imprimerie A. Côté et Cie.

Chouinard, Honoré-Julien-Jean-Baptiste. 1890. *Fête nationale des Canadiens-Français célébrée à Québec, 1881–1889: Histoire, discours, rapports, statistiques, documents, messe, procession, banquet, convention*. Québec: Imprimerie Belleau et Cie.

Conseil de la langue française. 1994. "Indicateurs de la langue de travail au Québec." http://www.cslf.gouv.qc.ca/bibliotheque-virtuelle/publication-html/?tx_iggcpplus_pi4%5bfile%5d=publications/pubf148/section3/sect3.htm#3.1

D'Allemagne, André. 1974. *Le RIN et les débuts du mouvement indépendantiste québécois*. Montréal: L'Étincelle.

de Carufel, Hélène, Maxime Pierre Ayotte, and Corporation des fêtes du 24 juin. 1980. *À la redécouverte de notre fête nationale*. Québec: Corporation des fêtes du 24 juin.

De Tocqueville, Alexis. (1831) 2003. *Regards sur le Bas-Canada* (selection of texts by Claude Corbo). Montréal: Typo.

Dugré, Alexandre. 1923. "Saint Jean-Baptiste: Le Saint, la fête, la Société." *L'Oeuvre des tracts* 48: n.p.

Durham, Lord. 1839. *Report on the Affairs of British North America*. London: The House of Commons.

Garneau, François-Xavier. 1845. *Histoire du Canada depuis sa découverte jusqu'à nos jours*. Québec: Imprimerie de N. Aubin.

Lemay, Léon-Pamphile. 1898. *Fêtes et corvées*. Lévis: P. G. Roy.

Morin, Victor. 1924. "Les enseignements de la fête nationale." *La revue nationale* (June): n.p.

Paulette, Claude. 1980. *Je me souviens, depuis 1834*. Ottawa: Leméac.

Rose, Paul. 1968. *Le Lundi de la matraque, 24 juin 1968*. Montréal: Éditions Parti pris.

Saguenay (ville de) c. Mouvement laïque québécois. 2013 QCCA 936. Greffe de Québec 200-09-007328-112 (150-53-000016-081).

Société Saint-Jean-Baptiste. 1926. *Processions de la Saint-Jean-Baptiste en 1924 et 1925*. Montréal: Beauchemin.

Sulte, Benjamin. 1929. *Mélanges historiques: La Saint-Jean-Baptiste*. Montréal: Éd. Édouard Garand.

Thibault, Charles. (1884) 1905. *La croix, l'épée et la charrue. Les trois symboles du peuple canadien*. Montréal: Bibliothèque religieuse et nationale (approuvée par Mgr L'Évêque de Montréal).

Turcotte, Gérard. 1987. "Pourquoi Saint Jean-Baptiste?" *L'information nationale* (June): n.p.

Vallières, Pierre. 1968. *White Niggers of America: The Precocious Autobiography of a Quebec Terrorist*. Toronto: McClelland and Stewart.

Vaultier, Roger. 1946. "Les feux de la Saint-Jean." In *Les fêtes populaires à Paris*, 131–43. Paris: Albin Michel.

Voltaire. (1758) 1957. *Candide*. Paris: Librairie de M. Didier.

Secondary Literature

Agulhon, Maurice. 1981. *Marianne into Battle: Republican Imagery and Symbolism in France, 1789–1880*. Cambridge: Cambridge University Press.

Alexander, Jeffrey C. 2008. "Iconic Consciousness: The Material Feeling of Meaning." *Environment and Planning D: Society and Space* 26: 782–94.

Alexander, Jeffrey C., Dominik Bartmański, and Bernard Giesen, eds. 2012. *Iconic Power: Materiality and Meaning in Social Life*. New York: Palgrave.

Anderson, Benedict. (1983) 1991. *Imagined Communities: Reflections on the Origins and Spread of Nationalism*. New York: Verso.

Angers, François-Albert. 1939. *La position économique des Canadiens français dans le Québec*. École des Hautes Études Commerciales, Université de Montréal. http://classiques.uqac.ca/contemporains/angers_francois_albert/position_can_fr_industrie/position_can_fr_industrie.pdf

Appadurai, Arjun, ed. 1986. *The Social Life of Things: Commodities in Cultural Perspective*. Cambridge: Cambridge University Press.

Armstrong, Elizabeth A., and Suzanna M. Crage. 2006. "Movements and Memory: The Making of the Stonewall Myth." *American Sociological Review* 71 (5): 724–51.

Asad, Talal. 1999. "Religion, Nation-State, Secularism." In *Nation and Religion: Perspectives on Europe and Asia*, edited by Peter van der Veer and Hartmut Lehmann, 178–96. Princeton, NJ: Princeton University Press.

Asad, Talal. 2003. *Formations of the Secular: Christianity, Islam, Modernity*. Stanford, CA: Stanford University Press.

Balthazar, Louis. 1986. *Bilan du nationalisme au Québec*. Montréal: L'Hexagone.

Baril, Daniel. 2007. "Les accommodements religieux pavent la voie à l'intégrisme." *Éthique publique* 9 (1): 174–81.

Barthes, Roland. 1957. *Mythologies*. Paris: Éditions du Seuil.

Bartmański, Dominik, and Jeffrey C. Alexander. 2012. "Introduction: Materiality and Meaning in Social Life, Toward an Iconic Turn in Cultural Sociology." In *Iconic Power: Materiality and Meaning in Social Life*, edited by Jeffrey Alexander, Dominik Bartmański, and Bernard Giesen, 1–12. New York: Palgrave.

Baubérot, Jean. 2007. *Les laïcités dans le monde*. Paris: Presses Universitaires de France.

Baum, Gregory. 1991. *The Church in Quebec*. Outremont: Novalis.

Beauchemin, Jacques, Gilles Bourque, and Jules Duchastel. 1991. "L'Église, la tradition et la modernité." *Recherches sociographiques* 32: 175–97.

Beauchemin, Jacques. 1995. "Nationalisme québécois et crise du lien social." *Les cahiers de recherche sociologique* 25: 101–23.

Beauchemin, Jacques. 2002. *L'histoire en trop: La mauvaise conscience des souverainistes québécois*. Montréal: VLB éditeur.

Bédard, Éric. 2005. "De la difficulté à penser le conservatisme canadien-français." *Recherches sociographiques* 46: 453–71.

Bégin, Paul. 2007. "Laïcité et accommodements raisonnables." *Éthique publique* 9 (1): 158–65.

Behiels, Michael D. 1985. *Prelude to Quebec's Quiet Revolution: Liberalism versus Neo-nationalism, 1945–1960*. Montréal: McGill-Queen's University Press.

Béland, Nicolas, Éric Forgues, and Maurice Beaudin. 2010. "Inégalités salariales et bilinguisme au Québec et au Nouveau-Brunswick, 1970–2000." *Recherches sociographiques* 51: 75–101.

Bélanger, Yves, Robert Comeau, and Céline Métivier, eds. 2000. *La Révolution tranquille 40 ans plus tard: Un bilan*. Montréal: VLB éditeur.

Bellavance, Marcel. 2000. "La rébellion de 1837 et les modèles théoriques de l'émergence de la nation et du nationalisme." *Revue d'histoire de l'Amérique française* 53: 367–400.

Bellavance, Marcel. 2004. *Le Québec au siècle des nationalités (1791–1918): Essai d'histoire comparée*. Montréal: VLB éditeur.

Bender, Courtney, and Pamela E. Klassen, eds. 2010. *After Pluralism: Reimagining Religious Engagement*. New York: Columbia University Press.

Berezin, Mabel. 1994. "Cultural Form and Political Meaning: State-subsidized Theater, Ideology, and the Language of Style in Fascist Italy." *The American Journal of Sociology* 99 (5): 1237–86.

Berger, Peter L., ed. 1999. *The Desecularization of the World*. Grand Rapids: Wm. B. Eerdmans.

Bernard, Jean-Paul. 1971. *Les Rouges: Libéralisme, nationalisme et anticléricalisme au milieu du XIXe siècle*. Montréal: Presses de l'Université du Québec.

Bernard, Jean-Paul. 1983. *Les rébellions de 1837 et de 1838 dans le Bas-Canada: Les Patriotes du Bas-Canada dans la mémoire collective et chez les historiens*. Montréal: Boréal Express.

Billig, Michael. 1995. *Banal Nationalism*. London: Sage.

Bizier, Hélène-Andrée, and Claude Paulette. 1997. *Fleur de lys: D'hier à aujourd'hui*. Montréal: Art global.

Blain, Jean-Pierre. 1964. *L'idéologie nationaliste de la Société Saint-Jean-Baptiste de Montréal*. Unpublished master's thesis, Université de Montréal.

Bock-Coté, Mathieu. 2007. "Behind Secularism, the Nation: Looking Back at the Controversy of Reasonable Accommodations and the Crisis of Québécois Multiculturalism." *GLOBE: Revue internationale d'études québécoises* 10 (2): 95–113.

Boisvert, Donald Luc. 1990. *Religion and Nationalism in Quebec: The Saint-Jean-Baptiste Celebrations in Sociological Perspective*. Unpublished Ph.D. dissertation, University of Ottawa.

Bonnell, Victoria. 1997. *Iconography of Power: Soviet Political Posters under Lenin and Stalin*. Berkeley: University of California Press.

Bosset, Pierre. 2005. "Le droit et la régulation de la diversité religieuse en France et au Québec: Une même problématique, deux approches." *Bulletin d'histoire politique* 13 (3): 79–96.

Bouchard, Gérard. 1999. *La nation québécoise au futur et au passé*. Montréal: VLB éditeur.

Bouchard, Gérard. 2004. *La pensée impuissante. Échecs et mythes nationaux canadiens-français, 1850–1960*. Montréal: Boréal.

Bouchard, Gérard. 2005. "L'imaginaire de la Grande Noirceur et de la Révolution tranquille: Fictions identitaires et jeux de mémoire au Québec." *Recherches sociographiques* 46 (3): 411–36.

Bouchard, Gérard. 2012. *L'interculturalisme. Un point de vue québécois*. Montréal: Les éditions du Boréal.

Bouchard, Gérard, ed. 2014. *National Myths: Constructed Pasts, Contested Presents*. London: Routledge.

Bourque, Gilles, Jules Duchastel, and Jacques Beauchemin. 1994. *La société libérale duplessiste*. Montréal: Les presses de l'Université de Montréal.

Bourque, Gilles, and Jules Duchastel. 1996. *L'identité fragmentée: Nation et citoyenneté dans les débats constitutionnels canadiens, 1941–1992*. Montréal: Éditions Fidès.

Breton, Raymond. 1988. "From Ethnic to Civic nationalism: English Canada and Quebec." *Ethnic and Racial Studies* 11 (1): 85–102.

Brubaker, Rogers. 1996. *Reframing Nationalism: Nationhood and the National Question in the New Europe*. New York: Cambridge University Press.

Brubaker, Rogers, and Frederick Cooper. 2000. "Beyond 'Identity.'" *Theory and Society* 29: 1–47.

Brubaker, Rogers, Margit Feischmidt, Jon Fox, and Liana Grancea. 2006. *Nationalist Politics and Everyday Ethnicity in a Transylvanian Town*. Princeton, NJ: Princeton University Press.

Bryan, Dominic. 2000. *Orange Parades: The Politics of Ritual Tradition and Control*. London: Pluto Press.

Carroll-Burke, Patrick. 2002. "Material Designs: Engineering cultures and engineering states—Ireland 1650–1900." *Theory and Society* 31: 75–114.

Casanova, José. 1994. *Public Religions in the Modern World*. Chicago: University of Chicago Press.

Chaves, Mark. 1994. "Secularization as Declining Religious Authority." *Social Forces* 72: 749–74.

Chennells, David. 2001. *The Politics of Nationalism in Canada: Cultural Conflict since 1760*. Toronto: University of Toronto Press.

Christiano, Kevin J. 2007. "The Trajectory of Catholicism in Twentieth-Century Quebec." In *The Church Confronts Modernity: Catholicism since 1950 in the United States, Ireland, and Quebec*, edited by Leslie Woodcock Tentler, 21–61. Washington, DC: The Catholic University of America Press.

Clément, Éric, and Marc-Alain Wolfe, eds. 2008. *Québec sur le divan: Raisonnements de psys à l'heure des accommodements*. Montréal: Voix Paralelles.

Cohen, Abner. 1993. *Masquerade Politics: Explorations in the Structure of Urban Cultural Movements*. Oxford: Berg.

Corbo, Claude. 2002. *L'Éducation pour tous. Une anthologie du Rapport Parent*. Montréal: Les Presses de l'Université de Montréal.

Cushing, Lincoln, and Ann Tompkins. 2007. *Chinese Posters: Art from the Great Proletarian Cultural Revolution*. San Francisco: Chronicle Books.

Davis, Susan G. 1986. *Parades and Power: Street Theater in Nineteenth Century Philadelphia*. Philadelphia: Temple University Press.

De Sève, Micheline. 1998. "Féminisme et nationalisme au Québec, une alliance inattendue." *Revue internationale d'études canadiennes* 17: 193–212.

DeNora, Tia. 2000. *Music in Everyday Life*. Cambridge: Cambridge University Press.

Deschênes, Gaston. 2007. "Duplessis, le crucifix, et le garagiste de Rouyn." http://

blogue.septentrion.qc.ca/gaston-deschenes/2007/04/03/duplessis-le-crucifix-et-le-garagiste-de-rouyn/

Desdouits, Anne-Marie. 1987. *La vie traditionnelle, au pays de Caux et au Canada français: Le cycle des saisons*. Sainte-Foy: Presses de l'Université Laval.

Dillon, Michele. 2007. "Decline and Continuity: Catholicism since 1950 in the United States, Ireland, and Quebec." In *The Church Confronts Modernity: Catholicism since 1950 in the United States, Ireland, and Quebec*, edited by Leslie Woodcock Tentler, 239–67. Washington, DC: The Catholic University of America Press.

Dufour, Valérie, and Jeff Heinrich. 2008. *Circus Quebecus: Sous le chapiteau de la commission Bouchard-Taylor*. Montréal: Les éditions du Boréal.

Dumont, Fernand. 1971. *Idéologies au Canada français*. Sainte-Foy: Presses de l'Université Laval.

Dumont, Fernand. 1986. "Histoire du catholicisme québécois, histoire d'une société." *Recherches sociographiques* 27: 115–25.

Dumont, Fernand. 1993. *Genèse de la société québécoise*. Montréal: Les éditions du Boréal.

Durkheim, Émile. (1912) 1995. *The Elementary Forms of Religious Life*. New York: Free Press.

Durkheim, Émile. 2010. "Value Judgments and Judgments of Reality." In *Sociology and Philosophy*, translated by D. F. Pocock, 42–51. New York: Routledge.

Eid, Nadia F. 1978. *Le clergé et le pouvoir politique au Québec: Une analyse de l'idéologie ultramontaine au milieu du XIXe siècle*. Montréal: Hurtubise.

Fehérváry, Krisztina. 2009. "Goods and States: The Political Logic of State-Socialist Material Culture." *Comparative Studies in Society and History* 51 (2): 426–59.

Fehérváry, Krisztina. 2013. *Politics in Color and Concrete: Socialist Materialities and the Middle Class in Hungary*. Bloomington: Indiana University Press.

Ferretti, Lucia. 1999. *Brève histoire de l'Église catholique au Québec*. Montréal: Les éditions du Boréal.

Foisy-Geoffroy, Dominique. 2004. *Esdras Minville: Nationalisme économique et catholicisme social au Québec durant l'entre-deux-guerres*. Sillery: Septentrion.

Fournier, Marcel. 2001. "Quebec Sociology and Quebec Society: The Construction of a Collective Identity." *Canadian Journal of Sociology* 26 (3): 333–46.

Fox, Jon E., and Cynthia Miller-Idriss. 2008. "Everyday Nationhood." *Ethnicities* 8 (4): 536–63.

Freedberg, David. 1991. *The Power of Images: Studies in the History and Theory of Response*. Chicago: University of Chicago Press.

Frenette, Yves. 1998. *Brève histoire des Canadiens français*. Montréal: Les éditions du Boréal.

Gagné, Gilles. 2007. "Les identifications nationales en question: Le Québec en trois questions faciles." In *Actualités de la fonction symbolique*, edited by Paul-Laurent Assoun and Markos Zafiropoulos, 67–95. Paris: Economica / Anthropos.

Gagné, Gilles, Simon Langlois, Sami Jalbert, and Catherine Poulin. 2007. *Effectifs du clergé catholique au Québec: 1901–2006*. Québec: Université Laval, Département de sociologie.

Gagnon, Alain-G., and Michel Sarra-Bournet, eds. 1997. *Entre la Grande Noirceur et la société libérale*. Montréal: Éditions Québec-Amérique.

Gagnon, Bernard, and Françoise Paradis Simpson. 2013. "Une migration silencieuse. Paroles de prêtres laïcisés dans le diocèse de Rimouski." *Études d'histoire religieuse* 79 (2): 55–70.

Gagnon, Nicole. 2000. "Comment peut-on être Québécois?" *Recherches sociographiques* 12 (3): 515–66.

Gaudreault-Desbiens, Jean-Francois. 2009. "Religious Challenges to the Secularized Identity of an Insecure Polity: A Tentative Sociology of Quebec's Reasonable Accommodation Debate." In *Legal Practice and Cultural Diversity*, edited by Ralph Grillo, 151–75. Burlington, VT: Ashgate.

Gauvreau, Danielle, and Peter Gossage. 2000. "Avoir moins d'enfants au tournant du XXeme siècle: Une réalité même au Québec." *Revue d'histoire de l'Amérique française* 54 (1): 39–65.

Gauvreau, Michael. 2008. *The Catholic Origins of Quebec's Quiet Revolution, 1931–1970*. Montréal: McGill-Queens University Press.

Geadah, Yolande. 2007. *Accommodements raisonnables: Droit à la différence et non différence des droits*. Montréal: VLB éditeur.

Geertz, Clifford. 1973. *The Interpretation of Cultures*. New York: Basic Books.

Geertz, Clifford. 1985. "Centers, Kings, and Charisma: Reflections on the Symbolics of Power." In *Rites of Power: Symbols, Ritual, and Politics Since the Middle Ages*, edited by Sean Wilentz, 13–32. Philadelphia: University of Pennsylvania Press.

Gell, Alfred. 1998. *Art and Agency*. London: Oxford University Press.

Gellner, Ernest. 1964. *Thought and Change*. London: Weidenfeld and Nicolson.

Gellner, Ernest. 1983. *Nations and Nationalism*. New York: Cornell University Press.

Giguère, Guy. 1975. *Le défilé de la Saint-Jean-Baptiste à Ste-Anne-de-Beaupré*. Québec: CELAT.

Glaeser, Andreas. 1999. *Divided in Unity: Identity, Germany, and the Berlin Police*. Chicago: University of Chicago Press.

Glassberg, David. 1990. *American Historical Pageantry: The Use of Tradition in the Early Twentieth Century*. Chapel Hill: University of North Carolina Press.

Gorski, Philip S. 2000. "Historicizing the Secularization Debate: Church, State, and Society in Late Medieval and Early Modern Europe, ca. 1300 to 1700." *American Sociological Review* 65: 138–67.

Gorski, Philip S., and Ateş Altınordu. 2008. "After Secularization?" *Annual Review of Sociology* 34: 55–85.

Greer, Allan. 1993. *The Patriots and the People: The Rebellion of 1837 in Rural Lower Canada*. Toronto: University of Toronto Press.

Griswold, Wendy. 1987. "A Methodological Framework for the Sociology of Culture." *Sociological Methodology* 17: 1–35.

Grzymała-Busse, Anna. 2015. *Nations Under God: How Churches Use Moral Authority to Influence Policy*. Princeton, NJ: Princeton University Press.

Guay, Michèle. 1973. *La fête de la Saint-Jean-Baptiste à Montréal: 1834–1909*. Unpublished master's thesis, University of Ottawa.

Guindon, Hubert. 1988. *Quebec Society: Tradition, Modernity, and Nationhood*. Toronto: University of Toronto Press.

Guss, David M. 2000. *The Festive State: Race, Ethnicity, and Nationalism as Cultural Performance*. Berkeley: University of California Press.

Hall, John A. 2001. "Liberalism and Statelessness: Québec in Contexts." In "Stateless Nations in the 21st Century: Scotland, Catalonia and Quebec," edited by John MacInnes and David McCrone, special issue, *Scottish Affairs* 37 (2): 42–53.

Hall, John R., Blake Stimson, and Lisa Tamiris Becker, eds. 2006. *Visual Worlds*. New York: Routledge.

Hamelin, Jean. 1984. *Histoire du catholicisme québécois: Le XXe siècle, Vol. 2 (De 1940 à nos jours)*. Montréal: Les éditions du Boréal.

Handler, Richard. 1988. *Nationalism and the Politics of Culture in Quebec*. Madison: University of Wisconsin Press.

Harvey, George. 2005. *Le Printemps de l'Amérique française*. Montréal: Les éditions du Boréal.

Hayes, Carlton. 1960. *Nationalism: A Religion*. New York: Macmillan.

Heap, Ruby, Pierre Savard, Fernand Dumont, Jean Hamelin, and Nicole Gagnon. 1986. "Débat: Le catholicisme au XXe siècle." *Recherches sociographiques* 27: 101–31.

Hechter, Michael. 1975. *Internal Colonialism: The Celtic Fringe in British National Development*. Berkeley: University of California Press.

Hechter, Michael. 2001. *Containing Nationalism*. New York: Oxford University Press.

Hobsbawm, Eric J. 1983. "Mass-Producing Traditions: Europe, 1870–1914." In *The Invention of Tradition*, edited by Eric J. Hobsbawm and Terence Ranger, 263–307. Cambridge: Cambridge University Press.

Hobsbawm, Eric J. (1992) 1995. *Nations and Nationalism Since 1780*. New revised edition. New York: Cambridge University Press.

Hughes, Everett C. (1943) 2009. *French Canada in Transition*. Chicago: University of Chicago Press.

Hunt, Lynn. 1986. *Politics, Culture and Class in the French Revolution*. Berkeley: University of California Press.

Hunt, Lynn. 1998. "The Sacred and the French Revolution." In *Durkheimian Sociology: Cultural Studies*, edited by Jeffrey Alexander, 25–43. New York: Cambridge University Press.

Jarman, Neil. 1997. *Material Conflicts: Parades and Visual Displays in Northern Ireland*. Oxford: Berg.

Jewsiewicki, Bogumil. 1995. "The Identity of Memory and the Memory of Identity in the Age of Commodification and Democratization." *Social Identities* 1 (2): 227–62.

Johnson, Paul Christopher. 2008. "Vodou Purchase: The Louisiana Purchase in a Caribbean Perspective." In *New Territories, New Perspectives: The Religious Impact of the Louisiana Purchase*, edited by Richard J. Callahan, 146–67. Columbia: University of Missouri Press.

Keane, Webb. 2003. "Semiotics and the Social Analysis of Material Things." *Language and Communication* 23: 403–25.

Keane, Webb. 2006. "Subjects and Objects." In *Handbook of Material Culture*, edited by Chris Tilley, Webb Keane, Susanne Küchler, Mike Rowlands, and Patricia Spyer, 197–202. London: Sage Publications.

Keane, Webb. 2008. "The Evidence of the Senses and the Materiality of Religion." *Journal of the Royal Anthropology Institute* 14: 110–27.

Keating, Michael. 1996. *Nations Against the State: The New Politics of Nationalism in Quebec, Catalonia, and Scotland*. New York: St. Martin's Press.

Kenney, Mary Catherine. 1991. *Neighborhoods and Parades: The Social and Symbolic Organization of Conflict in Northern Ireland*. Unpublished Ph.D. dissertation, University of Michigan.

Kertzer, David I. 1988. *Ritual, Politics, and Power*. New Haven, CT: Yale University Press.

Kirkland, Richard. 2002. *Identity Parades: Northern Irish Culture and Dissident Subjects*. Liverpool: Liverpool University Press.

Kohn, Hans. 1946. *The Idea of Nationalism: A Study in Its Origins and Background*. New York: Macmillan.

Koussens, David. 2009. "Neutrality of the State and Regulation of Religious Symbols in Schools in Québec and France." *Social Compass* 56 (2): 202–13.

Kröller, Eva-Marie. 1997. "Le Mouton de Troie: Changes in Quebec Cultural Symbolism." *American Review of Canadian Studies* 27 (4, Winter): 523–544.

Kuru, Ahmet T. 2007. "Passive and Assertive Secularism: Historical Conditions, Ideological Struggles, and State Policies toward Religion." *World Politics* 59 (4): 568–94.

Lamonde, Yvan, and Claude Corbo, eds. 1999. *Le rouge et le bleu: Une anthologie de la pensée politique au Québec de la Conquête à la Révolution tranquille*. Montréal: Presses de l'Université de Montréal.

Lamonde, Yvan. 2000. *Histoire sociale des idées au Québec*. Saint-Laurent: Éditions Fidès.

Lamont, Michèle, and Christopher A. Bail. 2005. "Les frontières de la reconnaissance: Les catégories internes et externes de l'identité collective." *Revue européenne des migrations internationales* 21 (2): 61–90.

Lamoureux, Diane. 1983. "Nationalisme et féminisme: Impasse et coïncidences." *Possibles* 8 (1): 43–59.

Langlois, Simon. 1999. "Une revolution sociale et culturelle." In *Québec 2000. Rétrospective du XXe siècle*, edited by Roch Coté, 125–99. Montréal: Fidès.

Langlois, Simon, and Jocelyn Létourneau, eds. 2004. *Aspects de la nouvelle francophonie canadienne*. Sainte-Foy: Presses de l'Université Laval.

Latour, Bruno. 2002. "What is Iconoclash? Or is there a World Beyond the Image Wars?" In *Iconoclash: Beyond the Image Wars in Science, Religion and Art*, edited by Bruno Latour and Peter Wiebel, 16–40. Cambridge, MA: MIT Press.

Latour, Bruno. 2007. "Can we get our Materialism Back, Please?" *Isis* 98 (1): 138–42.

Lemay, Léon-Pamphile. 1898. *Fêtes et corvées*. Lévis: P. G. Roy.

Lemieux, Raymond. 1990. "Le catholicisme québécois: Une question de culture." *Sociologie et sociétés* 22: 145–64.

Lemieux, Raymond. 2006. "Catholicisme et fonction identitaire: Du 'Canada français' au Québec contemporain." In *Le Canada français: Son temps, sa nature, son héritage*, edited by Gilles Gagné, 29–41. Montréal: Nota Bene.

Létourneau, Jocelyn. 1997. "La Révolution tranquille, catégorie identitaire du Québec contemporain." In *Duplessis: Entre la Grande Noirceur et la société libérale*, edited by Alain-G. Gagnon and Michel Sarra-Bournet, 95–108. Montréal: Québec/Amérique.

Lincoln, Bruce. 2003. *Holy Terrors: Thinking about Religion after September 11*. Chicago: University of Chicago Press.

Linteau, Paul-André, René Durocher, and Jean-Claude Robert. 1983. *Quebec, a History*. Toronto: J. Lorimer.

Linteau, Paul-André, René Durocher, Jean-Claude Robert, and François Ricard. 1991. *Quebec Since 1930: A History*. Toronto: J. Lorimer.

Linteau, Paul-André. 1999. "Les francophones reconquièrent l'économie." In *Québec 2000*, edited by Roch Coté, 97–111. Montréal: Éditions Fidès.

Mann, Susan. 1988. *The Dream of Nation: A Social and Intellectual History of Quebec*. Montréal: McGill-Queen's University Press.

Martin, David. 1978. *A General Theory of Secularization*. New York: Blackwell and Oxford.

Martin, David. 2005. *On Secularization: Towards A Revised General Theory*. Burlington, VT: Ashgate.

Mathieu, Jacques-Pierre. 1969. "L'idéologie des Annales de la Société Saint-Jean-Baptiste de Québec, 1880–1902." *Recherches sociographiques* 10: 438–48.

McDannell, Colleen. 1995. *Material Christianity: Religion and Popular Culture in America*. New Haven, CT: Yale University Press.

McDonnell, Terence E. 2010. "Cultural Objects as Objects: Materiality, Urban Space, and the Interpretation of AIDS Campaigns in Accra, Ghana." *The American Journal of Sociology* 115 (6): 1800–1852.

McRoberts, Kenneth. 1979. "Internal Colonialism: The Case of Quebec." *Ethnic and Racial Studies* 2: 293–318.

McRoberts, Kenneth. 1993. *Quebec: Social Change and Political Crisis*. 3rd ed. Toronto: McClelland and Stewart.

Meunier, É.-Martin, and Jean-Philippe Warren. 1999. "L'horizon 'personnaliste' de la Révolution tranquille." *Société* (20–21): 347–448.

Meunier, É.-Martin, and Sarah Wilkins-Laflamme. 2011. "Sécularisation et transformation du régime de religiosité au Québec: Étude comparative avec le catholicisme au Canada (1968–2007)." *Recherches sociographiques* 52 (3): 683–729.

Meunier, É.-Martin. 2011. "Présentation: Catholicisme et laïcité dans le Québec contemporain." *Recherches sociographiques* 52 (3): 673–82.

Meunier, É.-Martin. 2015. "L'ancrage du catholicisme au Québec et sa déliaison progressive. Une sociologie historique de l'exculturation." In *Catholicisme et cultures. Regards croisés Québec-France*, edited by Solange Lefebvre, Céline Béraud, and E.-Martin Meunier, 21–44. Sainte-Foy: Presses de l'Université Laval.

Miles, Margaret R. 1985. *Image as Insight: Visual Understanding in Western Christianity and Secular Culture*. Boston: Beacon Press.

Miller, Daniel, ed. 2005. *Materiality*. Durham, NC: Duke University Press.

Milot, Micheline. 2002. *Laïcité dans le nouveau monde. Le cas du Québec*. Turnhout: Brepols.

Milot, Micheline. 2005. "Les principes de laïcité politique au Québec et au Canada." *Bulletin d'histoire politique* 13 (3): 13–27.

Miner, Horace. 1939. *St. Denis: A French-Canadian Parish*. Chicago: University of Chicago Press.

Mitchell, W. J. T. 1986. *Iconology: Image, Text, Ideology*. Chicago: University of Chicago Press.

Mitchell, W. J. T. 1998. "Showing Seeing: A Critique of Visual Culture." In *The Visual Culture Reader*, 2nd ed., edited by Nicholas Mirzoeff, 86–101. New York: Routledge.

Mitchell, W. J. T. 2005. *What do Pictures Want? The Lives and Loves of Images*. Chicago: University of Chicago Press.

Morgan, David. 1999. *Visual Piety: A History and Theory of Popular Religious Images*. Berkeley: University of California Press.

Morgan, David. 2005. *The Sacred Gaze: Religious Visual Culture in Theory and Practice*. Berkeley: University of California Press.

Mukerji, Chandra. 1994. "Toward a Sociology of Material Culture: Science Studies, Cultural Studies and the Meanings of Things." In *The Sociology of Culture: Emerging Theoretical Perspectives*, edited by Diana Crane, 143–62. New York: Blackwell.

Mukerji, Chandra. 1997. *Territorial Ambitions and the Gardens of Versailles*. New York: Cambridge University Press.

Mukerji, Chandra. 2012. "Space and Political Pedagogy at the Gardens of Versailles." *Public Culture* 24 (3): 509–34.

Nelles, H. V. 1999. *The Art of Nation-Building: Pageantry and Spectacle at Quebec's Tercentenary*. Toronto: University of Toronto Press.

Newman, Simon P. 1999. *Parades and the Politics of the Street: Festive Culture in the Early American Republic*. Philadelphia: University of Pennsylvania Press.

Nora, Pierre, ed. 1997. *Les lieux de mémoire. vol. 1 (La République, La Nation)*. Paris: Gallimard (Quarto).

O'Sullivan See, Katherine. 1986. *First World Nationalisms: Class and Ethnic Politics in Northern Ireland and Quebec*. Chicago: University of Chicago Press.

Orsi, Robert. (1985) 2010. *The Madonna of 115th Street: Faith and Community in Italian Harlem, 1880–1950*. 3rd ed. New Haven, CT: Yale University Press.

Ozouf, Mona. 1988. *Festivals and the French Revolution*. Cambridge, MA: Harvard University Press.

Ozouf, Mona. 2005. *Varennes. La mort de la royauté. 21 juin 1791*. Paris: Gallimard.

Palmer, Bryan D. 2009. *Canada's 1960s: The Ironies of Identity in a Rebellious Era*. Toronto: University of Toronto Press.

Pasieka, Agnieszka. 2015. *Hierarchy and Pluralism: Living Religious Difference in Catholic Poland*. New York: Palgrave.

Pelletier, Jean-Guy. 1988. *Bulletin de la bibliothèque de l'assemblée nationale du Québec*, nos. 3–4.

Pettinicchio, David. 2012. "Migration and ethnic nationalism: Anglophone exit and the 'decolonisation' of Québec." *Nations and Nationalism* 18 (4): 719–43.

Potvin, Maryse. 2008. *Crise des accommodements raisonnables: Une fiction médiatique?* Outremont: Athena.

Promey, Sally, ed. 2014. *Sensational Religion: Sensory Cultures in Material Practice.* New Haven, CT: Yale University Press.

Provencher, Jean. 1982. *C'était l'été: La vie rurale traditionnelle dans la vallée du Saint-Laurent.* Montréal: Boréal express.

Reid, Philippe. 1980. "L'émergence du nationalisme canadien-français: L'idéologie du *Canadien* (1806–1842)." *Recherches sociographiques* 21: 11–53.

Ricoeur, Paul. 2004. *Memory, History, Forgetting.* Translated by Kathleen Blamey and David Pellauer. Chicago: University of Chicago Press.

Riesebrodt, Martin. 2010. *The Promise of Salvation: A Theory of Religion.* Chicago: University of Chicago Press.

Rioux, Marcel, and Yves Martin, eds. 1971. *La société canadienne-française.* Montréal: Hurtubise HMH.

Rochefort, Martin. 2008. "L'introduction de la prière et du crucifix de l'Assemblée nationale du Québec." *Bulletin. Bibliothèque de l'Assemblée nationale. Québec: Assemblée nationale,* 37 (2): 18–23.

Rogoff, Irit. 1998. "Studying Visual Culture." In *The Visual Culture Reader,* 2nd ed., edited by Nicholas Mirzoeff, 24–36. New York: Routledge.

Ross, Marc Howard. 2007. *Cultural Contestation in Ethnic Conflict.* New York: Cambridge University Press.

Rousseau, Louis. 2005. "La construction religieuse de la nation." *Recherches sociographiques* 46: 437–52.

Routhier, Gilles. 1997. *L'Église canadienne et Vatican II.* Saint-Laurent: Éditions Fidès.

Roy, Fernande. 1993. *Histoire des idéologies au Québec aux XIXe et XXe siècles.* Montréal: Les éditions du Boréal.

Rumilly, Robert. 1975. *Histoire de la Société Saint-Jean-Baptiste de Montréal: Des Patriotes au Fleurdelisé, 1834–1948.* Montréal: L'Aurore.

Ryan, Mary. 1989. "The American Parade: Representations of the Nineteenth-Century Social Order." In *The New Cultural History,* edited by Lynn Hunt, 131–53. Berkeley: University of California Press.

Sarra-Bournet, Michel, ed. 2001. *Les nationalismes au Québec, du XIXe au XXIe siècle.* Sainte-Foy: Presses de l'Université Laval.

Seljak, David. 1996. "Why the Quiet Revolution was 'Quiet': The Catholic Church's Reaction to the Secularization of Nationalism in Quebec after 1960." *Historical Studies* 62: 109–24.

Sewell, William H., Jr. 1996. "Historical Events as Transformations of Structures: Inventing Revolution at the Bastille." *Theory and Society* 25: 841–81.

Sewell, William H., Jr. 2005. *Logics of History: Social Theory and Social Transformation.* Chicago: University of Chicago Press.

Simard, Jacques. 2000. "Ce siècle où le Québec est venu au monde." In *Québec 2000,* edited by Roch Coté, 17–77. Montréal: Éditions Fidès.

Smith, Anthony D. 2003. *Chosen Peoples: Sacred Sources of National Identity.* Oxford: Oxford University Press.

Smith, Jonathan Z. 1998. "Religion, Religions, Religious." In *Critical Terms for Reli-*

gious Studies, edited by Mark C. Taylor, 269–85. Chicago: University of Chicago Press.

Smithey, Lee A. 2011. *Unionists, Loyalists, and Conflict Transformation in Northern Ireland*. New York: Oxford University Press.

Stevenson, Garth. 2006. *Parallel Paths: The Development of Nationalism in Ireland and Quebec*. Montréal: McGill-Queen's University Press.

Stoker, Valerie. 2003. "Drawing the Line: Hasidic Jews, Eruvim, and the Public Space of Outremont, Quebec." *History of Religions* 43 (1): 18–49.

Stoker, Valerie. 2007. "Zero Tolerance? Sikh Swords, School Safety, and Secularism in Québec." *Journal of the American Academy of Religion* 75 (4): 814–39.

Stolow, Jeremy. 2010. *Orthodox by Design: Judaism, Print Politics, and the ArtScroll Revolution*. Berkeley: University of California Press.

Swidler, Ann. 1986. "Culture in Action: Symbols and Strategies." *American Sociological Review* 51: 273–86.

Sztompka, Piotr. 1993. *The Sociology of Social Change*. Cambridge, MA: Blackwell Publishing.

Sztompka, Piotr. 2012. "Visual Meanings." In *Iconic Power: Materiality and Meaning in Social Life*, edited by Jeffrey Alexander, Dominik Bartmański, and Bernard Giesen, 233–45. New York: Palgrave.

Taylor, Charles. 2007. *A Secular Age*. Cambridge, MA: Belknap Press.

Tentler, Leslie Woodcock, ed. 2007. *The Church Confronts Modernity: Catholicism since 1950 in the United States, Ireland, and Quebec*. Washington, DC: The Catholic University of America Press.

Thériault, Joseph-Yvon. 1994. "Entre la nation et l'ethnie: Sociologie, société et communautés minoritaires francophones." *Sociologie et sociétés* 26 (1): 15–32.

Thériault, Joseph-Yvon. 1999. "La nation francophone d'Amérique: Canadiens, Canadiens français, Québécois." In *Dislocation et permanence: L'invention du Canada au quotidien*, edited by Caroline Andrew, 111–37. Ottawa: Ottawa University Press.

Thompson, Bernard. 2007. *Le Syndrome Hérouxville ou les accommodements raisonnables*. Boisbriand: Momentum.

Tilley, Chris, Webb Keane, Susanne Küchler, Mike Rowlands, and Patricia Spyer, eds. 2006. *Handbook of Material Culture*. London: Sage.

Turner, Victor. 1967. *The Forest of Symbols: Aspects of Ndembu Ritual*. Ithaca: Cornell University Press.

Vaillancourt, François, Dominique Lemay, and Luc Vaillancourt. 2007. "Le français plus payant: L'évolution du statut socio-économique des francophones du Québec." Institut C.D. Howe, Bulletin de recherche, 103: 1–14.

Van Gennep, Arnold. 1949. "Cérémonies périodiques et cycliques: Cycles de mai et de la Saint-Jean." In *Manuel de folklore français contemporain*, tome 1, vol. 4, 1927–2135. Paris: Éditions A. et J. Picard.

Venne, Michel, ed. 2000. *Penser la nation québécoise*. Montréal: Québec-Amérique.

Ville de Montréal. 2014. *Profil sociodémographique: Agglomération de Montréal, 2014*. Montréal: Ville de Montréal.

Vloberg, Maurice. 1942. *Les fêtes de France: Coutumes religieuses et populaires*. Grenoble: Arthaud.

Voisine, Nive. 1984. *Histoire du catholicisme québécois*. Montréal: Boréal express.

Wagner-Pacifici, Robin. 2005. *The Art of Surrender: Decomposing Sovereignty at Conflict's End*. Chicago: University of Chicago Press.

Wagner-Pacifici, Robin. 2010. "The Cultural Sociological Experience of Cultural Objects." In *Sociology of Culture: A Handbook*, edited by Laura Grindstaff, John R. Hall, and Ming-cheng Lo, 109–17. New York: Routledge.

Warner, Michael, Jonathan VanAntwerpen, and Craig Calhoun, eds. 2010. *Varieties of Secularism in a Secular Age*. Cambridge, MA: Harvard University Press.

Warner, W. Lloyd. 1959. *The Living and the Dead: A Study of the Symbolic Life of Americans*. New Haven, CT: Yale University Press.

Woodward, Ian. 2007. *Understanding Material Culture*. London: Sage.

Wuthnow, Robert. 1994. *Producing the Sacred: An Essay on Public Religion*. Champaign: University of Illinois Press.

Zubrzycki, Geneviève. 2006. *The Crosses of Auschwitz: Nationalism and Religion in Post-Communist Poland*. Chicago: University of Chicago Press.

Zubrzycki, Geneviève. 2011. "History and the National Sensorium: Making Sense of Polish Mythology." *Qualitative Sociology* 34: 21–57.

Zubrzycki, Geneviève. 2012a. "Negotiating Pluralism in Québec: Identity, Religion and Secularism in the Debate over 'Reasonable Accommodation.'" In *Religion at the Edge: Toward a New Sociology of Religion*, edited by Courtney Bender, Wendy Cadge, Peggy Levitt, and David Smilde, 215–37. New York: Oxford University Press.

Zubrzycki, Geneviève. 2012b. "Religion, Religious Tradition and Nationalism: Jewish Revival in Poland and 'Cultural Heritage' in Quebec." *Journal for the Scientific Study of Religion* 51 (3): 442–55.

Zubrzycki, Geneviève. 2013. "Aesthetic Revolt and the Transformation of National Identity in Quebec, 1960–1969." *Theory and Society* 42 (5): 423–75.

Zylberberg, Jacques. 1984. "Religions and Nationalisms: Canada and Quebec." *Social Compass* 31 (4): 331–37.

INDEX

Page numbers in italic refer to figures.